The Imperial Discipline

D1280726

The Imperial Discipline

Race and the Founding
of International Relations

Alexander E. Davis, Vineet Thakur
and Peter Vale

PLUTO PRESS

First published 2020 by Pluto Press
345 Archway Road, London N6 5AA

www.plutobooks.com

British Library Cataloguing in Publication Data
A catalogue record for this book is available from the British Library

ISBN   978 0 7453 4060 9   Hardback
ISBN   978 0 7453 4062 3   Paperback
ISBN   978 1 7868 0659 8   PDF eBook
ISBN   978 1 7868 0661 1   Kindle eBook
ISBN   978 1 7868 0660 4   EPUB eBook

This book is printed on paper suitable for recycling and made from fully managed
and sustained forest sources. Logging, pulping and manufacturing processes are
expected to conform to the environmental standards of the country of origin.

Typeset by Stanford DTP Services, Northampton, England

Simultaneously printed in the United Kingdom and United States of America

Contents

Acknowledgements

This has been a long-term project between researchers based at various times in South Africa, the UK, the Netherlands, Australia and India. Such a project is only possible with a great deal of support from multiple institutions. First of all, we would like to thank the University of Johannesburg, where we were all employed concurrently for a short time when much of the research for this book was done, and many of the ideas were thrashed out. We also received great financial and moral support from the University of Western Australia, Institute for History (Leiden University), Gratama Foundation and Leiden University Fund, the Netherlands Institute for Advanced Study in the Humanities and Social Sciences (Amsterdam), the University of Pretoria, La Trobe University and the University of Adelaide.

We would like to thank *Millennium: Journal of International Studies*, and its editors Sarah Bertrand, Kerry Goettlich and Christopher Murray, for publishing our initial article from this project, 'Imperial Mission, "Scientific" Method: An Alternative Account of the Origins of IR', *Millennium: Journal of International Studies* 46, no. 1 (2017), 3–23.

We are also grateful to the journal *South Asia: Journal of South Asian Studies* for allowing us to reproduce parts of the article 'A Communal Affair over International Affairs: The Arrival of IR in Late Colonial India', *South Asia: Journal of South Asian Studies* 40, no. 4 (2017), 689–705.

The staff members at the following libraries and archives were exceedingly helpful in our archival research: Bodleian Library (Oxford), Chatham House Archives (London), the Barr-Smith Library Special Collections Room (University of Adelaide), Library and Archives Canada (Ottawa), the JC Beaglehole Reading Room (Victoria University of Wellington), Archives New Zealand (Wellington), the British Library (London), National Archives of India (New Delhi), Nehru Memorial and Museum Library (New Delhi), Cory Library (Rhodes University, Grahamstown), Wits Historical Papers (Johannesburg), University of Cape Town Archives (Cape Town) and National Archives of Scotland (Edinburgh).

We would like to thank our families and our partners, Petra Mosmann, Melissa Nefdt and Louise Vale for their support over the years it took to write this book.

In particular, thanks to Petra Mosmann for her careful reading of the final draft of the manuscript.

Peter Vale would like to recognise and remember the late John Barratt, who directed the South African Institute of International Affairs for nearly three decades.

Several of our colleagues were especially helpful in putting together the book and performing the research. We are particularly indebted to Ruth Gamble, Rebecca Strating, Estelle Prinsloo, George Barrett, Luisa Calvete, Karen Smith, Ian Patel and Sanchi Rai.

Finally, we would like to thank Jakob Horstmann and everyone at Pluto Press for their support for this project.

Abbreviations

AIIA – Australian Institute of International Affairs
ANU – Australian National University
CIIA – Canadian Institute of International Affairs
ICWA – Indian Council on World Affairs
IIIA – Indian Institute of International Affairs
INC – Indian National Congress
IPR – Institute of Pacific Relations
IR – International Relations
LoN – League of Nations
NZIIA – New Zealand Institute of International Affairs
PIIA – Pakistan Institute of International Affairs
RIIA – Royal Institute of International Affairs
SAIIA – South African Institute of International Affairs
SAIRR – South African Institute of Race Relations
UN – United Nations
WWI – World War I
WWII – World War II
VUW – Victoria University of Wellington

Introduction: Race, Empire and the Founding of International Relations

At the end of a long and busy day in the frenetic weeks of activity leading up to signing of the Treaty of Versailles, 33 men gathered in the Paris' Hotel Majestic on 30 May 1919.[1] While the bare bones of the League of Nations (LoN) were being thrashed out and debated in every corner of the city, this gathering of men was invited by a British delegate, Lionel Curtis (1872–1955), to discuss an institution quite different from the League. Focusing solely on an inter-state institution like the League, Curtis reasoned, was no guarantee of peace. The text on pages of treaties was often an unreliable barometer of the state of the world. The mind of the public, not the ink on the pages, shaped the future. Hence, he argued, efforts towards peace would eventually have to be directed towards shaping the minds of the public.

Attending this meeting were members of the American and British delegations. The meeting, presided over by General Tasker H. Bliss (1853–1930), American Plenipotentiary to the Peace Conference, was presented with a memorandum, co-written by Curtis and his one-time student at Oxford but now secretary of the LoN Commission, W.H. Shepardson. The memorandum proposed setting up a joint Institute of International Affairs with a branch each in Britain and America. It argued that the interest of the international society at large ought to become the primary factor in inter-national affairs, an interest that required thinking beyond just the nation or the state. As such, universal interest subsumed and surpassed national interest, and in that spirit the memorandum urged that a joint institute with branches across the Atlantic would demonstrate the possibility of embody-ing such thinking in concrete institutions.

Curtis had been asked to become part of the British delegation by Robert Cecil, the chief of the LoN section of the British delegation. He was selected because he had published an article titled 'Windows of Freedom' in the journal *The Round Table*, where he had argued that the prospective LoN must ultimately strive for a world government, and suggested that the British Commonwealth could provide a model. Curtis was no arm-chair academic. In the aftermath of the South African War, he had been recruited by Alfred Milner, the High Commissioner to South Africa, as one of a group of youngsters brought to the-then Transvaal to bring administrative efficiency. In 1907, Curtis, who later became one of the central pillars of this group called 'Milner's Kindergarten', made the case for a federated South Africa in a document titled 'Selborne Memorandum'. For the next two and a half years, along with his Kindergarten group, Curtis devoted his energies towards propagandising the need for a unified state in South Africa through publications and 'Closer Union' societies. When the Union of South Africa was finally declared in 1910, the Kindergarten took credit, and going further, made plans to create a federated global empire. The organisation, The Round Table, of which both Curtis and Cecil, as well as several of those present in this meeting were part, was established in 1910 with the purpose of finding a scheme for the organic union of the British empire. Before, and to some extent during, the war, the Round Table had carried out propaganda for a larger federated organisation of the British empire, which Curtis had notched up further with his proposals for a world government. In this period, Curtis had served as the roving ambassador of the Round Table movement.

Almost a year after the meetings in Paris and Versailles, on 5 July 1920, when said institute was inaugurated, it was reduced to only one leg. After waiting for the Americans for a considerable period, the British Committee went ahead on its own. The institute was now called the British Institute for International Affairs. Three years later, in 1923, through a generous grant from a Canadian benefactor, Colonel R.W. Leonard (1860–1930), the institute moved to a Georgian house at 10 James Square whose past occupants included three former British prime ministers. It was named Chatham House, after the first of those prime ministerial occupants. In 1926, the institute received a Royal Charter, and became the Royal Institute of International Affairs (RIIA). Although the American Committee had finally been able to start the Council for Foreign Relations, the idea for a joint institute was by then dropped. However, the two institutes have shared a close relationship ever since. On 1 January 1928, the first Chatham House affiliated institute was opened in Canada, followed closely by institutes in Australia (February 1933), South Africa (May 1934), New Zealand (July 1934) and India (March 1936). A branch of Chatham House was opened in Newfoundland in April 1936.

These institutions may well be very familiar to those engaged in the study of international relations (IR). Considerably fewer IR students and scholars would be familiar with the imperial and world-making purposes of their founders. As we explore the stories of origins and developments of each of these institutes, we want to use this introduction to explore the linkages between knowledge production and world-making that came to define the mandate of these institutes of international affairs. In particular, we will string our subsequent discussion through three key themes which are central to this kind of knowledge production: understanding of the 'scientific method'; tracing the development of an epistemic community which is sympathetic to such ideas of knowledge; and race-thinking – which we argue was the central concern of world-making in this period.

The centenary of the institutional 'birth' of IR took place in 2019. The occasion prompted celebration, reflection and navel gazing about what the discipline had accomplished (if anything) since its foundation. The idea of 2019 as IR's centenary is ultimately grounded in the idea that the discipline was founded at the University College of Wales, Aberystwyth, and Chatham House, two institutional initiatives that began in 1919. A disciplinary lore has formed around this story – that IR was inspired by a demand for the 'scientific study of international politics' as a project for global peace after the horrors or World War I (WWI). We call this lore the Aberystwyth narrative: the tale IR tells itself about its origins, in which it was begun by well-meaning liberal thinkers who hoped to prevent the nightmare of global conflict from repeating. Following this, we are told, was the 'great debate' between realists and idealists, over whether we should analyse the world as it is or how we would like it to be.

In discussing the sclenticisiation of political philosophy, Peter Lassman has suggested that 'if a social science were possible then ... politics in its normal sense would become unnecessary'.[2] The academic as the knower of truth and laws authors the future, while politics and politicians follow. To redirect a claim about philosophers to politicians, made by Peter Lasslet in 1956, the horrors of war had made politics too serious a task to be left to politicians.[3] Consequently, the 'science' of the political was meant to elevate the academic over the politician – the former charted the future, while the latter dabbled in the present. Just as sociology was driven by the desire to achieve 'positive polity',[4] IR was designed as an intellectual project for realising 'world peace'. The nature of this world peace, however, was not nearly as idyllic as the Aberystwyth narrative would have us believe. Rather, we argue here that the origins of IR lie far more in imperial debates about race and racial hierarchies, and the structure of empire. The world peace in question, then, was to be a permanent imperial control under the British empire. Within this, racial categorisations were central to the thinking of interwar IR.

In this book we argue that the 'science' of studying international politics, the method of doing it, and the implacable belief that knowledge created, not just explained, reality came from initiatives undertaken by the group of people who were part of a society called 'The Round Table', and that these initiatives were key to the founding of IR. The Round Table was founded in September 1909. It was based on the Closer Union Societies formed a year previously in South Africa. *The Round Table*, the first journal of IR started in 1910, was the journal of the Round Table movement and was modelled on a journal started in South Africa two years previously, *The State*. Alfred Zimmern (1879–1957), Lionel Curtis and Philip Kerr (1882–1940) – the first IR Chair at Aberystwyth, the founder of Chatham House, and the first editor of the journal *Round Table*, respectively – were close academic collaborators but also active participants of the Round Table movement.

In the last few decades, an increasing number of scholars have turned their critical eye on the field's history,[5] challenging the standard narrative of IR's origins.[6] Highlighting the linkages between imperialism and the origins of IR, they have dismissed the 'great debates' narrative of the discipline which argues that IR begins with the efforts of the 'idealists' to 'scientifically study' international affairs in the aftermath of WWI. Instead, they argue that the 'birth of the discipline' not only precedes WWI, but also that it emerged out of discussions about race and empire, not peace and war.[7]

Despite this re-writing of the discipline's history, we remain stuck with a sense that IR began in the US and the UK: the great imperial centres of the time. As this re-writing has taken place, a number of scholars have sought to uncover non-Western ways of thinking about IR, so as to draw them in to the discipline to challenge eurocentrism.[8] For such efforts to be fully realised, however, we need to understand the disciplinary history of IR, and how it thought about coloniser and colonised. If the origins of IR are imperial, though, surely to complete our understanding of them we need to think beyond the power centres of empire, and consider ideas which emerged from the colonies and the colonised. IR does not have one single history. As Robert Vitalis has suggested, it is a 'mongrel' discipline, drawing on elements from politics, philosophy and colonial anthropology, to create a new discipline.[9] It has a great plurality of origin stories across the world. As such, we do not aim to fully dispel the Aberystwyth narrative. It is accurate in so far as Chatham House and the Aberystwyth School were founded in 1919. Rather, we seek to re-write its context and content, while adding more stories to IR's origins from other geographic and social contexts. The addition of these stories can only deepen and add complexity to our understanding of the discipline of IR, and the world it seeks to explain.

IR is often thought of, following Stanley Hoffman's famous formulation, as an 'American social science'.[10] This speaks to a US-centrism which has been prevalent within much of the discipline's thought. The discipline's largest academic organisation, which hosts its flagship annual conference, the International Studies Association, rarely ventures outside of the continental US. When it does, it only goes as far as Toronto and Hawaii. Much of the critical work on IR's disciplinary history has likewise centred on the US story. We are mostly appreciative of this work, and as such, the US is not an explicit case study in the book. This is partly because we feel the US story has been covered excellently elsewhere.[11] Aside from Vitalis, Jessica Blatt has looked at race in the making of American political science, the founding of the *Journal of Race Development*, which was a predecessor journal to *Foreign Affairs*.[12] Perry Anderson has shown the ways in which American foreign policy thinkers have sought imperial control throughout US international history.[13] In our case, however, taking the emphasis off the US experience is also for institutional reasons. The Round Table were not directly responsible for the foundation of IR in the US in the way that they were around the British empire. Throughout, we seek to document the ways in which US IR and the British imperial IR were connected and influenced one another.[14] The Round Table and its key thinkers all spent time in the US, and were absorbed in particular with its racial politics. As such, our story will engage with that of the US, and it will contextualise the US story by placing it in a transnational context. But when we consider IR's development outside of the US, the analogy of IR as a mongrel becomes even more appropriate. IR developed in various cultural and imperial contexts simultaneously and transnationally. To decolonise the field, then, and the knowledge it produces, we must understand these plural histories and take the discipline's history out of the hands of the imperial centres.

We intervene by revealing the centrality of the empire's frontiers to the emergence of IR and by writing its history in new contexts. We take up Long and Schmidt's challenge to get our 'hands dirty by reading texts, journals, memoirs, and other sources that have been standing dormant on library shelves'.[15] We study the unexplored archives of IR outside of its imperial centres to argue that, ever since its foundation, IR has concealed an agenda of transforming the 'Empire' into the 'International'.[16] Within this, debates about race and hierarchy were crucial. This can be seen, for example, in discussions about imperial futures that took place in the mid-1800s, such as the idea of 'Greater Britain'. Precisely who is inside and who is outside of 'Greater Britain' was itself always a murky question. This reveals to us some of the racial ideas that were part of the discipline's founding, the UK and its settler colonies almost always included, but colonies such as India and South Africa only occasionally considered. This was the case with the institutes examined here, with India in particular on the margins of their project. The Round Table took inspiration from these ideas and this discursive context. The foundational anxiety of IR in this context, then, was not so much the creation of 'world peace', but the successful maintenance of Britain's empire. This archival excavation helps us locate the origins of the discipline at the interstices of the three levels of imperial being – empire, state and society – and the developing conceptions of sovereignty in the Edwardian era.

This did not just happen in national, geocultural contexts, although these can be useful units of analysis. We argue that IR began in a fundamentally transnational fashion: it developed around the British empire by a network of committed imperialists seeking to develop a new 'objective' perspective on international affairs. This group – a thought collective, in the terms of Philip Mirowski and Dieter Plehwe[17] – developed IR's original methodology, its first journal and its first institutes. Led by Lionel Curtis, the Round Table created an academic discipline with a political and imperial goal in mind. In this book, we chart the story of IR's emergence through the British Dominions and in India. We argue that Anglo-American IR did not spring forth out of nowhere in Aberystwyth or in the US. Rather, it developed at least in part through the periphery's interactions with the imperial centre. The development of ideas in distant frontiers was central, beginning with the politics of race and the process of state-making in South Africa. This means that, rather than the imperial centres of Washington and London, we focus on the far-flung British settler colonies and on late colonial India. IR, then, developed at least in part by interaction and travel between the empire's capital and its edges. In these diverse geographical locations, IR was created with an imperial mission in mind: the binding of the empire together through a shared outlook on world events.

None of this is to say that these are the only contexts or the only histories that matter, or that the US and UK centred stories are wrong or ahistorical. Rather, central to the premise of the book is that the inclusion of more diverse and plural origin stories of IR is essential in decolonising the discipline.

In this book, we take an archival journey into the founding of the Round Table, the movement as well as its journal, and its subsequent institutions. We trace the emergence of ideas and methods through two of this collective's initiatives. We begin with the formation of the South African Union (1906–1910) and follow this with its global iteration through Curtis' Dominion tour from September 1909 to March 1911, on which they sought to take forward their method of study. It is this tour that we argue was formative for IR. Following this, we look at the ideas and institutions produced by the various national contexts in which this mission and method were embedded: Canada, Australia, South Africa, New Zealand and India. This collective developed a stream of ideas about Empire and the International, but also about questions of scientific methodology and its relationship to shaping the future. In this formative period, the 'scientific study' was connected not so much to creation of world peace (though this was desired), but fostering greater connections between the imperial centre and the Dominions. The goal was not so much world peace as it was fostering an 'organic unity' that would bind Britain and the settler colonies together.

This historical tale also allows us to thrash out another of the central concerns of the 'founding fathers' of academic IR – the issue of race. The more one reads interwar 'idealist' texts, the more the centrality of race and empire in the worldviews of British thinkers becomes clear.[18] However, IR's compulsive framing of notions such as world peace and world state around the idealist/realist binary ignores their obvious racial and imperial overtones.

HISTORY, THEORY, MEMORY: WHAT IS AT STAKE?

Long and Schmidt noted over a decade ago that 'Disciplinary history is rarely a neutral or impartial undertaking. Rather, it is often closely tied to intellectual struggles to determine and legitimate the contemporary identity of the field.'[19] We would take this slightly further: understanding and contesting the history of the discipline cannot be neutral. Indeed, if it were not tied to some theoretical concern or some debate, what would be the purpose of writing such a history? These histories are inexorably tied to dictating the identity of the field and the terrain it covers. Whether or not we begin with anarchy or, as Vitalis suggests we should in his recent disciplinary history, with empire, depends on how one sees the history of the discipline.[20]

To that end, some excellent disciplinary histories have been produced in the past few years that have begun to reshape the IR memory-bank, which have begun to emphasise imperialism, race and hierarchy as foundational concerns.[21]

And yet, these histories, in their own paradoxical way, focus primarily on the US and Europe. This is not meant as a criticism, and not to suggest the works are themselves Eurocentric. Vitalis focuses on America, but produces an outstanding documentation of an African-American school of thought that resisted the dominant white world order. One criticism that Hobson has addressed of his work is that it could be conceived of as Eurocentric as it does not go into detail into the non-Western origins of some of the thought he discusses.[22] Our goal here, however, is merely to point out that the focus of these histories still lies on the US and European origins of IR. This implicitly shapes the identity of the field. Even though they are critical, and they bring race, imperialism and hierarchy to the fore, they are not enough in and of themselves to decentre the discipline's focus on Europe. Disciplinary histories of course struggle to take in the entirety of the history of a discipline across different global/national/local scales, and so it is relatively common for a disciplinary history to be limited to a particular geographically focused area. As we show here, however, IR's history was ultimately not based just in Europe and/or America, but developed in a transnationally networked fashion, with particular nodes operating in localised contexts.

That the discipline has forgotten the origins that we uncover here is an example of its deep and enduring Eurocentrism. In this sense, it is not just the history of ideas or the history of events in IR which shape the way we think, but the way in which we remember them. The way in which we remember the field today tends to emphasise IR as developed simultaneously as a Western set of ideas, focused on two particular states: the US and the UK. Just as writing national history constructs national identities and reflects contemporary political concerns, writing a disciplinary history constructs the identity of a discipline. If we write the history of the discipline through a Eurocentric model, or as emerging solely from the 'West', even if it is to critique these models, we still fail to look at the racial and colonial origins of IR as it developed elsewhere. The colonial origins of IR outside of the imperial metropoles, and the influences of the imperial frontier on their thought, however, were important in the global development of the discipline. IR was transnational and colonial at its origins. This history, then, is another reason why Eurocentrism in IR has been so difficult to shift, because non-Western voices were excluded from the beginning as a central concern of the project.

As will be seen throughout the following chapters, concepts such as race, racism, empire, hierarchy, culture, civilisation were central to the foundation of IR. At the same time, the imperial frontier was also central, not just the great imperial powers of the US and the UK. Contemporary IR theories often avoid these concepts. Despite this forgetting, these concepts have become targets for analysis in the past few years. Hierarchy has been analysed from various theoretical perspectives. These include postcolonial, constructivist, Marxist and even English School approaches. Race and racism have become areas of critique and interest,[23] despite what Sankaran Krishna called in 1999 a 'wilful amnesia' and a systematic politics of forgetting.[24] Culture and civilisation, as exemplified by Samuel Huntington's *Clash of Civilizations* thesis, have longer and more obvious histories within IR, but are often handled in a manner which scholars attentive to race and racism have criticised. Indeed, as we will see, colonial, racialised, essentialist and hierarchical ideas of culture and civilisation were central to the Round Table's original project.

When we are told that the study of IR, and its practice, are predicated on anarchy, on the state system, that it began with Westphalia and that colonial societies were outside of it, we erase imperialism from our analysis. When we remember IR as we know it as beginning with the Peace of Westphalia, we limit it to Europe and America, and dismiss the majority of peoples from engaging in (and with) its study. This is particularly troubling when we remember that the international and its affairs were themselves the site of colonial domination and expansion. What is at stake, then, is the decolonisation of IR's knowledge production.

IR as a discipline, as argued by Navnita Behera, produces and privileges particular kinds of knowledge through its universal claims and key concepts of borders, sovereignty, anarchy and the state.[25] This focus needs to be replaced by 'diverse notions and understandings, informed by varied geo-cultural epistemologies derived from across the globe ... and develop plural traditions depending on the local context [and] histories'.[26] In order to accomplish this goal, we need to flood IR with new stories of origin, which go beyond the discipline's origins in the US and the UK. As only two of our stories (those of South Africa and India) come from the Global South – our South African story is certainly the whitest of all – we do not claim to be re-writing the discipline in quite this manner. Rather, we seek to tell a limited number of new stories of IR's origins from around the British empire, while calling on more diverse scholars from different backgrounds to add to these stories from other contexts.

It is worth pausing here to note that this knowledge production is not just to do with race, empire and hierarchy, but also with gender. With the possible, if unlikely, exception of some of the anonymous articles in *The Round Table*, the authors examined here are overwhelmingly white and male. Patricia Owens has rightly pointed out that women have played important roles in international thought, but that their influences have been obscured or even purposefully erased.[27] Here, we present an institutional history of a deeply patriarchal organisation. Our focus is on the explicit manifestations of racial thought within that organisation. Women's exclusion from the Round Table, and from this form of international thought, was so germane to its purpose as to not have been often commented upon. We do not seek to present our story of disciplinary origins as the sole story. Rather, we urge that more stories of origin are told. Within this, women's role in the history of international thought and IR is the untold story most urgently in need of telling.[28]

The circulation and dispersion of ideas around the empire led to distinct traditions of IR in each of the societies to which it travelled. These traditions of thought still exist today. They reflect the contemporary strategic culture of these societies. Australian IR remains often dedicated to the study of Asia. Anti-colonial thought from India is still common, though it emerged from foreign policy elites who might have neglected India's own social hierarchies and maintained forms of colonial governance. Today, though, Indian think tanks seeking political influence produce a great deal of analysis which celebrates the Indian state, its inherent historical unity and the eternal nature of its borders. IR works produced by mainstream think tanks are seldom theoretically incisive, nor even concretely historical. Much of the policy end of Indian IR treats its university counterparts with active disdain.[29] IR in New Zealand and Canada remain more distinctly liberal internationalist, and often celebrate the ability of these states to 'punch above their weight'. In South Africa, as we will show, 'race' was the core concern of early institutions. For anyone conversant with the history of South Africa this is not startling, but what indeed is startling is that during apartheid, the country's sole IR institute managed to evade race completely in the name of impartiality. For all the conflicts – the staple of IR – that South Africa generated in the second half of the twentieth century, it was obvious that their resolution would have to go through the race question even if the local IR community kept the issue at arm's length.

Although we suggest that imperialism was the key foundational concern of IR, and that it was the abiding ideology of the Round Table, this is not to argue that it was solely imperialistic. There are occasional moments of resistance which appear throughout this history. As Vitalis identifies a black power politics strand of resistance through the Howard School in America, there are important moments of resistance to imperial forms of IR that permeate our narrative here. In India, those critical of India's alignment with the colonial worldview opposed the Indian Institute for International Affairs (IIIA), leading to the formation of the Indian Council on World Affairs (ICWA). This rival institute was then able to host the Asian Relations Conference of 1947, which gave voice to anti-colonial concerns.

Ultimately, we argue that this history still shapes the way that we think even as the discipline largely failed to remember it. The discipline's ideas are predicated on a historical forgetting of the context from which they emerged. If, as we argue here, IR began as a thought collective that went global, with the aim of producing a perpetual peace based on a permanent empire, this needs to be acknowledged in order for it to be expunged.

There is, however, a deeper reason for why the disciplinary origins of IR need sustained interrogation. IR has long hinged itself on Martin Wight's claim of the International being the zone of exception.[30] As calls for decolonising the discipline grow, IR's centre has used this logic of insularity from the everyday to foreclose on debates about IR's theoretical and empirical agenda. Decolonising IR would thus first need stripping the discipline of its historical certainty, and this means challenging the foundational assumptions of what it means to do IR. The historical antecedent to the 'international', as the discipline tells us, is not 'anarchy'. Rather as we will argue throughout, it is 'empire'.

This is where our investigation begins.

OUTLINE OF THE BOOK

The main argument of the book is that IR began partly as an imperial 'science', which emerged out of the racial anxieties of South Africa and the settler colonies and was exported around the empire. The book dates the emergence of IR's original ideas and institutions, tracing them back to Milner's Kindergarten in Johannesburg, South Africa. An intellectual group of young imperialists brought to South Africa by the High Commissioner Alfred Milner after the Anglo-Boer War to form a new Transvaal administration, the Kindergarten included, among others, Curtis, Kerr and Robert Brand. In South Africa, the Kindergarten played a crucial role in the formation of the Union of South Africa. Soon after this, they moved to London and constituted the core group of the highly influential Round Table movement. These thinkers, we argue, crafted a method of study of the international which sought to create a shared frame of reference for looking at the empire and charting its future.

Their ideas were soaked in imperial racial thought and sought the maintenance of imperial domination over world order. Their project failed, though, when it travelled outside of the white settler colonies.

The book first examines how they formulated their ideas through travel and study around the empire, and how this project was disseminated through its networks to the British empire in the form of a chain of 'Institutes of International Affairs'. Following this, we then discuss the transnational founding and development of IR institutions and the ways in which these patterns of thought were embedded and transformed in Canada, Australia, South Africa, New Zealand, and finally India. These five chapters each tell nationally located but globally moderated stories of IR's origin. Throughout we trace this history through the spread of IR around India and the 'Old Commonwealth', arguing that this began in South Africa, which was imagined to be a microcosm of empire, and was transported through imperial networks to Australia, Canada, New Zealand, returned to South Africa anew, and then to India.

The idea of binding the empire together through the study of international affairs might seem curious now, given how fractious and contested IR is today. And yet, the idea of English-speaking unity, or a shared global outlook on international affairs belonging to the Commonwealth or the Anglosphere remains a facet of international politics.[31] Their relationship is in some ways institutionalised, through the Five Eyes network. Influential conservative politicians in the UK, Canada and Australia have continuously drawn on this idea. Similarly, a theory such as the English School, which is based on a seemingly innocuous concept of 'international society', emerged out of similar strains of thought. Perhaps unsurprisingly, given the supposed 'objective' study of international events was itself driven by an identity-building project, the new discipline was subsumed within the imperial identities of each location. The goal of binding the empire together was not entirely fulfilled, though connections across Australia, Canada, the US and the UK remain a key part of IR's international establishment.

We begin our alternate narrative of IR's plural origins in Chapter 1 with the development of IR's original scientific method and the blueprint for the network associated with the RIIA. We begin in Johannesburg, South Africa, with Milner's Kindergarten seeking to build a South African state. Here, these imperialist thinkers built what we might call today a 'think tank' and an academic journal. Following their success in South Africa, Milner's Kindergarten, led by Lionel Curtis, set out to take their thought collective's method global, by creating Round Table societies around the British empire and to publish a journal called *The Round Table*. We look at our key protagonist Lionel Curtis' motivations, methods and personality. IR's first institutes were developed in these contexts through the work of the Round Table movement, who based their methods on what they saw as their successful project of state-building in South Africa. Their goal was to reconstruct the empire as an 'Organic Unity': bound together not by costly administration and naval power located in London, but by a shared identity and a shared outlook on international affairs.

Over the following years, this ideology resulted in the foundation of not only the journal *The Round Table*, but a network of institutes of international affairs. These were centred around the RIIA. As a result, IR's mission and method was attached to the goal of binding the British empire together permanently through the construction of a shared frame of reference for understanding 'the international'. We argue on this basis, then, that the idealist world peace associated with IR's founding could more accurately be described as perpetual empire.

Over subsequent chapters we examine the foundation and development of IR in each of the colonial contexts targeted by Curtis and his thought collective: Canada, Australia, South Africa, New Zealand and India. The mood of the times was favourable to the notion that 'institutes' (of 'International Affairs', or other applied social categories) were in vogue. It was commonsensical to the Round Tablers, therefore, that the imperial metropole should have an interest in promoting this idea in the periphery. This relationship was no longer that of the 'mother' to 'daughter' variety which had marked the Victorian age, but the vocabulary around the relationship had matured into a sibling-type linkage. Each chapter traces the ideational context in which IR was founded, the foundation of institutes for international affairs, and the style of scholarship which emerged in each colony. Each story is slightly different in terms of structure, due to the vagaries of history, what historiography has been produced, how these histories have been remembered in national contexts. Still, the stories are unified in their discussion of how each of these colonies took up IR within the framework of the Round Table and Chatham House, wrestled with Curtis' original vision for the scientific study of international affairs as a means of binding the empire together, and eventually transforming it and making it their own within a global study of the international. Each colony was studied in each issue of *The Round Table*, with articles published from London and disseminated through the empire. The articles were written from the colonies themselves – often in workgroups, so the Dominions felt ownership of the journal. The anxiety that provoked these foundations of IR – the possible fracturing of the empire – can be seen in ideational battles over the study of international affairs in each colony. Although the circulation of ideas was deeply embedded in transnational colonial networks, we argue that different streams of thought emerged in each national context, as the Round Table's project failed to produce the organic union that was imagined.

We close each chapter not at a specific moment in time, but with two inter-related events in each context: the founding of a journal and the broader taking up of IR scholarship entering university institutions.[32] With these moments, IR entered a qualitatively different stage, it moved out of politically active think tanks such as the Round Table, and into the form we recognise today: university-based researchers not necessarily beholden to the ideology of a think tank and its publishing. This means that each chapter ends at a different moment in time, as the discipline found its way into university departments unevenly across different national and social contexts.

Even our focus on these specific institutes is imperfect. There were traditions of international thought that pre-existed Curtis' project. There were people studying the empire and the international outside of these institutional contexts. This is not to say these are the sole origins of IR in these state contexts. Rather, we argue the Round Table, and its affiliated institutes, were significant in founding IR in each of these contexts, in ways which have not been fully appreciated. Moreover, the Round Table itself has important South African roots which have not been appreciated elsewhere. Focusing on these institutes reveals to us the depth and extent of racialised and imperialist thought in the origins of IR.

To put it another way, it tells how deep the colonial rot is in today's IR. And this allows us to better understand the task ahead of us in decolonising the discipline.

We begin our state-specific histories in Canada in Chapter 2, beginning with *The Round Table* through to the foundation of *International Journal*. It examines the streams of thought which emerged in early Canadian IR, the role of the Canadian Institute of International Affairs, and the relationship between Canadian and IR in the US. Here, the Canadian Institute of International Affairs (CIIA), founded in 1933, worked closely with the Institute of Pacific Relations (IPR). Curtis' vision was limited by Canada's bilingualism. With the need to maintain the relationship between anglophone and francophone Canada, IR scholarship could not be as comfortably tethered to Anglo-Saxonism as it was in Australia. A clash emerged between the imperialist 'old guard' of the institute, and a younger, energetic liberal idealist stream of thought that saw for Canada an outsized, activist role in the world, in which Canadian ideas and interventions could improve international organisation, and save the world from conflict. This chapter in particular thinks through the connections between the US and the British imperial origins of IR. There was consistent interaction between the CIIA and institutions based in the US. At the end of World War II (WWII),

Canadian international thought and the foundational journal of CIIA, *International Journal*, emphasised Canada's liberal imperial perspective on world affairs, and its potential to have an outsized impact on the course of international affairs.

Chapter 3 examines the forms of international thought that developed in Australia. Here, the study of international affairs focused on events in Asia, something which remains true today, and the maintenance of Australia's colonies, Nauru and New Guinea. Moreover, a great deal of analysis was focused on settling Australia, the use of land, and Australia's tropical North. The White Australia policy and racial anxieties over Australia's proximity to Asia were a consistent subject for analysis. This chapter looks at the early international thought in Australia from the arrival of the Round Table to the founding of the Australian Institute of International Affairs (AIIA) through to the founding of Australia's first IR journal, *Australian Outlook*. The AIIA was founded in 1933, and began to craft a more national focus. Its four main research priorities were the 'peopling of Australia', 'problems of tropical Australia' with 'special reference to settlement', the management of Australia's colonial possessions of New Guinea and Nauru, and politics in East Asia. These topics were all frequently discussed in Australia's first IR journal, *The Austral-Asiatic Bulletin*. With WWII, though, Australian IR changed significantly. *The Austral-Asiatic Bulletin* was remade as *Australian Outlook*, which became the *Australian Journal of International Affairs* in 1973. On each occasion, the journal's opening editorial reflected Curtis' original mission and method. The chapter closes with IR entering the Australian university system and the Australian National University creating Australia's first school of IR, with the first Chair in the subject going to former colonial administrator Walter Crocker (1902–2002).

We argue that much of the early emphasis in Australian IR was on the issue of colonisation, with research priorities focused on settler colonialism and racialised concerns about immigration. The settlement of the Northern Territory by white Australians was a common focus of research, as it was seen as a suspicious 'foreign' borderland. Research then shifted to focus on Asian politics, often motivated by racialised concerns about security and invasion. Australia's 'international' priorities at this stage were deeply intertwined with the domestic. They radiated outwards from the key cities of Australia, looking at land tenure, the Northern Territory, colonial territories, and eventually to the empire and to Asia.

Chapter 4 traces the return journey of the Round Table to South Africa. The Round Table had managed to create a network of imperial enthusiasts across the empire who helped in founding local IR institutes. However, the group found little success in the country of its origin – South Africa. In fact, unlike other parts of the empire the Round Table movement had almost no presence in the country. South Africa's universities were too busy investigating race to study the emergent concept of the 'international'. This was despite the continual and clear intermingling of the two categories in other contexts. In the late 1920s, efforts to revive the Round Table societies in South Africa were made through an initiative to open the South African Institute of International Affairs (SAIIA). This chapter looks at the formation of SAIIA, in a context in which the South African segregation model – peddled by Jan Smuts – was also sought to be transformed into a global model of 'native/colonial administration'.

We discuss the early years of SAIIA's work and how it struggled to find a mandate especially as South Africa's liberals cohered around the South African Institute of Race Relations. Race and the International – in South Africa's imaginary – were entwined, rather than two different spheres of thinking. We also trace SAIIA's revival immediately after WWII, in the context of the coming to power of the apartheid government. With these two events, we argue that SAIIA used the idea of impartiality and the international to avoid talking about the topic of race, even as the issue overtook all areas of South African domestic life. In this chapter, as well as using archival material, we also draw on the memories of our co-author Peter Vale, one of South Africa's best-known respected IR thinkers.

Chapter 5 looks at IR in New Zealand and at the discipline's struggles to find its footing in a smaller society which saw itself as having a special genius for colonisation. We chart IR in New Zealand from the founding of the Round Table through to the establishment of the New Zealand Institute of International Affairs (NZIIA) in 1934, through to NZIIA joining Victoria University of Wellington. A stream of scholarship emerged which focused narrowly on New Zealand's domestic politics of race and racism, as well as its role in Samoa, which it held as a mandated territory. In part due to the small population of the colony, though, the institute found it hard to obtain funds and patronage. It produced a few publications, particularly studying New Zealand's colonial possessions, and discussing New Zealand's particular skills at colonisation. The institute struggled on until the 1950s, when it was incorporated into Victoria University of Wellington (VUW). It eventually started a journal, the *New Zealand International Review*, in the 1970s.

The final chapter of the book looks at the arrival of the imperial IR project in late colonial India. It is here that we see even more flaws in Curtis' original scheme, and greater signs of resistance. The study of the international was quickly subsumed into the secrecy and surveillance of the late colonial state, with discussion (and funding) limited to pro-imperial topics. The study of international affairs was also split by the political currents of Indian independence. The Indian National Congress (INC) was unwilling to work with the IIIA's discussions, and so created the Indian Council on World Affairs (ICWA) in 1943. The IIIA became seen as dominated by the Muslim League. Split along communal lines, the two institutes fought one another over which could produce the most research, and which could better represent India at international conferences. Finally, just before Independence and Partition, the IIIA was moved to Karachi, where it briefly co-existed with the Pakistan Institute of International Affairs (PIIA), while the ICWA stayed in Delhi. Despite South Asia's well-established and rich traditions of international thought, the IIIA was barely able to produce any research using Curtis' model in the context of late colonial India.

To conclude the book, we return to the idea of decolonising IR, by thinking through what IR's past says about its future. We argue for the return of the idea of IR as an interdiscipline that takes studies of the 'international' or 'global' as its point of departure. Within this, though, we emphasise the need for plural stories of origin and knowledge from any or all cultural backgrounds, arranged without producing hierarchies. As we will see, in each of our geocultural contexts, the goal of the scientific study remained improving world order by studying it. And yet, the imperial and ideational politics of each colony profoundly shaped the way in which scholarship was produced, and race was a central and continual concern. A greater understanding of how imperial ideology historically informed IR's knowledge production allows us to rethink the discipline's history, its purpose, and its present. This breaking open and transformation of IR, though, will only be possible with a sustained and critical engagement with the discipline's imperial history across different cultural and historical contexts.

1

An Edwardian Fantasy: The Empire-Wide Origins of International Relations

When Union [of South Africa] was achieved, more rapidly than ever we had hoped, we felt that it was up to us to apply the same process of imperial relations, especially in view of the German menace. The Round Table Groups and the magazine were the result ... In the course of the war, the Dominions as well as the British Government seized on men trained in the Round Table Groups to help them with the Imperial relations and Foreign Affairs, with the result that a large number of us found ourselves together at the Conference in Paris in 1919. Our years of Round Table experience had taught us the supreme importance of genuine research; but it had also taught us that genuine research is hampered in so far as it was connected with any element of propaganda. The Round Table, founded by people who believed intensely in the British Empire, necessarily suffered from this limitation. We, therefore, set out to establish a separate organ of research in which people of all differences of opinion, however great, could unite: an organ debarred from all propaganda. All this was settled in 1919 [with the establishment of the joint institute] ... the time is gone, when we need to be afraid of admitting ... that Chatham House was the outcome of Round Table network. I have always lived in hope that a day would come when my Round Table colleagues would acknowledge their child and drop the habit of imputing its sole parentage to me.

Lionel Curtis to Phillip Kerr[1]

In the second decade of the twentieth century, the Round Table movement became one of the most influential epistemic groups across the empire. The imperial enthusiasts of this epistemic collective pushed the idea of an imperial federation – a polity with an imperial parliament – with unrelenting devotion and energy. Copious histories of the Round Table movement have detailed how the idea was not only too far-fetched but also held little relevance after the Imperial Conference of 1921 when the idea of imperial parliament was formally killed.[2] But while the broader aim of the movement may have failed, the other key aspect of the Round Table proposals – equality of status between the Dominions and the UK – was carried with success.[3]

The connections between the Round Table movement and Chatham House are fairly well established.[4] The quote above from Curtis himself is one sample, but the works of Andrea Bosco and Alex May, among others, have convincingly explored the Round Table's role in the making of Chatham House. Scholars have also gestured enough towards the trans-Atlantic connections of the Round Table, and indeed how instrumental the Round Table networks were in fashioning ideas about Anglo-American relations as well as studies on international affairs. While in this book we focus primarily on the Dominion side of the story, and locate how the Commonwealth Institutes of International Affairs were shaped, this chapter explores the motivations for two broader themes. First, we explore the Round Table's creation of an empiricist methodology for studying world affairs. Second, within the Round Table's methodology, we also explore the role of epistemic communities or networks in the propagation of ideas, and particularly ideas connected to race relations. These two themes broadly bind the institutes in the Dominions to Chatham House and the Round Table movement.[5]

LIONEL CURTIS AND THE INVENTION OF A 'METHOD'

Curtis brought a religious zeal to his world-making project, believing fully in the mission of empire. Even the title of his key text on world government, *Civitas Dei* (The City of God), implies a sense of Christianity as part of his project and motivation. He was widely known as the 'Prophet of Empire', and Christian theology was a key element of his motivation, and found its way into his thought, particularly after the Round Table was established. His thought blended beliefs in empire, federalism, racial hierarchy, Christianity and democracy. His self-claimed expertise lay in shaping the minds of people. He was motivated by a devotion to the British empire, and a desire to remake world politics. And he had, indeed, developed a distinct methodology for it. So, his proposal argued that propaganda may seem like an obvious answer to infiltrate the minds of people, but that alone was not enough. Indeed, propaganda alone is devious; nothing sells better than lies. As important as propaganda might be, Curtis also focused on developing ideas that he saw were in need of propagation. Developing such ideas, however, needed commitment to knowledge, rigour and dispassionate inquiry – characteristics inversely related to the ideals of propaganda.

Curtis saw universities as the sites where ideas were developed, yet believed that universities' commitment to following the truth was often compromised by their distance from the 'real world'. University professors were flourishing in isolation from their surroundings, and their inveterate excitement at mindscapes rather than landscapes. Between the university professor and the newspaper journalist – the knowledgeable and the propagandist – there was a large gap, Curtis argued. This gap was the space in which knowledge could be produced for public consumption.

But, additionally, who were the publics? For Curtis, it was futile to think of publics in abstract or multitudes. The 'elites' were the public; they were the ones who decided on policies and led public opinion. To him, capturing the minds of the elites was in effect capturing the minds of the publics.

Thus, institutes – or in our current day parlance, think tanks – served the middle role. In international affairs, Curtis argued, there was a need for institutes that would occupy the space between knowledge and propaganda. The designation 'Fellow' was thus not only an intermediary between the professor and the journalist, but also someone who was attentive to both knowledge-making and its world-making function.

It was at the intersection of truth and propaganda that the 'scientific method' of the Round Table first emerged. This method understood knowledge production in a very specific way; with particular connotations about who can create knowledge, how it ought to be created, who must be its primary consumers, and the ends for which knowledge is created. In order to explore these dimensions, we need to go to the origins of the Round Table movement itself, which are not in London, but in Johannesburg.

The Union of South Africa came into existence in May 1910. Eight years earlier the two defeated Boer Republics – the Transvaal and the Orange Free State – had surrendered their sovereignty to the British empire. The idea of a unified state in Southern Africa, a colonial fetish since the 1850s, came to fruition in the eight years between surrender and union. Alfred Milner (1854–1925), then the British High Commissioner, and his 'young men' (as Walter Nimocks called them) played a great part in this change.[6]

Milner viewed the British empire as a group of white, self-governing communities bound by a common 'civilisation'. The ultimate goal of the idea of empire, he argued, could only be a 'permanent organic union'. The notion of 'Organic Union' drew from the contemporary assumptions about social Darwinism, Burke's theory of Organic Unity and superiority of the Anglo-Saxon race.[7] It follows that each element in the organism had a specific role and would gravitate towards the others in a 'natural' way. Each had a part to play in sustaining the whole.

At the end of the Boer War, Milner had become the Governor of the Transvaal and Orange River Colony from where he embarked on the project of state-building in Southern Africa. He overhauled the first institution of the state, the bureaucracy, and in the building of the Weberian ideal of an efficient bureaucracy, Milner recruited young men from his alma mater, Oxford. In the years following the Boer War, he recruited a group of young men – mainly, from New College and Balliol – who were fervently drawn to Milner's call for a united Southern Africa. Derisively called 'Milner's 'Kindergarten' (originally by William Marriot), the group included Robert Brand (1878–1963), Patrick Duncan (1870–1943), Geoffrey Robinson (later Dawson) (1874–1944), Richard Feetham (1874–1965), Dougal O. Malcolm (1877–1955), Hugh Wyndham (1877–1963), Lionel Hitchens (1874–1940), F. (Peter) Perry (1873–1935), Philip Kerr, John Dove (1872–1934) and Lionel Curtis. When Milner left South Africa in 1905, this group carried forward his project with the willing assistance of his successor, Lord Selborne (1859–1942).[8]

Unlike Milner, who gave only a broad outline, Curtis and others added more details of a unified Southern Africa through a series of initiatives. In September 1906, they established a private thought collective called the 'Fortnightly Club'. This was the site where Milner's Kindergarten and other like-minded devotees of empire met to discuss issues relating to the creation of a unified state in South Africa, and flesh out its possible relations with, and ramifications for, the greater imperial project.[9]

The Fortnightly Club papers reveal discussions on sovereign statehood, racial segregation, the immigration of Asians and, more generally, imperial politics. A preoccupation of the Club was the absence of an empire-wide theory of government. The existing British empire, as Curtis argued in an early presentation, was the outcome of a series of contingencies from Canada to Australia to South Africa to India. As a result, questions on the relationship between empire, state and society, the three constituents of imperial life, were fuzzy. It was unclear what sovereignty for the Dominions might mean or look like. Consequently, political authority within the empire was fragmented and the relationship between these entities was unclear.[10] What would, for instance, be the relationship between two otherwise exclusive political concepts, empire and state, when they were organised along two different axes of political rule – allegiance and sovereignty? There was no coherent theory of imperial rule.

For these concerns, South Africa was a microcosm of the empire. Germany was a threat both at the imperial level as well as in Southern Africa. Furthermore, the Southern African colonies were perhaps the most representative of the racial and immigrant 'problems' of the empire as a whole. They encapsulated the intra-civilisational European conflict of the Irish question, through the conflict between Boer and Brit. Southern Africa also reflected the 'inter-civilisational' interface between Europeans and non-Europeans. The two 'civilisational extremes' were juxtaposed: the English and the Africans. Added to this mix was the question of Asians who occupied the liminal space between these two extremes. As immigrants, too, the presence of Asians had raised the question of rights of the subjects of empire, most vociferously by Mohandas Gandhi (1869–1948).

However, underlying all these concerns was a firm belief in the genius of the Anglo-Saxon mind, spirit and institutions. The genius of Britain lay in fashioning institutions for each population according to their stage.[11] Consequently, the empire was slowly progressing towards a better version of itself. This was a process of continuous progress and evolution towards a teleological end. The Kindergarten saw Southern Africa as a political laboratory that pre-figured this future of the empire. The course of change in South Africa was both a precursor and the model for the grander project of creating an 'Organic Union'.

Imagining South Africa in this way, the Kindergarten saw their own role as political engineers. While they subscribed to a teleological view of history, history on its own was an inefficient, if not careless, moderator of progress. Following Seeley's injunction that the British empire was a series of accidents, the Kindergarten balked at the haphazard way in which the empire developed. In South Africa, they viewed their own role as midwives of history, ably curating the destinies of four distinct polities towards an Organic Union. In this understanding, their role was to reveal and then propagate the truth. Knowledge was nothing but an objective unearthing of this truth. In other words, in the teleological scheme of things, the ultimate truth was both pre-destined and revealed to those who followed the currents of history closely. Truth was only a logical deduction from the progress of history. Who can access this knowledge or truth? Those who were willing to submit themselves to the linearity of history, and pursue its ends with an unflinching commitment to objectivity. Objectivity, in this understanding, did not mean an uncommitted worldview, but a commitment to nothing but historical progression. Knowledge creators, or the seekers of truth, were thus agents of history, who hastened this long progression by weeding out the irregularities and pushing out ideas which are meant to be defeated in the long run.

The Kindergarten in South Africa thus busied themselves in first creating and then propagating this knowledge. Curtis, with the help of other members of the Kindergarten, prepared a missive which was finally published in the name of Lord Selborne, entitled *The Selborne Memorandum*.[12] This was a statement on the interdependent and mutually reinforcing relations of the Southern African colonies which recommended the creation of a federal state. In 1908, the members of the Kindergarten published a series of studies along this theme. The most important for our purposes was a two-volume book titled *The Government of South Africa* which set out the need to form a single government in South Africa. Again, this book was written mostly by Curtis.[13] The argument had begun with the assumption that federation was suited to South Africa. However, Curtis argued that his 'enquiries into the actual facts' revealed to him that the Union was more desirable in South Africa.

Here, Curtis emphasised that objective research had pulled the Kindergarten in the opposite direction, 'in spite of their pre-conceived ideas'.[14] This signposting is crucial, because here Curtis suggests that a thorough and objective investigation into South Africa had worked against his own preconceived ideas. Curtis would often cite this exercise as an example of 'scientific research' and how objective enquiry had pushed the Kindergarten towards achieving the Union of South Africa. Indeed, from here on, *The Government of South Africa* volumes served as methodological primers for all of his later works, including *The Commonwealth of Nations* and *Civitas Dei*.[15]

In 1908, the Kindergarten began two further projects, which later would prove instrumental in their evolving 'scientific' method. These were the establishment of a public association known collectively as the 'Closer Union Societies' and the launching of a journal called *The State*. The purpose of these societies was to propagate the establishment of a single South African state within the British empire encompassing all four colonies.[16] The organ which carried these ideas on behalf of the Closer Union Societies was *The State*, ironically founded before the South African state came into existence.

And this is the second important aspect of knowledge creation. For the Kindergarten, knowledge creation was not an interpretative exercise. Knowledge was the pursuit of truth – a singular truth – and once that was revealed, all efforts must be made to turn the truth into reality. Once this truth was revealed, as Curtis once wrote to Kerr, he could 'do missionary work with real effect'.[17] He added, 'until I have got a doctrine I can preach, I am conscious of being utterly paralysed so far as influencing the current course of affairs is concerned'.[18] But once the 'facts' had been written down and 'tested by the criticism of men like themselves in all the countries concerned',[19] the missionary work could start. Thereafter, propaganda work was as central to knowledge creation as the truth itself. Propaganda was how the truth became the driver of history, and not its end. Hence, the creation of a network of believers – those who believe in this truth – a wide epistemic community consisting of those who would partake in its dissemination was another central feature of knowledge production. Both the Kindergarten and the Round Table movement were very careful about involving only like-minded people in the movement. This meant that the work the group produced tended to be ideologically coherent, and with little dissent.

The founding of South Africa, and the lore the Kindergarten built around it, served as the legitimising canon for the Kindergarten when its core members moved to England to set up the Round Table movement. In a moment of self-congratulation, Lord Selbourne wrote to Curtis:

> I am quite sure that had it not been for 'The Government of South Africa', we never should have got such an excellent form of constitution and, although you had many splendid helpers, the main credit for this work must always be yours ... Milner's Kindergarten will have more profoundly influenced the history of South Africa than any combination of Afrikanders (sic) has ever done.[20]

Indeed, the Kindergarten's legitimacy for their subsequent efforts in developing a theory and a practice of IR rested almost entirely on the work they did in South Africa. In other Dominions, a belief took hold about how '30–40 men went and planted themselves in the different colonies in South Africa' and 'accomplished (the South African) union' through research and propaganda.[21]

As soon as it was clear that the Union of South African was an established fact, Curtis and the Kindergarten shifted their ambitions to the empire. In a letter that Curtis wrote to Leo Amery in March 1909, he acknowledged that in South Africa, the Kindergarten had 'acted as an advance party of sappers sent out to build a vital section of the road over which the main force will have to travel later on'.[22] He was now ready to construct the main road. Curtis laid out his plans: the first task was, as with the *Selborne Memorandum*, to identify and 'state the Imperial problem'. This was to be done through a well-researched 'memorandum' that would serve as a common reference for all Imperial Union enthusiasts. As Curtis had studied Southern Africa to write the *Selborne Memorandum*, he would visit all the Dominions to prepare the new document. Curtis also insisted on launching publications, along the lines of *The State*, which would circulate the gospel of Imperial Union.

Their plans were then sold to sympathetic ears in London, in particular to their patriarch and patron, Alfred Milner. In July and August 1909, Milner presided over a series of meetings in and around London, attended by F.S. Oliver (1864–1934), Lord Lovat (1871–1933), Leo Amery (1873–1955), Leander Starr Jameson (1853–1917) and the South African High Commissioner Lord Selborne.[23] This is where Curtis, Brand, Kerr and Robinson tried to convince the others of their plans. These events and ideas led to the weekend retreat at Plas Newydd, where Curtis' 'scheme' was discussed and consensus evolved over the idea that the empire needed to be re-calibrated as an 'Organic Union'. This task required following the same methodology used in South Africa: (a) careful selection of a small group of imperial devotees across the Dominions;[24] (b) creation of a central office in London to coordinate propaganda; (c) appointing an iterant delegate who would visit various groups in order to collect, digest and disseminate ideas about Organic Union; (d) preparing the final Imperial Statement – the truth – in consultation with all the groups in the Dominions which would set out 'the alternatives involved, the real problem of disruption, the sacrifices needed to avoid it, and the successive stages through which the ultimate goal is to be sought'; and (e) once this was issued, its goals would be taken up by all groups as 'a creed to which all have contributed and all have subscribed'.[25] The Imperial Statement was the bible, or the truth, whose dissemination would facilitate the Organic Union of the empire. Indeed, it was discussed as if 'the whole world were hanging on it', Arthur Steel-Maitland joked once.[26]

Another key aspect of propaganda was a journal that the Round Table launched in 1910, called *The Round Table*. Modelled on *The State* in South Africa, *The Round Table* was to become the premier organ of imperial affairs. As we will see, it increasingly shifted attention to discussing international, rather than imperial, issues in the interwar period.[27] Like *The State*, the key idea was that the journal would be read by 'a great majority of men (sic) of real influence in politics, journalism, business, etc.' and that efforts were underway to inculcate a readership among the 'people who count "in order that from the outset it may reach a large number of readers"'.[28]

In its early years, two people were central to this project – Philip Kerr and Lionel Curtis. Reprising their roles in South Africa, Kerr organised the affairs of the Round Table in London and efficiently helmed the journal for the first few years. In contrast, Curtis became the iterant delegate who toured the Dominions to collect information but more importantly to preach the gospel. Called the 'prophet', Curtis' devotion to the imperial project was total. He visited Canada in 1909, 1913 and 1916, South Africa in 1910, and Australia and New Zealand in 1910 and 1916. He set up the Round Table groups across the Dominions. At the start of the WWI, there were 36 Round Table groups across the empire with a membership of over 300 people.[29] For Curtis, these tours acted as 'fact-finding' missions, during which he studied the Dominions and allowed them to help shape both his broader political goals and means for achieving them.

Soon after returning from Canada in 1910, Curtis started writing a memorandum, known as *The Green Memorandum*, where he presented his first sketch of ideas about the Organic Union. The memorandum was sent for review to the different Round Table groups that he helped to set up during his tour. By now, he had arrived at a set methodology. Driven by an overall belief in the organic evolution of political condition, Curtis would study secondary sources and conduct extensive interviews with influential and 'knowledgeable' individuals. On the basis of the 'facts' gleaned from these sources, he would draft a report for circulation among a select group across the Dominions. Following this, wider self-selecting groups would discuss the draft and enter their comments into interleaved copies. These copies would be sent back to Curtis, who would then prepare the next draft. At every iteration, the 'method' involved fieldwork, interviewing, library research, drafting, and an early form of peer review. The final draft was only completed after this long process. The draft was commented upon by almost 200 members across the Dominions.

This method was distinctly reminiscent of the Closer Union Societies in South Africa. Following the first round, Curtis then went on to write a larger study on the Commonwealth. It was meant to be a three-part work, but came out in two volumes titled *The Problem of the Commonwealth* (for the more general audience) and *The Commonwealth of Nations*. But the journey of his ideas was not as smooth as in South Africa. Some of the proposals – a separate home parliament for the UK, an imperial parliament, imperial taxation, and the place of colonies – were met with stringent opposition, as a consequence of which Curtis published these books under his own name, rather than the broader rubric of the Round Table studies. Anonymity, or rather joint ownership of the fruits of research, had until then been a core principle of objectivity. It encapsulated the idea that the product of this research was not an individual's truth, but truth itself. However, faced with strong opposition when Curtis published these drafts under his own name, it seems the method itself had come undone.

This point of departure allows us to reflect back on the epigraph, and distil more clearly the point we are making about methodology whose claims are further fleshed out in the course of this book.

In the epigraph, Curtis complains that while Chatham House was a natural progression from the Round Table, one aspect of the Round Table's work which needed careful vetting was propaganda. He had come to see propaganda as inimical to the force of the truth. This was potentially driven by the failure of the Round Table project of Organic Union. Curtis believed that the vehement criticisms *The Problem of the Commonwealth* and *The Commonwealth of Nations* received came not from an opposition to the ideas of the Round Table per se but to the perceived nature of the organisation as a secretive, propagandist network. While the Round Table had projected itself as a non-partisan body, it had been attacked by both the conservatives and liberals. Conservatives railed against its decentralising imperative, while the liberals saw the Round Tablers as Little Englanders trying to impose an imperial parliament. The idea of appealing to the public through propaganda and creation of a larger movement was sceptically viewed. The idea that once the truth had been revealed through the Imperial Statement, a few publicly spirited 'men' in each Dominion would 'shout "harooh" (sic) in a spontaneous manner' to create a movement for the end goal, and the imperial centre would be compelled to agree was too naive. Instead, the focus ought to become more inward, driven towards influencing public policy directly. The truth – in this case the reconfiguration of empire – does not need to be whispered through networks in a secretive fashion on a pan-imperial scale. Rather, the creation of an institutionalised foreign policy elite would help in achieving the same strategic objects of the Round Table.[30]

The change, however, was only of tactics, not of an understanding of knowledge or the eventual objectives of the Round Table. This is what then Curtis and the Institute of International Affairs came to define as 'scientific study of International Relations'. What came to be defined and imitated as 'Chatham House Method' – 'keeping abreast of the facts, discussing the issues in private study groups and publicly communicating the results'[31] – was driven by a form of empiricism where 'facts' revealed teleology – they lay bare the mechanisms of history moving headlong towards, as Francis Fukuyama would term it in the 1990s, its end. There were indeed no theories to be found, unearthed or debated; that question was subsumed by the flow of history itself. Facts helped us to anticipate and hasten the movement of history towards a British Commonwealth of Nations, which would eventually 'organically' evolve into a World Commonwealth.[32] This understanding was still rooted in the nineteenth-century British tradition of 'knowing', primarily reflected in (and influenced by) Herbert Spencer's belief that human nature was constantly evolving and that human history reflected the eternal march of progress. In this understanding, the purpose of science was to empirically establish this history of progress and authenticate its telos.

VISIONS OF RACE IN THE COMMONWEALTH

The project for the Organic Union of the empire, as we have identified above, had started in the background of South Africa. As a microcosm of the politics of empire, South Africa also provided a particular way out of the racial issues confronting the empire, as all the Dominions increasingly emphasised the racially exclusive nature of their polities.[33] W.E.B. Du Bois' 'colour line', as Marilyn Lake and Henry Reynolds have shown, had primarily emerged in the form of a transnational white solidarity.[34] As a key practitioner-philosopher of the empire, Milner's view of the new political unity of the empire was sutured around the identity of a 'British Race'.[35]

The Round Table's efforts were not the first efforts to federate the empire. Movements for Imperial Federation and Greater Britain had earlier envisioned similar ideas. But they had often been roundly critiqued for being impositions from London. The imposition of these ideas was seen with cynical scepticism – if not outright opposition – by opponents in the white settler colonies. In the Round Table project, Curtis and others, however, explicitly positioned their ideas coming from the imperial margins, that is, the white settler states themselves. In his Dominion tours, in fact, Curtis deliberately positioned himself as a 'South African'. The Round Table groups established across the empire were indeed a way of generating a groundswell of movement towards an imperial federation. However, the motivation for a federated empire was not merely for the sake of external defence.

In the first iteration of the Round Table's thinking towards the Organic Union, a document titled 'Memoranda on Canada and the British Commonwealth' (or the 'Green Memorandum', as it was internally called), Curtis had argued that the primary purpose of creating a new federal scheme for the empire was the need for defence not only from external dangers, but also from internal threats of unrest in the colonies. The colonies, he argued, were 'volcanoes upon which Great Britain was doomed to sit … [as they] remain an eternal danger to the peace of the Empire'.[36] Indeed, if Great Britain were to withdraw from India and Egypt, such anarchy and bloodshed would plunge the whole world in tumult and compel the intervention of some other civilised power.[37] So while Great Britain must remain a constable in the dependencies,[38] he called upon the Dominions to share the burden of both internal and external threats to the empire with Britain. Amery had similarly argued, in an internal Round Table memo, that imperial organisation requires two different kinds of governance models.[39] While disagreeing with Richard Jebb's 'Colonial Nationalism' thesis which conceptualised the British empire as a hydra-headed empire, with fairly autonomous white settler communities,[40] the Round Table schemes were more in sympathy with Jebb's other argument that one way to develop a sense of imperial partnership was to invite the Dominions to participate in colonial governance. A collective imperialism, Jebb had argued, was the way forward to cultivate a sense of white solidarity across the empire.[41] Evidently, in these schemes, India and other dependencies appeared primarily as conduits for building closer bonds among white citizens of the empire.

However, as Curtis later relayed, William Marris (1873–1945) – Curtis' fellow traveller on his first Dominion tour – differed. On an evening in Canada in 1909 discussing the unrest in India, Marris has argued to Curtis that India was too important a part of empire to be merely seen as a laboratory for facilitating white bonds. India, on its own, was an empire in itself. Marris explained this further in an article in *The Round Table* in its inaugural issue. He reminded his readers that India already paid for its defence and maintained a huge army. India was not only England's biggest trading partner, but also a key strategic ally providing an army of more than 240,000 fighting men employed for contingencies across the empire.[42] Indeed, India provided the British empire with stability and strength. The word 'Empire' in British Empire, he suggested, was mostly just India. Any scheme of Organic Union hence cannot exclude India, or include it merely as a secondary concern. But contingency alone was not the reason for why India must be included in any conception of Organic Union. He wrote:

> Because we hold and govern three hundred millions of another race, we are without a rival among the nations of the world. Take India from us, and we sink to the level of a trade competitor with Germany and the United States ... To hold India, with its hundreds of races and religions and languages, and castes and customs, to be possessed of such a heritage of history, learning and romance, is an achievement for which the world's records show but one parallel ... Only Rome in her greatest days did what England has been doing, as a matter of course, for one hundred years.[43]

In other words, what separated the British empire from other competing empires, and great empires of the past, were the multitudes of India, which made the British empire an immensely diverse empire, and the sense of duty with which the empire governed India. If there was no progress to show in the hundred years of British rule, then the British empire in India would be morally the same as other despotic empires. Hence, he reasoned that the historic task of educating and uplifting Indians towards self-government was Britain's true contribution to world history. Governing India was 'the common privilege of the race', but a logical end of that process will be to eventually turn India into a self-governing dominion.[44]

It was an unusual suggestion to make at the time, and faced stiff opposition from most members. But these views impelled Marris' fellow travellers on the Canadian tour, Curtis and Kerr, to reconsider their own ideas on India and its importance for their scheme of Organic Union. While on a Dominion tour of the Antipodes to promote the work of the Round Table, Curtis considered making a tour of India and Egypt, for he agreed with Marris that they needed to be incorporated in some manner in their scheme. This was prevented when he was asked by the Round Table to visit Canada instead. In July 1911, Marris further wrote to Kerr warning that Indians would protest strongly against any proposal to bring the Indian government under an imperial body that the Round Table was proposing. The Dominions held strong racial views against Indians, especially on account of their opposition to Indian immigration into the Dominions. Any imperial assembly that had a large Dominions' representation, without any concomitant Indian representation, would likely be strongly anti-Indian in character and hence foment trouble in India.[45] He convinced Kerr to visit India to assess the situation.

Kerr shortly made a visit to India. After four months of travelling in the country, he wrote to Curtis in April 1912, 'I have gradually become convinced that we cannot, in the interests of Empire treat India as originally proposed. I only reached this conclusion recently, and after doing my best to resist it for I know what difficulties it means in the dominions.' He concluded, 'I believe I have reached the truth.'[46] The 'truth' was presented in the form of an article for the journal and a separate internal memorandum with proposals for inclusion of India in the scheme of the Organic Union. In the journal article, Kerr agreed with Marris that the British rule in India may have begun as an instrumental venture of trade, but its purpose now was more intuitive and moral. The primary purpose of British rule in India, he argued, was the welfare of Indians themselves. The 'ideal goal' would be that India should acquire the status of a self-governing dominion, 'independent in the control of her own affairs, a loyal and willing partner with the other units of the Empire in their common concerns'.[47] He added that India would remain within the empire because 'her people wish to do so'. He concluded with a warning:

> Only one thing can make the rupture inevitable – if the British in India or elsewhere should allow their policy to be swayed from the paths of enquiry and justice by pride of colour or race. The belief that we treat them inferior or inherently incapable of development, not on their true merits, but because of their blood or the pigment of their skins, will unite all Indians, Mohammedans with Hindu, high caste and low caste, north and south, in revolt against our rule, as nothing else will do.[48]

In his internal memorandum to the London Moot, Kerr was more direct. His memorandum, as he confessed to his deputy editor, Paterson, 'alter[ed] the fundamental preposition of the "egg" [the Imperial Statement]'.[49] As we have noted, until now the Round Table had considered India peripheral to concerns about Organic Union; Kerr instead argued that India was central to the future stability of the empire. He wrote: 'we must disabuse ourselves of the notion that India can be dismissed under the label, dependency. It is an empire as large as Europe ...'. Considering this, India's fate cannot be left to an imperial Assembly which would 'constitute of people not only ignorant of Indian affairs, but bitterly and selectively hostile themselves [Dominion representatives]'. Hence, he proposed giving representation to India in this new imperial body. His preference was for two elected Indian members – one Hindu, one Muslim – with a right to vote. Anything else, he argued, 'will be an insult' to educated Indians.[50]

Thinking about India also allowed Kerr to think more expansively about the objectives of the British empire. In a speech he made in Toronto, Kerr argued that the British empire was attempting to solve two of the most important political dividing factors of modern times: nation and race. By generating post-national solidarities in the Dominions and bridging the East-West divide in India[51] – and, even if inadvertently, through the combination of these two objectives – the British empire had embarked on a third one, universal peace.[52] He said:

> If by reconstruction of the Constitutional edifice of the Empire, we can reconcile the conflicting claims of the five white nations of the British Empire, and also contrive an enduring agreement between those of its peoples who are of dark colour and of white colour, we shall have proved

to the world that there is some other way than war by which disputes between nations and disputes between black, yellow and white can be settled. That is to say, we shall have shown the world the road by which it can attain universal peace.[53]

While Kerr was in India, Curtis was working on a 'short gospel',[54] a draft of what was the first volume of Round Table studies. In March 1912, he wrote to Valentine Chirol, the *Times* journalist and author of *Indian Unrest*,[55] that

the attempt to force democracy on India would mean ... that it would not be self-government at all; but merely a ruthless exploitation of 300 million voiceless laborious people by perhaps at most fifteen million or less ... India wants time – any amount of time, to absorb the new wine of European civilization without being burst into pieces.[56]

Maintenance of British supremacy at sea, he argued, was of primary importance and hence a middle way was needed to assuage the ongoing Indian unrest without giving in to demands of self-government. Both Kerr and Marris wrote to Curtis to reconsider his opinion of India; and Marris argued that it was important that proposals on India be included in the 'egg' 'to make it impossible for South Africa or Australia to look on India as another collection of blackmen'.[57]

Kerr and Marris seem to have convinced Curtis of not only taking India more seriously, but also considering the idea of self-government in India a real possibility.[58] But the central problem of these proposals for Curtis was that India could not be treated solely as an exception. In response to Kerr's memorandum, he had argued that if India was represented in the Imperial Assembly as a voting member, by what logic could other dependencies in Asia and Africa be kept out?

The idea of the British empire needed to be fundamentally rethought so as to provide a more sure-footed philosophical basis to Kerr's and Marris' proposals. As his friends and foes agreed, Curtis had a knack for broad generalisations, often (mis)using both history and theory to serve his own ends. In attempting to – using H.G. Wells' phrase – 'hurry on to wholes',[59] Curtis focused on the philosophical principle, which according to him essentially reframed the conception of the empire.

In late June 1912, he circulated the first two chapters of his work, which contained the crux of the argument of his proposed three-volume study.[60] It is here that Curtis uses the concept of the 'Commonwealth' for the first time.[61] He began by provocatively discarding the liberal conception of state as a social contract. In contrast, he argued that all states are founded on the willingness of certain members of their subjects to sacrifice their individual interests. The ultimate basis of state was thus sacramental, not contractual.[62] Ultimate authority always rested with the state.[63] Hence, all rights are vested in the state, and citizens only have duties. The state has sovereignty – ultimate authority over the individual – while the individual has allegiance – total obedience to the state.

Having set it up thus, he elaborated that there are two kinds of states – Autocratic and Commonwealth. In an autocracy, the authority of the state is either divine (theocracy) or rests with one individual (Monarch), who acts as vice-regent or mouthpiece of God. The other, which he called 'the Commonwealth', is a state founded on the idea of general will. This means that individuals have obligations not to one individual, but to each other. To be able to sacrifice self-interest for duty towards others was true patriotism. In a Commonwealth, each individual's interests are subordinate to the interests of others; collectively expressed in the general will. The general will was represented in the rule of law. However, the general will had to change with the conditions of its application, and hence there had to be some recognised organ which could change the law in harmony with the general will.

This conception of a Commonwealth also allowed Curtis to rope in what were clearly different political communities into one state. As argued in a later memorandum for the Round Table, the British empire was one state, not many, since the British rule of law is applicable across the Dominions as well as dependencies, implying a sense of shared duty. Indeed, the British empire ought to be seen not as a horizontal territorial entity, but as a 'vertical section bringing together every section of civilization and every form of human life.'[64]

The prime objective of the Commonwealth, Curtis argued, was to cultivate this faculty of patriotism in its citizens. He identifies three types of citizens in the Commonwealth, according to their levels of 'patriotism': active, latent and non-active. Those with non-active patriotism, that is, those who promote self-interest over the general will, such as criminals, should always be excluded from franchise. Latent patriots were those whose patriotism was not fully developed. He argued that since such faculties are developed by practising them, an 'educational franchise' should be extended to those with latent patriotism. He adds; '[h]ow far it is safe to extend this educational franchise will depend upon how far the patriots are numerous enough and their patriotism active enough to secure that in the long run private and sectional will not prevail over public and common interests.'[65]

Consequently, he identified three principles of political conduct in the Commonwealth: (a) strengthening the mutual sense of duty upon which the Commonwealth rests; (b) increasing the circle to whom this duty is owed; and (c) making sure that the Commonwealth is suitably equipped with an organ competent to express and enforce the general will.

In concrete terms, the first principle would call for cultivating a pan-Commonwealth identity, against the sectional national identities, within the British empire; the second would ensure that dependencies with latent patriotism like India would be increasingly incorporated into the Commonwealth; and finally, the Commonwealth must create both political and military organs that ensure the expression and enforcement of the general will.

Through invocation of the Commonwealth, Curtis was able to resolve two major issues with the Organic Union scheme. First, by making allegiance a sacramental and not contractual duty, he nipped in the bud arguments about the responsibilities of the British state and corresponding rights of the white Dominions in the empire. Instead, he argued now that the allegiance to the empire was a duty owed by one to all others in the Commonwealth. In doing this, he also shifted the source of sacramental duty from the monarch (which would make the empire an autocratic state, in his conception) towards political institutions as referents of loyalty in the Commonwealth.

Second, and perhaps more importantly, through his 'latent citizenship' he was able to incorporate non-white constituents (primarily Asians as we will see below) into the scheme of the Commonwealth. In addition, the Commonwealth idea also separated British rule from its continental (primarily Germany) and American counterparts. Continental states were non-organic (since owing to the incessant conflicts, rule of law could not develop) while America was riven by self-interest as it refused to share its Commonwealth with those outside – both white and non-white. The British empire was organic and it had invested in cultivating a sense of citizenship among the continuously expanding sphere of latent citizens. As such, Curtis saw the British empire as the embodiment of 'a great white, black and yellow Commonwealth' that was unique in world history and provided a strong basis for fashioning a greater world unity in future.[66]

Kerr and Marris, even if gesturing towards the duty that the British owed to Indians, had primarily emphasised India's strategic importance to the empire. Curtis, in contrast, took a predominantly moral and philosophical approach by reconceptualising the basis of the empire.[67] In doing this, he turned the colour line into a non-racial, hierarchical distinction of different

types of patriotism. This non-racial racialism defined the political education of its latent patriots as the primary purpose of the Commonwealth.

The Curtis memorandum was vastly criticised within the London Moot,
which led him to abandon inclusion of these ideas in his 1916 tract, *The
Problem of the Commonwealth*. But, instead, in his role as prophet, he went
to India in 1916 and 1917, and authored a thick tome called *Dyarchy*, which
was a key influence in the Montagu-Chelmsford reforms of 1919 in the
country. We will return to this in Chapter 6.

Furthermore, as he was to argue later in his magnum opus published in
three volumes in the 1930s, *Civitas Dei*, the primary reason for the failure of
the first Commonwealth in ancient Greece was its inability to organically
include the excluded ('barbarians' and 'gentiles') into the Commonwealth.[68]
Since the idea of sovereignty in the Commonwealth was neither territorial
nor divine, but institutional, it meant that the deepening of political institutions was dependent on their capacity for horizontal expansion – in the
power to bring more and more people within their fold. This is what made
Curtis later the champion of World State in the 1920s and 1930s, which he
argued was an organic expansion of the British Commonwealth.[69]

CURTIS AND THE THREE EMPIRES

Commenting on Curtis' Commonwealth scheme, the Indian scholar S.R.
Mehrotra has argued that his conception was truly revolutionary, as it
turned the prevailing conceptions of two empires (White and Non-White)
and roped the empire into a singular thread.[70] Curtis was able to erase the
colour line that separated the white and the non-white empire. Arnold
Toynbee, Curtis' colleague at Chatham House, agreed. He argued that the
Commonwealth and the universality of democracy were Curtis' two greatest
acts of imagination.[71] The idea of Commonwealth was not entirely original.
However, the notion that mutual duty is extended to all irrespective of
colour made it a fundamental contribution. Toynbee argues that 'Lionel was
surely the first political thinker in the Western World to hold and declare
that non-western peoples had the same human right to self-government as
Western peoples and also the same inherent human capacity for governing
themselves… '.[72] More importantly, while Curtis' ideas were vehemently
debated in the Round Table Moot in London, and were dismissed by most
members, they found gradual acceptance in the 1930s, so much so that this
became the standard liberal conception of the empire, particularly with
Chatham House. When positioning early IR debates as being between
'imperialists' and 'internationalists', then, we need to be careful to bear in

mind the colonial and racial nature of internationalism. We will explore this particularly when we turn to Canada, Australia and New Zealand.

Postcolonial scholars have amply critiqued such social Darwinist ideas of progress. Notionally, equality of non-Western peoples with their Western counterparts some time in future was recognised, the future itself however was suspended in perpetuity as non-Western peoples were held in the 'waiting room of history'.[73] As Curtis acknowledged, the possibility of India becoming an equal nation in the Commonwealth was 'too far in future'.[74]

Our eye must, however, fall on the third category in Curtis' schema that was not discussed at all within the Round Table, but came to define much of the liberal view on Africa, and its scholarship, in the interwar period: non-active citizenship. 'Non-Active Patriotism' included those categories of people who could be permanently excluded from citizenship. Curtis mentioned Criminals for instance; but this could also potentially include the African and other Indigenous subjects of the empire. Indeed, in a letter to Kerr, he acknowledged that 'the Kaffirs and the Maoris' constituted the third level of imperial hierarchy, who could not be elevated to civilisation.[75]

Reading Curtis' Commonwealth formulation more closely, especially with regard to his view on Africans, it becomes clear that Curtis actually doesn't think of the empire as one, but rather three, empires. This is elaborated in a separate memorandum in 1914, originally written by Curtis but then revised by Edward Grigg, then the co-editor of *The Round Table* who later became the Governor of Colonial Kenya, in 1914.[76]

The 1914 memorandum, called Whitsuntide Memorandum, refers to Africans and Indigenous Americans as 'child-races' and argue that they were so low on the scale of civilisation that 'it was difficult to treat them as members of the same human family'.[77] While Asians had lived for thousands of years under organised government – even if despotic – the primary form of political community for Africans was the tribe. The duty of the British in such lands thus was not one of dispensing the rule of law but 'secur[ing] to [the Africans] in perpetuity the just enjoyment of their own lands, while opening those lands to the necessary process of development, and to graft upon the present codes of law and custom, which we cannot destroy without destroying them [sic], the slips of higher form of government'.[78] What becomes clear here is that Curtis and Grigg did not think that Africans could be raised to civilisation. Indeed, without naming it, the memorandum proposes a political system that Curtis and his Kindergarten colleagues had fleshed out in much greater detail in South Africa – segregation.

It is important, here, to take a detour through the history of such racial thought, before coming to our conclusion. In South Africa, there were two fundamental motivations behind segregation. Howard Pim (1862–1934), the first one to sketch out the theory of segregation in South Africa, had argued that any prolonged contact between whites and Africans was detrimental to both.[79] In a paper presented at the Fortnightly Club we have briefly mentioned earlier, Pim noted that Africans were 'mentally and morally' inferior. Indeed, 'each race in succession has left the negroid peoples where it found them, and no civilized race has transmitted to them the distinctive features of its religion, society or knowledge'.[80] In the same club, William Honnold (1866–1950), later a close aide of Herbert Hoover and the co-founder of the South African company 'The Anglo-American' with Ernest Oppenheimer, argued that the Africans had an internal trait of 'retrograde development'. Left to themselves, the black individual is a debased being whose instincts are 'inimical to survival' and knowing 'little self-control, obligation and cooperation' is constantly moving towards self-annihilation.[81] He used this logic to argue that slavery, whatever its ills, actually saved the black population in America from self-inflicted extinction through the intervention of the 'parental' hand of the white man. However, wherever the native population resisted this parental hand, extinction was natural and sometimes the white colonisers had to push through changes quickly in the service of civilisation.

This extinction was so unnoticeable, unremarkable and ironically *extinct* for the coloniser, that in their renditions they seemed to have merely populated empty lands, or *terra nullius*. It is here that our origin story of IR takes on a genocidal turn. As we will see in Australia, *terra nullius* was continually assumed, and settlement and peopling of Australia with white subjects was seen as a key arena for foreign policy analysis.

W.S. Weber brought both of these elements – racial degeneration and retrograde development – to present an apocalyptic picture for South Africa. He argued that close contact between whites and Africans in a context where Africans were in great majority (unlike America) made the continuation of white civilisation impossible.[82] Prolonged contact between whites and Africans, both Weber and Pim argued, would lead to the extinction of the white race in South Africa.

For these writers, there were key differences between the South African version of segregation and the American one. While segregation in the US was primarily driven by racial notions of superiority of the white majority, the South African one played on cataclysmic scenarios of white extinction.[83] Hence, while the American segregation pertained mostly to access to facilities, the South African version saw territorial separation as the key element. When moved up to the pan-imperial/global scale, the South

African version allowed for imagining separate forms of political and territorial communities. It therefore provided a better model for the British Commonwealth, and even an idea for a world state, because the South African demographic composition reflected the commonwealth/global reality, where non-Europeans were in majority.

Pim, Honnold and Weber were thus key inspirations when Curtis sketched out his own scheme of segregation in a volume titled *The Government of South Africa*, and Kerr similarly endorsed it in a journal he edited, *The State*.[84] Reading Honnold's paper, Curtis later wrote that the 'longer experience of the United States has a bearing on the future composition of society in South Africa, the importance of which is difficult to overrate'.[85] In the *Government of South Africa*, Curtis acknowledged that 'the degree of liberty which acts like a tonic on European society, becomes an intoxicant when administered to a race of children endowed with the passions of grown men'.[86] In sum, the argument was that Africans were not only unlikely to cultivate Western civilisation, but also were more prone to debasing the white civilisation through their continuous contact. However, if they were completely left alone, they exhibited signs of 'retrograde development' or self-annihilation. Hence, segregation – a form of rule that allowed Africans to live within their own tribal systems with a parental hand of the whites – became seen as the best form of government.

The Whitsuntide Memorandum and the two Commonwealth books of Curtis make the same argument. The Whitsuntide Memorandum reads: 'the salvation of the more backward races [Africans] is not to be achieved by Europeans repudiating the task of control, but only by exercising control from first to last in the interest of the lower races as well as the higher'.[87] So, while Indians were the latent patriots who could be included in the Commonwealth, Africans were the non-active patriots, who, like criminals, needed to be kept under permanent supervision. This view married as it were with Boasian notions of relative development, as we will explore further in Chapter 4 on South Africa and the SAIIA, which emerged as the primary liberal ideology of the time: segregation.

For Curtis, this three-fold distinction was also reflected in the key features of each community. The dominant feature of European society was politics, and, as such, a state founded on deliberative principles was the dominant institution. Asian societies were fundamentally driven by either religion or a notion of society, meaning that their political institutions replicated the conservative, mostly authoritarian, structures of society. Africans and Indigenous populations, in contrast, were still seen as at the 'primitive' stage of social development where political institutions were absent. Politics implied a shared mutual duty beyond the bonds of blood. However, in African and Indigenous societies, ties of family and kinship underwrote what were seen as fundamentally tribal institutions. Politics, society and kinship were the governing features of the three races, European, Asian and African, respectively, making the empire 'a section of humanity cut from top to bottom' containing 'a sample of every typical layer ... under its jurisdiction'.[88] The tribal nature of African and other Indigenous peoples meant that unlike Indians (and Asians) they exhibited no trace of politics. So, Indians were to be slowly introduced to self-government, but the only salvation for Africans was permanent subjection. By bringing together two competing racial ideas of the time – social Darwnisim and segregation; racial progress and cultural (relative) development – Curtis imagined a future British Commonwealth as a segregationist racist utopia.

As we will now see throughout the rest of the book, this vision, and its analysis of race, empire and hierarchy, was the basis of much interwar IR thought. This could not be much further from the imagined idea of world peace that the Aberystwyth narrative propagates today.

THE ORIGINS OF IR'S KNOWLEDGE PRODUCTION

In this chapter, we have focused on two themes which string together this book: ideas of knowledge production and understandings of race. The Round Table movement played a considerable role in establishing them as the key ideas around which the birth of IR as a discipline is situated. Turning the 'imperial' into the 'international' required making key methodological as well as epistemological moves. The scientific method, which was strongly informed by Spencerian pretensions, helped to fashion a field which views the Commonwealth and later the World State not just as desirable outcomes, but also as teleological certainties. In this scheme, epistemic networks and their specific role in propaganda was fleshed out. Epistemologically, the greatest challenge in turning the imperial into the international is how to include those who are excluded as either equals or as exceptions. Curtis' tripartite scheme works this out by proposing a sacramental notion of the Commonwealth, imagined as the new international, as against a social contractual one. This allowed him to imagine a Commonwealth based on racial hierarchy that excluded by way of inclusion. As a result, the study of international affairs that was pioneered by the Round Table took race, racism and racialised hierarchies as their starting assumption. These ideas of race development then played out in each context in which the Round Table, and its later institutes of international affairs, was embedded.

2

Canada: From Imperial Federationism to Liberal Imperialism

With Curtis' scheme and mission determined, he set about building the Round Table network of Canada, Australia, New Zealand. Canada was the first place that Curtis visited on his Dominion tours. It was also the first of these societies to form an 'institute of international affairs', the Canadian Institute of International Affairs (CIIA). Within CIIA there was a tussle between two competing ideas: one which was basically that of Curtis, which argued that Canada should be permanently allied to the British empire. The second vision, which we call liberal exceptionalism, emerged during the 1930s and considered Canada as its own special force in the world that should be independent from the UK. Throughout the 1930s, after CIIA was established, the institution became the scene of conflict between liberal exceptionalists and the imperialist old guard. This battle extended to key financial backers of CIIA, all of whom were wealthy industrialists. Some of the old guard even withdrew their funding when the institute became more staunchly internationalist. By the beginning of the Cold War, Canada's sense of its own liberal exceptionalism had begun to dominate, limiting its sense of commitment to any idea of a greater British empire. As it did so, however, it also erased discussion of Canada's own settler imperialism from the agenda.

In this chapter, we treat this battle within the CIIA as part of IR's disciplinary history in Canada. Very few histories of IR's arrival in Canada have been written, as it is usually treated as a footnote in the discipline's history in the US. Discussion of 'Anglo-American' IR seems to refer solely to the US and the UK, even though Canada is arguably both 'Anglo' and 'American'. Sometimes, such as within Ole Waever's or Groom and Mandeville's history of 'North American' IR, Canadian (and, for that matter, Mexican) scholars, theories and ideas, though included in the geographical vision, are not cited or discussed as part of the record.[1] Holsti described the UK and the US as the 'core' of IR theory, but when critiquing a lack of diversity in IR theory, he described Australia and Canada as 'small appendages' of IR 'in other anglophone countries'.[2] Stanley Hoffman's influential piece, 'An American Social Science', refers the to the US, and not the continent.[3] When we emphasise IR's history in Canada, there is an important blurring between the establishment of IR in the US, as described by Robert Vitalis, and the Organic Unity project of Lionel Curtis which we consider here.[4]

Curtis' original imperial mission was partly aimed at drawing the US closer to the empire. Although the US was rapidly estranged from his original project after WWI, the linkages between the US and Canada take on a greater significance than that of a mere appendage. Canada, due to its position in the empire and indeed in Curtis' project, produced some distinctive work. The journal *Pacific Affairs*, produced by the IPR, published a great deal of Canadian work and was eventually moved to the University of British Columbia in the 1960s. Even before this, though, it published quite extensively on matters in Canada, Australia and New Zealand.

Although the specifics of the discipline's arrival in Canada are largely unexamined, some useful histories of Canadian international thought, strategic culture, and the historical ideologies and identities that guide its foreign policy have been produced, which gives us a base from which to proceed. Priscilla Roberts, a historian of US foreign policy, has produced one article on Canada, looking at the role of Edgar J. Tarr (1881–1950), a wealthy backer and president of Monarch Life Assurance Company, in funding CIIA.[5] Elsewhere, historians of Canadian foreign policy have written about Canadian diplomatic history, covering the ideas and ideologies of the movement including various key figures in the Canadian foreign policy establishment.[6] Here we see some detailed discussion of how Canada dealt with decolonisation, seeing itself as an anti-racist and anti-imperial power, with a special ability to engage with the postcolonial world. As Davis has argued elsewhere, however, this vision was still ultimately premised on the idea of the colonised and post-colonised world as irrational and ungrateful, and cannot be seen as straightforwardly anti-imperial or anti-racist.[7]

Kim Richard Nossal has argued that English-speaking Canadians always saw their loyalty as something broader than just Canada, and looks at how Canadian international thought and foreign policy shifted from 1867 through the Cold War.[8] From 1867 to 1918, this meant mostly British empire. After WWI, however, Canada turned isolationist, desperately hoping to avoid involvement in another European war. This was, of course, made ambivalent due to the resistance of French Canadians, meaning the 'British empire' was insufficient in describing Canadian loyalty. In this sense, the existence of different language groups has long shaped Canada's international identity and its international thought.

After WWI, Nossal displayed a loss of enthusiasm for the empire and for international engagements. Canada was a member of the LoN but sought to avoid excessive commitments to it, due to the fear of being dragged into another European war. Despite the sense of isolation, imperial connections were still central to Canada's foreign policy, and at the advent of WWII, support for Britain was still seen as a moral duty.[9] Not joining the war would have been unthinkable. Although Nossal primarily places Canada's identification within its foreign policy, these patterns of thought very much played out in the earliest versions of IR in Canada. After WWII, Canada's perception of its role in the world and a greater sense of activism expanded under Louis St. Laurent. As we will see, a more overtly racialised identity hardened in Australia partly due to its proximity to Asia, while Canada had a different experience.[10] Canada was able to unwind its racialised policies due to its distance and so had less anxiety over decolonisation in Asia. We should not, however, allow this to erase Canada's own history of settlement. Before we discuss the development of these themes in Canadian IR scholarship though, we will return to Curtis' role in founding the Round Table in Canada.

FOUNDING THE ROUND TABLE IN CANADA

Canada was the first mission of Curtis and Kerr in founding Round Table groups. Indeed, even before Curtis, Kerr and Marris travelled to Canada in September 1909, Milner went on a Canadian trip in 1908 where he discussed at length plans for establishing an empire-wide organisation with his friend Arthur J. Glazebrook, a notable financial broker in Toronto, Lord Grey, the governor general, John Willison, *The Times* correspondent in Canada, Edward Peacock, a merchant banker, and Edward Kylie, a recently returned Balliol graduate (who had become the first colonial to head the Oxford Debating Society – and unfortunately died on the front during WWI). So, when Curtis and others landed in Canada, they were received by a sympathetic group of imperial devotees. Soon after returning from Canada, Curtis started preparing *The Green Memorandum*, where he elaborated his plans for an Organic Union. He suggested that the empire had three options: cooperation, independence and Organic Union. For him, cooperation was not a viable future strategy for the empire; independence would negate it; and so Organic Union was the only possible way forward. In the Memorandum he proposed a constitutional convention (along the lines of South Africa), with the possibility of creating a federation with an imperial parliament.[11] Expecting Canadians to be the most unresponsive to his scheme, Curtis attempted to please them by predicting that 'the hegemony would inevitably pass from Great Britain to Canada' in an imperial federation, and added the incentive of being able to co-govern colonies like India.[12]

The Memorandum was debated in the Round Table groups he created in South Africa, Australia, New Zealand and Canada. He returned to Canada in early 1911 to establish more Round Table groups. Over the course of the next few years, he came to Canada two more times – in 1913 and 1916.

One of the reasons for why Curtis visited Canada more than the other Dominions was that the opposition to his scheme of imperial federation was the staunchest amongst French Canadians. Wilfred Laurier (1841–1919), Canada's first francophone premier from 1896 to 1911, was one of the strongest critics of the Round Table and their imperial ideas. He instead preferred a closer Canadian relationship with America. Later, during WWI, he bitterly criticised the Round Table 'as the junta sitting in London' which governed Canada.[13] Very few French Canadians joined the Round Table groups spread across the country. Western Canada was also more sceptical than East. Even in the East, one Toronto group, otherwise more sympathetic to the Round Table, issued a statement against what was referred to as the 'pistol policy' of either federation or separation. Robert Borden (1854–1937), who replaced Laurier in 1911 as Prime Minister and was actively courted by the Round Table, found the idea of *The Green Memorandum* 'impracticable and any advantage too remote and indirect'.[14] Borden was a 'theoretical imperialist' and remained close to the Round Table, although he could not be a federationist.[15]

The fact was that even staunch Canadian Round Tablers were never fully federationists. As one observer noted, 'even a Canadian Round Tabler was a nationalist when the chips were down'.[16] In 1915, when Curtis circulated his *The Problem of the Commonwealth*, which proposed an imperial tax to be levied by the new imperial government with portfolios of defence and foreign affairs, it was most staunchly opposed. Under Curtis' proposal, Canada's contribution for defence was to be 345 per cent of its 1913–14 level. On this, even English Canadian members of the Round Table were cautiously circumspect. They opposed the publication of the memorandum. A Montreal Round Tabler published a review of *The Problem* in a university magazine, which was picked up by a notable newspaper, *Toronto Daily Star*. *The Star* was scathing, which further sullied the Round Table's reputation as a secretive organisation plotting an imperial scheme. Facing strong opposition from the Canadian Round Table to his proposals which were to be published anonymously – as was the practice – in the name of the Round

Table collective, Curtis now resolved to publish *The Problem* in his own name. Even the staunchest of Canadian Round Tablers, such as Glazebrook and Vincent Massey (1887–1967) – a former student of Curtis at Oxford, who went on to key roles in both the CIIA and Canada's international affairs – distanced themselves from Curtis' proposals. John W. Dafoe (1866–1944), a critic of the Round Table, warned in private that 'the Canadian members of the Round Table were being shepherded along a definite path to a predetermined end … so skilfully that they realized neither the road that [they] were travelling, nor the end they were tending …'.[17]

Amidst the failure of Curtis' proposals to generate positive responses, let alone a consensus, came a significant success at the imperial level. David Lloyd George's government called an Imperial Conference in 1917, a proposal of which the London Round Table had been a strong proponent. Two of Lloyd George's key advisers were Phillip Kerr and Edward Grigg, both from the London Round Table. The Minister with whom he consulted to make this decision was Alfred Milner himself.

Robert Borden came to the Conference armed with a proposal, a significant part of which later became Resolution IX. This Resolution gave 'full recognition to the Dominions as autonomous nations of an Imperial Commonwealth'. The proposal was, as an observer noted, 'the epitaph of … Imperial Federation', as it ruled out any plans of a future imperial parliament or an imperial executive.[18] Ironically, Borden's proposal was based on a petition by the Canadian Round Table (minus a clause which proposed a new conference after the war to flesh out details of the imperial relationship),[19] which meant that London Round Table's plans had been killed by the Canadian Round Table.[20]

The key idea, imperial federation, for which the Round Table groups had been established, was now buried. This necessitated a rethinking on the purpose of the Round Table groups. London Round Table proposed a convention of the Round Table groups some time in 1917, but the idea was eventually shelved. This left little by way of energy or purpose to the Round Table groups. By 1921, most of the Canadian Round Table groups had disintegrated. In May 1921, six members – Glazebrook, Massey, J.M. Macdonnell, Percy Brown, George M. Smith and Archie Foulds – met in Toronto and acknowledged that it was not possible to revive local groups. They however agreed on supplying jointly written articles from Canada to *The Round Table*.[21]

But even in London, the main work of the Round Table had moved from plotting imperial federation to shaping institutions. Once Chatham House was established, members of the Round Table groups were also roped in to become members of the new institute. And when the London Institute opened its branches in the Commonwealth capitals, it drew on the existing networks of the Round Table. At the founding of Chatham House, ten Canadians were recruited as members.[22] By 1926 this number had increased to 26, when in a meeting in Toronto, in the presence of a representative of Chatham House, R. Wilson Harris, and John Nelson, a representative of the IPR, the group decided to form a Canadian organisation along the lines of Chatham House.

The origins of the IPR also go back to 1919 when members of the American YMCA met in Honolulu to explore a common Christian 'basis of understanding and motivations for the Pacific peoples'. After a few years of being consigned to cold storage, the effort was revived to organise another conference in Honolulu which would follow a Christian approach, but the participants need not be Christians or from the YMCA. A much more secularised form took birth in 1925 as an organisation primarily interested in studying and researching the Pacific region.[23]

Nelson travelled to London to discuss the formation of the Canadian Institute, and also extended an invitation to Chatham House to send a delegation to the next IPR Conference in Honolulu in 1927. Chatham House accepted the proposal of the Canadian Institute being affiliated to the IPR as well as of sending a delegation to Honolulu. In turn, Chatham House also became a national council of the IPR.

With all paths clear, CIIA was officially founded in January 1928 at Borden's house in Ottawa, who also became its first president. The subsequent three presidents were Newton Rowell, Vincent Massey and J.W. Dafoe, respectively. Glazebrook became honorary secretary. Borden and Rowell had been close associates of the Round Table, and Vincent Massey and Glazebrook its staunchest members.[24] Dafoe, while never a member or associate, had been in active conversation with the Round Table and indeed also contributed an article for the journal in 1926. The Pacific Council of the IPR itself came to be dominated by Round Table members or associates.[25] CIIA soon expanded into several branches. It already had 14 branches across Canada by January 1936 with a total membership of 77.[26]

THE ROUND TABLE AND CANADA

The Round Table, as we discussed in the previous chapter, was intended to circulate shared ideas around the Dominions so as to foster greater understanding and, ultimately, Organic Unity. The Round Table journal, though, did more than just report the news in these places. Each Dominion brought its own ideational discourse to this school of thought, with subtly different concerns and areas of specific interest. It was, perhaps, precisely this divide that Curtis and the Round Table were seeking to overcome. What developed, though, were subtly different schools of thought driven by the specific anxieties of each society. We might think of them as we do realism today: one broad school of thought with many variants (classical, neo, neoclassical, defensive or offensive) but still all associated with the same set of core concepts. In this case, though, rather than power, anarchy and the state, the key ingredients binding this school together were race, hierarchy and empire. In Canada, a school of thought on international and imperial affairs developed which was focused partly on its own settlement, its relationship with the US, and its place in imperial defence and later, its ability to shape world affairs as an 'activist' power.

Canada appeared in the first issue of *The Round Table*, beginning with an article covering three issues, which gives us a sense of what was important to the initial agenda. The first matter was the rebelliousness of the 'prairie provinces' in Western Canada, particularly in relation to tariff revisions. The author commented that: '[t]he social and political temper of Manitoba, Saskatchewan, Alberta and British Columbia is very like that of New Zealand and the Australian States'.[27] Following this domestic analysis, the piece moved on to discuss imperial cooperation between Canada and the empire, focused primarily on London. It closed with a consideration of the necessity of maintaining imperial naval dominance.[28] The second article took on a similar trajectory, looking at Canada's successful economic expansion, noting in particular its reliance on British capital. It then discussed Western farmer's concerns with tariffs and closed with analysis of the politics of the navy.[29] Here, there was some emphasis on the domestic settlement of Canada as shaping its international priorities.

Another article discussed the threat of republicanism in Canada and elsewhere, arguing that the monarch was central to imperial order and that without monarchy the empire would lose all meaning:

The Sovereign is the bond of Empire, the object towards which our devotion flows, the seat and centre of a common tradition and a common patriotism. With the Throne abolished and a party chief as President of a British Republic the party cleavage would run throughout the whole Empire and the Dominions become subject to the leader of a political majority in the British islands.[30]

Another author noted that the advent of WWI had led to a rise in Canadian patriotic sentiment for the empire and that this had reshaped some elements of Canadian identity. 'The war has disclosed a national spirit as intense and dominant in the West as in older Canada. It may be that in the West "Imperialism" is less vocal and that greater emphasis is laid upon the ideals of democracy. But the difference is in language rather than in spirit.' This was put down to the levels and history of settlement in Canada. In British Columbia, imperialism was different as 'for the time ... [British Columbia] is concerned to make itself rather than to remake the Empire. It has an Empire of its own to settle ...'.[31] The unity of Canada was a consistent concern in these early articles, including the differences between the Eastern and Western Canadian coasts and the settlement and opinions of the farming communities in central Canada.

The discussion of the British Imperial fleet was tied closely to racial anxieties. Another writer noted that 'the destruction of the Imperial fleet might imperil our existence as a British community or throw us upon the mercy of Washington.'[32] The author further argued that the people of British Columbia felt little connection to the people of South Africa and Australia. The protection of the British navy was linked also to fears of non-white settlement, with the author stating that 'There is no doubt that feeling on the Pacific coast runs strongly against Asiatic immigration' and '[T]here are those who fear that British Columbia is destined to become an industrial province of Japan.'[33]

A smaller stream of this thought was tied to immigration. Although there was a policy of blocking non-white immigration to Canada, as we will see in the subsequent chapter on Australia, this anxiety was less pronounced in Canada than other cases. A permanent Chinese population had been allowed to remain in British Columbia in numbers that greatly exceeded those in Australia. There were important moments where imperial defence was linked consistently to racial anxieties underpinning geopolitics. Despite the policy of blocking non-immigration, one author wrote that 'the masses of the Canadian people are essentially liberal and tolerant. They have been schooled in the wisdom of generous dealing with racial and religious minorities.'[34]

In 1921, one author commented that 'Most Canadians are ... content with the security of their isolation', and noted that the relationship with the US had become fairly easy 'as it would be highly inconvenient for the United States to have any European or Asiatic power secure a foothold in Canada.'[35] In 1923, one article discussed the matter of Asian immigration, stating that:

One is inclined to think, in a vague way, of Asiatic immigration as a Canadian problem, which causes anxiety to the people of Canada, and the peculiar difficulties of which lie in the necessity for reconciling national and Imperial objectives. But nine-tenths of the people of Canada care very little about the question ...[36]

In the same year, another author wrote that 'In British Columbia there would be energetic protest if the regulations affecting Asiatic immigration were relaxed.'[37] Although in policy terms Canada's approach to Asian immigration over this period was not that different to that of Australia and New Zealand, in emphasis and tone the matter was treated very differently. The issue featured far more often in Australian *Round Table* articles. And yet, as numerous authors have shown, Canada had quite severe restrictions placed on non-white immigration at the time.[38] There was, however, a consistent enough tethering of racial anxieties to the geopolitics of imperial defence. One author continued to argue that the 'problem' of Chinese immigration primarily affected those in Vancouver and British Columbia. The people of British Columbia, it was argued, were concerned that 'Asiatics' may gain a permanent foothold in the colony, particularly Chinese or Japanese people.[39] There was a small Indian community as well, but they were granted no specific legal status until the late 1940s.[40]

FOUNDING CIIA AND ITS INTERNAL DIVIDES

The CIIA was formally established on 30 January 1928.[41] It was the first institute that Curtis connected with Chatham House. Its founding gave a practical form to the hope that the latter's provisional committee had expressed in 1920 of the various existing groups in the Dominions and India 'hiv[ing] off' to open branches across the British empire.[42] The RIIA had indeed included in its list of original members public men from the Dominions and India – drawing largely from the pre-existing Round Table groups – precisely for this purpose. It was founded in 1928 with five branches, based in Montreal, Ottawa, Toronto, Vancouver and Winnipeg. At this stage, its membership was comprised of RIIA members, and the Round Table groups. Its national office was set up in Toronto in the early 1930s. It also developed connections with Canadian groups of the IPR. Today, the institution describes its history as arising out of the desire of its founders, Borden, Sir Arthur Currie (1875–1933) and J.W. Dafoe, to deal with 'the devastating consequences of the First World War [which] had awakened in them a strong desire to remedy a lack of public understanding of international affairs'.[43] As we will see throughout though, Canada's vision of international scholarship was defined by Curtis' original formulation, alongside the efforts of some of its key administrators and funders to produce a far more diverse, neutralist, even socialist, outlook for Canadian foreign policy, and with it the study of international affairs through CIIA. Members of the RIIA who believed in a tightly knit empire were dominant at its founding. However, younger and more social democratic members joined when the institute also became Canada's wing of the IPR. This ensured that, as its first national secretary, as Escott Reid put it, the institute had a 'divided personality'.[44]

Borden, Currie and Dafoe were indeed the three key founders of the institute. Together, they attracted a great number of Canada's intellectual, political and economic elite to join and support the study of international affairs. Currie was a journalist from Winnipeg who worked closely with Prime Minster Mackenzie King. Borden had previously been the Conservative Prime Minister of Canada from 1911 to 1920, before retiring. He was instrumental in Canada receiving Dominion status, and a strong advocate for the LoN. He also wrote a book on Canada and the Commonwealth. Currie was a Canadian General in WWI who had gained a reputation for standing up to his British superiors. Borden in particular was central, having led Canada to its ability to make its own foreign policy, and insisted upon Canada's own representation at the Paris Peace Conference. With his Chairmanship of CIIA, Borden began to look for new ways for Canada to engage with the world. Also crucial, in terms of funding, were wealthy backers like Tarr, Massey and Sir Joseph Flavelle (1858–1939). Some, such as Flavelle, believed strongly in imperial unity. Others, like Tarr, believed in Canadian neutrality.[45] Dafoe, a journalist with the Winnipeg Free Press, was the institute's first Vice-Chairman. Like Tarr, he rejected British dominance and believed in a more independent Canadian foreign policy.[46] Academic researchers Norman MacKenzie and Henry Angus, who wrote chiefly on immigration and continually published with CIIA throughout the period discussed in this chapter, were also central to the founding of the institute. As ever, the institute itself claimed a benign neutrality, seeking only to study international affairs. In practice, however, many of its leadership and funders were largely imperial-minded, wealthy and capitalist, with some important exceptions.

Unlike in Australia and New Zealand that we will examine in subsequent chapters, there was a great deal of debate and tension within the institute from the outset. Its various backers fought continually from its founding through to the 1940s over the purpose of the institute. Roberts has even argued that the institute 'championed Canadian national autonomy and sought to expand Canada's international role while challenging British imperialism, racism, and Anglo-Saxon dominance'.[47] Although we would stop short of calling this institute 'anti-racist', this does reflect a genuinely different Canadian foreign policy from that of dogmatic adherence to British imperial interests. This fight was very much political, with an emergent Canadian liberal internationalist vision of foreign policy coming through the institute, partly via the IPR. Tarr, however, sought to pull the institute in another direction entirely, along with Escott Reid, whom he backed as the institute's first key administrator.[48] The relationship between the IPR and CIIA was important in defining the character of Canadian IR scholarship in this period.

In Reid's formulation, the fight was between the crusty, imperialist old guard of the RIIA and the young, energetic leftists of the IPR, particularly himself. As shown by Roberts, Tarr's funding of the CIIA, his ideology, and indeed his support for Reid, were crucial to the contest within the institution.[49] Throughout the 1930s, debate on whether Canada should join imperial collective security or state openly a neutral foreign policy split the institute. According to Reid, in 1932, CIIA's 'sole activity' was to hold 'off-the-record talks' followed by informal discussion, for a wealthy, pro-empire elite. This was in line with the 'closed shop' approach of Curtis and the RIIA.[50] Although the debate was ultimately about what Canadian foreign policy should look like, it took the form of institutional infighting over membership, ideology and expansion. Some wished for the institute to remain small and ideologically committed, others wished for it to grow rapidly, and take in a far broader body of opinion.

Reid was a Rhodes Scholar, who had his Canadian nationalism hardened by his time in the UK and had become deeply interested in international affairs. He dropped out of a US-based PhD programme in order to take the job of the CIIA secretary.[51] As a PhD candidate he had published several articles on international affairs. He was also a ferocious networker. He had, however, a reputation for being difficult in the various positions his life in international affairs took him. Granatstein, in describing Reid's time at CIIA, noted that its leadership was largely at odds with his own style, stating that 'its leadership was politely nationalist but fundamentally imperial-minded, capitalist, anti-socialist, and far from neutralist'.[52] Reid, though, was an activist, a socialist and Canadian nationalist, and published in various magazines and journals calling for Canada to stay out of British wars. His reports on the institute's character, and his desires for it to become more diverse and open to minority opinion, further irritated the institute's funders. He urged Canadian neutrality. These positions put him quite directly in conflict with the CIIA's leadership.

Unlike many of his contemporaries who went on to high positions in Canada's international affairs (people like Humphrey Hume Wrong (1894–1954),[53] Lester Pearson (1897–1972)[54] and Arnold Heeney (1902–1970)),[55] Reid was not from such wealth that he could cover his own education. Rather, he had to go to night school and pay his own way at the University of Toronto. Only a Rhodes scholarship enabled his studies in Oxford. He became a committed socialist through these experiences.

CIIA was four years old when Reid took the job of national secretary, with one of its key goals being expansion. As Granatstein put it, he was a strong choice for the job, not just for his expertise, but because he was 'indefatigably energetic, imaginative, well connected, he spewed forth ideas for branches, meetings, speakers, conferences, and publications'.[56] His energy was useful in arranging conferences, producing research and expanding the institute. Rowell and Massey in particular were irritated that their secretary was openly partisan and calling for political positions that they disagreed with. Some were opposed to Reid's position that the institute should produce as much research as possible, finding academic debate to be overly theoretical and unnecessary.[57]

Reid, however, was so convinced that he was correct about what path the institute should take that he refused to moderate his writing or his approach to administering the institute.[58] Reid had enough backing from Tarr, however, to maintain his position, even as Massey refused to fund the institute for a year due to overemphasis on research.[59] Reid's own publications at this point even referred to imperial Canadian foreign policy as 'unintelligent', and called on Canada's armed forces to cut all links with Britain.[60]

In 1938, following seven months leave from the institute to teach at Dalhousie University, Reid wrote a special memorandum arguing for quite profound changes. He left the institute shortly after, and as such it reads as much as a resignation letter as a serious proposal for reimaging the institute. He urged that the institute should become far larger, more diverse, and more open to those who express strong opinions, both in its broader membership and in its publishing. This vision, though, was in opposition with Curtis' original framing. In his opening statement to the report he states: 'The faster the rate of the Institute development the better. The only important possible limiting factors are personnel and finance.' The 'most serious error of all', he argued, would be to become 'conservative, hide-bound, bureaucratic, afraid of new ideas in organization and policy'.[61]

Reid offered a critique, describing the institute as 'not only too predominantly, English-speaking, Protestant, of British racial origin and upper middle class, and male, its average age is also too high'. He carried on that it was too much based in major cities, and urged that the number of branches be doubled to include small cities. He also positioned the institute as excessively moderate, 'the Institute contains almost no representatives of the die-hard right or the "Lunatic-fringe" on the left. It contains few representatives of the schools of opinion next to these – the right-wing of the right, and the left-wing of the left'. In his mind, the institute contained the moderate conservatives, liberals, socialists, imperialists, nationalists and isolationists. This concerned him, though, as die-hard ideologues in Canadian society were not represented at all, stating that 'it is not only a question of getting French, the women, the immoderate, the lower middle class, the manual labourers, the farmers, etc. elected to membership of the institute, it is also a matter of getting them elected to the Institute's governing bodies'. For the institution to become properly representative, he argued, it had to include 'minority schools of opinion'.[62]

Reid noted that there may be difficulties of unity in the institute were it to grow so rapidly and become more open to different opinion, stating that 'the task of administration is difficult, thankless, and the monster of divisiveness is hydra-headed. But the attempt to maintain unity must be pursued even when it seems hopeless'.[63] The contest between ideological purity and growth, imperialism and exceptionalism, then, was a defining contest within the CIIA.

FROM *THE ROUND TABLE* TO *PACIFIC AFFAIRS* AND *INTERNATIONAL JOURNAL*

While fighting within the institute over its mission and purpose, the institute's foundational journals took shape. Throughout the 1930s, strategic analyses of international affairs, which look familiar to us today, became a more common facet of Canadian IR. In a piece of analysis that might not look out of place today, one author noted that the worst thing that could have happened to Canada would be the need to choose between 'co-operation with her oldest partner and continued good relations with her friendly neighbour'.[64] This linked Canada's role in imperial defences to its sentiments towards the Commonwealth, focusing on its particular geopolitical conditions and military skills.

Throughout this period, Canadian studies also began to appear continually in the IPR's journal *Pacific Affairs* as well as in *The Round Table*. Similar streams of thought emerged in this outlet. J.A. Stevenson argued that Canadian foreign policy as a field of study arose after WWI as, despite having already had the power to act independently, 'she had been content to allow the British Government to function as her trustee in the field of wider foreign policy'.[65] This narration of foreign policy as emerging gradually out of a process of decolonisation is telling as it draws on the colonial gradually giving way to the international. This led, in Stevenson's words, to a split in the attitude of the white Dominions, and which usefully summarise some of the differences of identity and interest we see here:

> At the Commonwealth Relations Conference, delegates from Australia and New Zealand, who lived under the shadow of possible Japanese aggression, were amazed at, and openly bewailed, the indifference of Canadian delegates to schemes of Imperial defense; but they came to realize that a sense of security, which they could only envy, was largely responsible for this attitude.[66]

As we will see in subsequent chapters, this anxiety played out in Australian and New Zealand international thought as well. The colonial projects of these two states as well as their anxieties about Asia's proximity were examined in far more detail in their emergent study of world affairs. Angus drew on this same stream of thought, commenting that 'It is probable that Canadians in general think of themselves as passive spectators of events for which they have no responsibility and from which they would do well to hold aloof.'[67] He continued that, still, Canada's influence in world affairs arguably had 'momentous consequences'. Here, we see a blending of narratives, in which Canada was both aloof in world affairs but had the potential to play a special and outsized role in world affairs due to its perceived liberal exceptionalism.

Despite the idea that Canada might not side with the UK and get involved in imperial wars, Canada joined WWII as soon as the UK did. As Nossal put it, this was still seen as an absolute moral imperative. Of course, the war took up most of Canada's international focus, with its publishing and analysis overwhelmed by military imperatives. The aftermath of WWII, though, saw the height of Canada's belief in its own liberal exceptionalism.

POST-WWII AND THE FOUNDING OF INTERNATIONAL JOURNAL

After WWII and with Canada's perception of its role in the world expanding, the CIIA expanded its own mission. It began new avenues of publication, planning a book series and creating the first wholly Canadian run journal: *International Journal*. As we will see in Australia, the corresponding journal there echoed Curtis' original imperial mission: the gathering of facts for the betterment of world order. This was not quite the case in Canada. *International Journal*'s opening editorial discussed its mission:

> Canada has a peculiar place in the community of nations and a unique opportunity to make a significant contribution to the cause of international understanding. We have escaped the physical destruction of the past six years; by our contribution to the victory, we have earned a right to be heard ...[68]

The mission statement of the journal reflected a sense of liberal exceptionalism and a desire for Canada to become more actively engaged with world affairs and as having a special ability to understand world politics. It continued:

> [W]e are so situated as to understand with sympathy both the purposes and the prejudices of the great nations; and, in general, we enjoy the trust and respect of great and small nations alike. Canada has today an opportunity for leadership in world affairs that comes seldom to a nation of twelve million people. But to be able to grasp this opportunity there must be more than action by our political leaders.[69]

This framing of the journal's role in this mission was to be a little different from that of *The Round Table* or, as we will see, the journal's Australian contemporary *Australian Outlook*. *International Journal* was focused on ensuring that the Canadian foreign policy was 'supported by the informed and thoughtful public opinion of Canadians generally',[70] and stated the hope that 'the *International Journal* may contribute in a substantial way to the knowledge of Canadians on problems of international relations and may also express to other countries the Canadian viewpoint on international questions'.[71] Canada could only implement its newfound activist foreign policy 'if it is able to reflect in its columns the vision and tolerance and leadership in ideas that Canada should contribute to world opinion today'.[72]

Given the mission of CIIA and *International Journal* in 1946 in improving and expanding Canada's role in the world, we will close this chapter with a consideration of ways in which this new Canadian journal dealt with imperial hierarchy in its first few years. Although there was some considerable debate and diversity in the first years of the journal, the majority of the articles were from English-speaking men, with the exception of articles in French by the *Quebecois*. However, there were, even in the first issue, considerable differences in approach to world affairs. There were articles supportive of colonialism, one urging socialism and decolonisation, a classical realist approach to the United Nations (UN), and those urging world government or strong international law.

To begin, Fowler followed up his editorial with a call for new forms of international law to 'repair the strained fabric of civilization'. The journal was to be politically neutral in the partisan sense, but had a quite clear foreign policy agenda. Canada, he argued, had a special role in the world, and CIIA had a special role in Canada's international policies. His earlier call for a more activist Canadian foreign policy was tied here to CIIA's two main activities, as through 'research and public education, facts and opinions are gathered and made available to the Canadian people for their assistance in the development of international policies'.[73] He carried on, 'what is needed are facts – some solid ground on which the law can have its chance. This study and collection of facts is the objective of the research activities of the institute'.[74] He continued that once the facts had been gathered, they had to be disseminated and discussed, hence the need for publication. The goal of his desired broadening of international law was to regulate the conduct of states. Even though the mission behind Curtis' method had dissipated and the imperial federation had been replaced with what would become a fairly loose Commonwealth and the UN, the method for the study of international affairs remained more or less the same.

Aside from calls for greater power for international law, calls for world government were fairly common in the first few years of *International Journal*. Willson Woodside similarly argued that the UN could not guarantee security unless it could set up a 'World Peace Force'.[75] G.V. Ferguson argued that a 'wide and enlightened' establishment of the Marshall Plan could bring a broad group of nations together to be a step towards world government'.[76]

Analyses and discussion of what Canada's role in this emergent world order should be were commonplace. Malcom MacDonald typified the liberal exceptionalist attitude, arguing that Canada could become a 'New Moral Force in the World'.[77] A slate of articles on Canada's role in the world were released in 1948. A.R.M. Lower wondered what Canada should do in the new 'non-British world' stating that 'Before 1940, Canada in a spiritual and emotional sense, was not much more than a new-born infant with its umbilical cord still unsevered.' Lower criticised the growing internationalist orthodoxy and critiqued new Prime Minister Louis St. Laurent's foreign policy, stating that 'Canadians must come to realize that their country, while capable of much, is not capable of conduct appropriate to a great power'.[78]

There were some commentaries by politicians published as well, which tended to follow this line of liberal internationalism and call for greater Canadian involvement in the world. Canada's Prime Minister Mackenzie King briefly discussed the nature of Canadian citizenship and the lessons of its experience for emerging world order. His analysis of the success of Canada drew on racial differences, but did so in a racialised manner:

> The nationhood of Canada is not based on the superiority of a single race, or of a single language. Canada was founded on the faith that two of the proudest races in the world, despite barriers of tongue and creed, could work together, in mutual tolerance and mutual respect, to develop a common nationality.[79]

King was referring not to a multiracial or multicultural Canada, but to the French and the English forging a common Canadian identity. He made the argument for a special role for Canada in international affairs on this basis:

But if the unity of Canada is vital to us it is also of great importance to the community of nations. Only by extending throughout the world the ideals of mutual tolerance, of racial co-operation, and of equality among men, which form the basis of Canada's nationhood, can nationality come to serve Humanity.[80]

Another MP, Gordon Graydon, called for Canada to 'deepen her roots in the soil of world affairs'.[81] In a more curious addition to this stream of thought, Daniel Spry, a Canadian Major General in WWII, argued that the establishment of the Boy Scouts globally would assist in the creation of One World.[82]

Although this liberal internationalism in which Canada could be crucial was perhaps the primary stream of thought, there was still diversity. Edmond Turcotte suggested that the foundation of peace lay not in 'pacts, treaties alliances or blocs. It lies only in respect and understanding amongst the peoples of the earth', and examined the role of UNESCO in achieving cultural understanding.[83] Malcolm Wallace's musings on 'The Human Situation Today', presented a dark vision of world affairs, but ultimately took this internationalist vision further. Noting the failure of the LoN, he argued that the newly founded UN would have to give way for world government if a permanent peace was to be achieved.[84] Although race was an undercurrent in his analysis, noting that 'Anglo-Saxons are an intensely practical race who are little given to philosophizing', what this world government would mean for the colonial world was not explored.[85]

There was dissent to this vision of imperialism and world order, as well, however. F.R. Scott wondered what the rise of socialism might do to the already decentralising British Commonwealth, noting that one of the more profound effects might be racial equality. He wondered whether socialism might prevent Australia and New Zealand from accepting UN trustee-ships.[86] The rise of socialism, he thought, 'means the end of old-style empire and the beginning of a new programme of economic and social planning for the benefit of the common people of every race and creed'. This leads to the question of whether or not, with the end of empire, the Commonwealth would hold together tightly. Scott's answer was that a multi-racial Com-monwealth would remain close because the institution went 'beyond nation and race' and drew on ideals that were 'common to all civilized and demo-cratic peoples'.[87] He concluded that 'In the new world that is in the making there is a greater opportunity than ever before for Commonwealth coun-tries to keep in the forefront of and to give leadership to the forces, both spiritual and material, which seek to establish a global system of peace based on social justice'.[88]

Though the focus on peace was common, the means of achieving it were of course contested. John Humphrey, a scholar at Magill University, empha-sised the state and anarchy, suggesting that, even if the UN could construct a detailed legal order, it could not have 'achieved its principal object of maintaining international peace and security. The simple fact is that the units would have been too strong for the whole, and the government, although legally supreme, could not have controlled its subjects'.[89] Another author suggested that 'Law and obedience are the results of pacification, not their basis'.[90]

Colonial matters were a fairly common concern in these early years. R.G. Trotter argued in 1946 that all the member states of the newly formed British Commonwealth were colonial powers and considered how Canada could be thought of in this way. Trotter mapped Canada's colonial expan-sion through Manitoba, the Yukon and the Northwest Territories, the last of which was still under a form of colonial governance. Trotter noted that most of the inhabitants of the Northwest Territories were of 'Aboriginal stock, Eskimo and Indian, and necessarily still dependent upon the Dominion'.[91] He continued that the Canadian government and people were responsible for lifting these groups 'from a primitive coulter to assimilation into the national society of Canada' and noted that this was an imperial responsibility. The argument, though, was framed in acknowledging the imperial nature of this relationship and around doing a better job at this responsibility. Canada had failed in its responsibility as an imperial power, and Trotter hoped that by acknowledging this Canada could 'observe more objectively and understand more sympathetically than sometimes they have done, the colonial problems of other powers'. The goal of this, for Trotter, was to allow Canada to engage more with the world and to 'discard the blinkers of North American complacency'.[92]

Issues of immigration were also part of the Canadian discipline, though not quite granted the significance they were in Australia. Angus discussed Canada's immigration policy, but did not discuss it in racial terms, leaving it unclear if he supported non-white immigration.[93] A similar argument was made by H.L.K. Keenleyside, who called for greater immigration to Canada to advance the nation, but did not delve into the further winding back of racialised restrictions.[94] A year later, Angus considered the possible costs and benefits of granting citizenship to the 1,700 strong population of Indians in Canada, and allowing a quota of Indians to emigrate, noting that such a decision might assist India remain in the Commonwealth.[95] He ultimately argued for the deracialisation of immigration, but for a quota system, stating that:

> Exclusion based on race is discourteous and so is racial disfranchisement. Rules applied to all races and nations alike are not insulting. Immigration can be controlled by national quotas and in Canada almost any method of calculation would accord to Asiatic races quotas so low that they would barely suffice for what might be called humanitarian immigration – the admission of wives and children of permanent residents of Canada.[96]

This is precisely the approach that the Canadian government eventually took, although, it should be noted, some Indian diplomats later found the quota and the use of it to bring husbands and wives to Canada to be insulting.[97]

The transnational circulation of ideas was evident too. An Australian author, prominent in the following chapter, Douglas Copland, published in the first year of the journal on Australia's attitude towards the British Commonwealth.[98] He argued that Australia was seeking greater autonomy for Dominions within the Commonwealth, but that this should not be seen as weakening the basic structure of the institution.[99] However, he also suggested that Australia was keen to use its new international status in order to promote liberal economic policy and to 'lift the living standards of backward people' in Australia's region.[100]

Canadian IR was no longer talking about settlement. The liberal exceptionalist vision had become dominant, which relied on the excision of colonial violence from Canadian history and identity. Canadian IR was fighting over the extent to which Canada should be enmeshed in the British empire, contrasted with Canada as an independent and activist international power. By the time *International Journal* was publishing regularly, this liberal internationalist stream of thought had turned to building strong international institutions to manage world order and bridge Cold War tensions.

CIIA AND THE LIMITS OF AN IMPERIAL IR

The CIIA, and the origins of IR in Canada, speak to the limits of Curtis' vision, and how the study of the international was transformed by the domestic and ideational conditions. The slow and incomplete overthrow of the pro-imperial thinkers within the Round Table and the CIIA by Reid, Tarr and their IPR-influenced colleagues represented how Canada's cultural context broke down the study of the international by a closed shop of imperialists. By the time *International Journal* was created, there was a great deal of intellectual diversity in Canada's IR community. There were the beginnings of the state-as-actor in anarchy model, but there were also imperial sentiments, and, more dominant, pleas for strong international laws, institutions, even world government. Importantly, though, this was still wrapped in an echo of Curtis' original vision through the initial editorial: the collection and dissemination of facts for the improvement of world order and imperial relations.

Canada's internationalist vision at the end of WWII, despite its supposed greater detachment from Britain and its fading empire, still included something fundamental to Curtis' vision for world order: a desire to control and maintain world affairs. In this vision, control was to be held by liberal international institutions rather than an empire. The liberal exceptionalist narrative which took over CIIA after WWII erased discussion of the settlement of Canada as part of international affairs. Ultimately, Reid and Tarr's vision was incomplete as anti-racist or anti-imperial. It saw the Canadian state as a benign and positive actor in international affairs that could play a 'special' role.

As we will see next, this stands in some considerable contrast to IR in Australia. Australia's frontier settlements were seen as perhaps the key international issue, a position which lasted well into the 1940s.

3

Australia: Race, Settlement and Understandings of the International

The Australian story of the Round Table dovetails neatly with that of Canada. There existed a similar debate to that in Canada, in which Australia considered the extent to which it should remain allied with the British empire. However, in this chapter we go deeper into the connection between race, empire and the early study of IR. In the Australian case, there were close, and as yet largely unacknowledged, ties between the study of the international in Australia and the Australian colonial project itself. Here, we look at the ways in which Australian international thought looked at race and the international, beginning with Curtis' efforts to set up the Round Table. Australia's international thought was deeply connected to 'domestic' concerns about race, empire and settlement. These concerns eventually radiated outwards into what we think of today as the international.

Australian disciplinary histories, with a few important exceptions, have tended to focus on the 1960s onwards, and thereby bypassed the colonial origins of the discipline.[1] Martin Indyk's history of Australian IR begins with J.D.B. Miller's taking up of Walter Crocker's vacant chair at the Australian National University (ANU) in 1962, and thus cuts out early Australian IR.[2] J.D.B. Miller begins his narrative with the establishment of the AIIA and wrote to celebrate 50 years since its establishment, though he highlights the quality of some books on Australia in the world produced prior to 1933.[3] Richard Devetak's brief survey of Australian IR's history mentions Curtis in passing to suggest that he was a vocal advocate for an imperial federation at a time when the idea had largely passed.[4] Cotton refers to Curtis and the Round Table in his summation of an Australian School of IR as having its heyday but describes this as having passed quickly.[5]

In perhaps the broadest and most useful contribution though, James Cotton argues that there were eight key thinkers who made up an 'Australian School' of IR prior to the 1960s and that they were engaged in teaching, thinking and writing throughout the 1930s. This school included Frederic Eggleston (1875–1954),[6] A.C.V. Melbourne (1888–1943),[7] W. Harrison

Moore (1867–1935), H. Duncan Hall (1891–1967),[8] W.K. Hancock (1896–1988),[9] Fred Alexander (1899–1996),[10] W. Macmahon Ball (1901–1896)[11] and Walter Crocker.[12] Although Cotton notes some of the racial doctrines discussed, particularly regarding the South Pacific, he tends to emphasise the international thinking and teaching that was done, largely through the analytical themes of imperialism and internationalism.[13] This work provides us with some considerable historiography from which to proceed.

Within these histories there is a tendency to look at the period through rose-tinted glasses, or to ignore domestic, racial and imperialist language as 'not IR'; to point to the quality of work that was done,[14] even to write in celebration,[15] rather than to interrogate critically the history of the discipline and what it means for how we think today. As we will see continuously throughout the chapter, ideas of empire, race and hierarchy were constant assumptions of Australia's early IR and not mere undercurrents to be forgotten or underplayed. As with Canada, there were important imperial notes to the prevalent 'internationalist' thought as well.

The depth of the forgotten history of imperialism buried in Australia's development of IR is troubling for a discipline whose foundational assumptions are being destabilised by critique of the Eurocentric and imperial origins.[16]

In Australia, the scientific study of international affairs immediately became connected with the deep-seated fears of non-white immigration which came with Australian settlement. This, of course, was also the case in Canada and New Zealand. The Australian case, though, was particularly intense. In the early 1900s, Australian identity was very much tethered to the British racial ideologies. The tropical regions of Northern Australia were thought of as 'foreign' or 'Asian', while the temperate South Eastern corner of Australia was seen as having a more hospitable climate for settlement. Australia had become a Dominion in 1901 and Curtis arrived just under ten years later. The 'Immigration Restriction Act', often known as the White Australia policy, was the first act to pass Australia's federal parliament once Dominion status was received. Though Curtis was struck by the possibility that Australia might drift away from the British empire, Australia saw itself as a vast outpost of British civilisation still requiring colonial settlements and threatened by 'overpopulated' Asia to the North. The idea which would go on to become *terra nullius* – that Australia was 'empty' and 'unsettled' – prior to the arrival of The First Fleet in 1788 still dominated Australia's identity discourse and the way it imagined the world. Unlike in New Zealand, Indigenous Australians were denied any place in 'civilised' society and did not receive acknowledgement of their humanity until a referendum in 1967. Their centuries of habitation remain unacknowledged in the Australian constitution. The Australian case, as we will discuss in Chapter 5, was looked upon scornfully in New Zealand's own thought on race and empire. These two societies in particular built their identities through comparison with the other, which was reflected in their international thought.

Here, we trace the founding of IR in Australia from Curtis' tour in Australia through to the institutional foundations of IR, including the establishment of the AIIA, Australia's first IR journals through to the establishment of the first Chair in International Relations at ANU in Canberra. Throughout, IR's arrival in Australia produced a school of thought in which hierarchy was not so much a category for critical analysis but a deeply ingrained assumption. As we might expect from our discussions in Chapter 1 about the Round Table's foundations in discussing segregation, immigration and race development in South Africa, civilisational and racial hierarchy were viewed as a natural and desirable element of international affairs. Caution, even hostility, towards decolonisation was also consistent after WWII. Scholarship and the knowledge it produced was tied to government and governance, with the belief commonly held that new knowledge would produce a better reality. The discipline was also an intellectual front for Australia's own colonial mission in New Guinea and Nauru. These elements of Australian international thought echo the Round Table's original premise, the identity project of Organic Union, and the scholarly means for accomplishing it, which were all present in the construction of Australia's IR scholarship.

THE ROUND TABLE IN AUSTRALIA

Lionel Curtis arrived in Sydney on 16 September 1910, directly from Canada, and toured Australia for three months. He spent his time primarily in New South Wales and Victoria, which were subsequently the two strongest bases for the Round Table movement and the first colonies to form the AIIA. Travelling with his Round Table colleague John Dove, he was also able to establish branches in Queensland and South Australia. They met with a prolific number of dignitaries over these three months, seemingly never eating a meal without some discussion and advocating for their project. Alfred Deakin (1856–1919), the former Prime Minister, by then in failing health, was the key facilitator for recruitments for the group in Melbourne. Thomas Davin, Deakin's private secretary and later the premier of New South Wales, was one of these 'suitable men'. A key recruit was

Eggleston, a lawyer, who became the central organising figure for the Round Table groups in Australia, and later the main force behind the Australian Institute.[17] Eggleston had been present in the foundational meeting at the Hotel Majestic, and was central until his death in 1954. The Melbourne branch went on to become one of the longest-surviving branches of the Round Table.[18]

Curtis met with a series of politicians, wealthy members of society, businessmen and academics. He met with the Prime Minister Andrew Fisher (1862–1928) and, believing he would not turn the discussion towards the possibilities of Organic Union, instead enquired about the possibilities of Asian immigration.[19] Although he gained many supporters on this tour, he was met with some resistance. He wrote of one Australian, a barrister called Mann, who had travelled back to England and been struck by 'how utterly foreign to himself was the social structure and the emotions of society there'. This person 'could not help thinking it was lucky there was 13,000 miles between the two countries, otherwise misunderstandings would be much more frequent … That they could be united in any kind of organic system of government seemed to him inconceivable'.[20]

Curtis ultimately found, however, that the idea of an Organic Unity between the British Dominions held some considerable appeal for Australia's intellectual classes.[21] He travelled again to Australia in 1916, where the Round Table network was both robust and expanding. His public lectures organised by the local Round Table groups were attended by audiences ranging from 200 to 600 people, which pleased Curtis. He felt vindicated at his method of organising only the elite and dedicated audience to the work of reorganising the empire, which was 'the only work which is worth doing', as opposed to changing opinions through mass media and publishing. His focus was on influencing 'one percent of the voters', those who were key influencers, 'provide that such men [w]ere sufficiently diffused and not confined to one political party'.[22] He was astounded by how quickly the public opinion had transformed in favour of the empire by these 'few dozen of men … and the few thousand readers of *The Round Table* magazine'.[23]

Australia did not make the first issue of *The Round Table*. It made its first appearance in the second issue. This article sought to provide a political update and description of the situation in Australia, but also included a full-throated defence of the White Australia policy. Such defences were commonplace in the Australian updates in the journal. This suggestion and its explanation were generally coupled with a narrative of Australian settlement as background to its necessity. 'To those unacquainted with local conditions the cry for a "White Australia" may seem somewhat hysterical, but there is no question upon which the people are more united and determined.'[24] This suggests not just an anxiety about Asian immigration but an anxiety that the other Dominions might not understand it. The justification continued that the entire Australian political community supported this, with the author stating that, after a consideration of the trouble caused by Chinese migrants, 'when outsiders appreciate the menace involved in the proximity to our empty north of hundreds of millions of land-hungry Asiatics, they will perhaps sympathize with the view held in common by all parties in Australia'.[25] Such tirades remained a common facet of this earliest form of Australian IR.[26]

The need for a White Australia policy was such common knowledge in Australia that a later article discussing imperial defence suggested it was not worth the time to make argument that Australia had to be wary of the '"the Yellow peril" [as] [a]ll thinking men now subscribe to defence policies which involves this assumption'. The author concluded that Australia sees 'peaceful immigration of eastern races as equally dangerous with conquest'.[27] An article that generated wide discussion within Round Table circles, written by Eggleston, summarising Australian views, explicitly stated that not only was 'White Australia' an article of faith for total exclusion, 'a peaceful penetration [of Australia by Asiatics] is more to be feared than real war'. If Germany or the US were to seek 'the vacant spaces of Australia, and Australia found it impossible to resist, she might, without seriously impairing her future, give up a portion of Australia'. There was no fundamental conflict with white races. But with 'an Eastern race [that is, Japan] the conflict of ideals and of civilization is fundamental'.[28]

Terra nullius was an inherent assumption as well, with another author writing on the labour movement that White Australia 'means the reservation of the whole Commonwealth territory for the exclusive occupancy of people of European stock'.[29] Within these early articles, the Northern Territory was narrated as foreign to Australia, with white settlement of the territory becoming a foreign policy goal.[30] This suggests very much that the Round Table's work in Australia was dominated by imperial racial ideologies and notions of racial development. We can see here that in the Australian context, the gathering and dissemination of international 'facts' is very much tied to its own domestic population and settlement.

Over the course of WWI, political and war reporting came to the fore of the journal's focus, with less discussion of immigration and identity. Support for the war was a constant. In 1915 *The Round Table* looked at conscription and the course of WWI, arguing that Australia had to understand that it is being defended from Gallipoli. Stating that 'Truly, if there is any part of the

British empire which ought to comprehend this fact, it is Australia, the one continent upon the globe which is governed by a homogeneous race.'[31] Interest in the South Pacific was also sparked by WWI, given the existence of some German colonies in the area. The Australian reports began to include detailed discussion of Australian policy towards the South Pacific.[32] This was maintained after WWI, when in 1920 Australia took possession of New Guinea as its first colony. The Australian mandate in New Guinea would continue to be a major subject in Australian IR. The policies discussed in *The Round Table* related to the best way to ensure the advancement of New Guinea's 'primitive' or 'stone age'[33] people while ensuring they did not settle in Australia. Nauru also became a focus, after becoming another Australian mandated territory.[34] Having received mandated territories, Australia's IR community began to look beyond just imperial politics of settlement in Australia and towards its own imperial projects in the South Pacific. At this point, Australia's international concerns were still colonial but the focus had moved beyond Australia's own settlement.

Aside from settlement, the other issue which consistently concerned Australia's IR community at this point was taking part in imperial conferences. Each imperial conference was met with a detailed report on the Australian perspective in *The Round Table*. This is unsurprising as, at this point, imperial conferences largely determined Australia's position in colonial, and therefore global, affairs. The 1926 report on Australia noted the difficulties between the Canadian and the British government as concerning and approved of the Australian government's approach of '[improving] by all practicable means the present system of consultation'.[35]

There were occasional moments of dissenting policy within these many anonymous reports on Australia's place in the world. One author, discussing the nature of Australia's maritime defence, noted 'the difficulty of reconciling the claim to racial equality with the White Australia dogma'.[36] Another focused on the problems created by the White Australia policy, without offering an endorsement or an explicit rejection of it limiting the development of some industries, as white colonisers had higher expectations of pay.[37]

These moments, however, were few and far between.

Australia's commentary on international affairs was framed around its engagement with the empire and Britain, imperial conferences and tropical Northern Australia. Over the first 20 years of articles in *The Round Table*, this gradually came to include Australia's engagement with the South Pacific, primarily through its new imperial obligations in its mandated territories. The Round Table continued to work on Empire-Commonwealth relations throughout the 1920s, with major contributions from Eggleston and Hancock.

FOUNDING THE AUSTRALIAN INSTITUTE FOR INTERNATIONAL AFFAIRS

The founding of the AIIA both reflected and further enabled a more global outlook on how Australia studied the rest of the world. At the same time, it offered deeper connections to London and the RIIA. Working from London, Curtis led the transformation, based on the model provided by Canada.[38] Though he was involved personally, of course much of the detail was ultimately down to the IPR and the RIIA groups in Victoria and New South Wales.

Discussions began in 1929 on merging the New South Wales branch of the RIIA with the IPR groups. It would then be affiliated with the RIIA, as had happened with the CIIA a few years before. This was to be done along the same lines as in Canada, with institutional subscriptions to continue and full privileges of membership of the RIIA provided to Australian members when they were in London.

There were some tensions within Australia over the name, with the secretary of the New South Wales branch of the RIIA concerned that the proposed institute 'could not properly be called the "Australian" Institute if it did not include the Victorian division of the existing Australian branch.'[39] Ian Clunies Ross (1899–1959), a Round Table member best known for his contribution to veterinary science, was also keen to ensure no rise in subscription price and a reciprocal membership for members of Australians and Canadian institutes. These terms were all thought of as tenable by the secretary of the RIIA in Victoria, Tristian Buesst, on the proviso that a similar arrangement be made in Victoria, though ensuring that the body would eventually become federalised.[40]

This was supported strongly by Ross, as he believed it would result in 'one strong and united body ... which will be able more effectively to stimulate and maintain interest in International Affairs.'[41] Chatham House reacted very positively to the news of negotiations and had only two conditions on these: that membership be confined to British subjects and that the institute not express any opinions on any aspect of international affairs.[42] This is very much in line with Curtis' original formulation: a narrow viewpoint on the world affairs (almost exclusively white Anglo-Saxon men) coupled with a sense of political objectivity that no one else could access. A few members were reluctant and, identifying more with London than with Australia, wished to maintain their Chatham House membership instead of joining the new institute.[43] It was decided that those members who had joined Chatham House prior to the existence of its branches in Australia could maintain their London-based membership.[44]

Following the successful establishment of the New South Wales branch of the AIIA, attention turned to creating a Victorian branch. The Victorians, though, were rather warier of the move, though they did not dismiss it out of hand. There were concerns that it may negatively affect other intellectual groups, such as the LoN Union and the Round Table groups. They cited the loss of revenue created by merging the IPR and the Victorian RIIA, as several people were members of both groups. They also questioned whether the move would foster greater cooperation between the Victorian branch and London given that they already cooperated substantially and shared a joint secretariat.[45] Still, these difficulties were overcome, and in early 1933 Victoria and Queensland branches joined the institute and a Common-wealth Council was formed.[46] With this merger, the body was formally constituted. The institute's first executive was made up of W. Harrison Moore,[47] K.H. Bailey, Edmund Piesse,[48] Tristan Buesst, Alfred Stirling, Douglas Copland,[49] Eggleston, P.D. Phillips, Ernest Scott and G.L. Wood.[50] Tasmania, South Australia and Western Australia would soon follow suit. Eggleston was also to represent the institute with the Pacific Council of the IPR. One woman, Eleanor Hinder, was involved at the high levels of the institute as the Australian member of the IPR programme committee.

At the meeting in which the AIIA was established, the three bodies selected their research priorities, which strongly reflected the direction that Australian IR was taking. Amidst all the administrative details, the priorities were telling. Victoria was to focus on the 'peopling of Australia' and land utilisation, Queensland was to focus on the issues relating to the 'problems of tropical Australia' with 'special reference to settlement', and New South Wales was to focus on the mandated territories of New Guinea and Nauru, with 'special reference to the Government of dependences in the Pacific'.[51] Another key research priority for the AIIA as a whole, worthy of a subcommittee of its own based in Canberra, was East Asian relations. Each of these priorities was related to Australia's own anxieties about its population and its colonial project. They reflected Australia's identity and issues with the international at the time. Within Australia's white identity discourse, the north of Australia has long been narrated as 'unsettled', 'foreign' or even as part of Asia. In this case, this was so strongly felt that managing the Northern Territory was placed within the remit of interna-tional affairs. Land management and the discussion of immigration procedures were Australia's key international priorities. The domestic, imperial, international and race were blurred by these priorities.

The final priority, though, the maintenance of Australia's imperial possessions reveals even more deeply the imperial nature of international affairs at this time. Australia's management of New Guinea and Nauru, today both used as secretive detention centres for housing refugees who arrive in Australia by boat, were Australia's colonial projects. Most of these issues were ever present subjects for discussion in *The Round Table*. The addition of East Asia was in some ways a departure from the purely colonial focus of Australian IR. As we will see below, these territories were frequent topics of Australia's first IR journal which was formed by the Victorian branch of the AIIA. This focus stood alongside the Northern Territory and Australia's colonial possessions as subjects for anthropological study under the banner of IR. We can see also, however, how East Asia was viewed as a key international issue for Australia.

AUSTRALIA'S FIRST IR JOURNAL:
THE AUSTRAL-ASIATIC BULLETIN

With the establishment of the AIIA, the Victorian arm of the institute decided to establish the first Australian IR journal. *The Austral-Asiatic Bulletin* was published by the Victorian branch of the AIIA from 1937 to 1946, before being replaced by a journal seeking to represent the institute nationally. Its editorial board was comprised of some familiar figures: Eggleston, Macmahon Ball, E.C. Dyason, P.D. Phillips and Ernest Scott. Its mission statement in the opening editorial, most likely written by some combination of the names above, discussed its goals, again describing them as apolitical:

> The 'Austral-Asiatic Bulletin', concerned as it is to review and comment upon current opinion regarding the Orient, does not espouse the easy solution of international problems – that of finding a scapegoat and assigning him to the wilderness. It is committed to the wider but less easy task of ascertaining the facts and summing up the evidence.[52]

The editorial continued, stating that this commitment to objectivity would not make the journal shy away from opinion. Indeed, it was hoped that the bulletin would lead to a greater mutual understanding between Australia and 'the Orient'. Australia was even deemed to be part of the Orient:

The Australian Institute of International Affairs, the Victorian Branch of which publishes 'The Austral-Asiatic Bulletin', is forbidden by its Constitution to pass judgment, but unless discussion is to become unreal and devitalized, complete freedom must be granted to informed personal opinion. Only thus can Australia become better acquainted with and more curious about the Orient, of which she is part. Only thus can the neighbour nations understand her better.[53]

The construction of Australia's relationship with Asia here is curious. Although it frames Australia as part of the 'Orient', there are clear divisions drawn as well, even in the hyphenation of the title of the journal. Within this, though, the knowledge produced was continually racialised, which was made even clearer when the focus fell on the White Australia policy and on the 'race development' in Australia's colonial possessions.

Although it was similar in terms of its method and mission, *Austral-Asiatic Bulletin* departed from *The Round Table* in some substantial ways. Rather than six or seven lengthy articles, the journal comprised of around 15 short articles each covering one to three pages. Almost all articles were published with the author's name attached, though some used pseudonyms. Some familiar topics were covered frequently, including the development of Northern Australia, colonisation in New Guinea and the pitfalls of immigration from Asia. Australia's place in imperial defences and the Commonwealth remained a subject, while a few discussions of Australia's relationship with the US took place. These connections, for the first few years prior to WWII at least, were the primary way in which the rest of the world was discussed in Australian IR.

The first article in the journal, by Charles Hawker, a politician in the Nationalist Party (a forerunner to today's Liberal Party) was titled 'Wanted: An Australian Policy'.[54] It discussed the occasional clashes between Australian interests and 'imperial patriotism', arguing that it would be beneficial to all parties if Australia was to take more responsibility for its own defence. He did so, though, with a slightly different justification to Curtis' original formulation of Organic Union: Australia could not 'treat British statesmen as super-men'.[55] Debate on the big picture of Australian foreign policy centred on the extent to which Australia could strike out on its own and develop its own international policy. Most, if not all, though, still saw themselves as part of a transnational network of Britishness, which offered Australia overwhelming benefits.

The study of New Guinea became even more common with the advent of the new journal. One anonymous article wondered what would become of

New Guinea if, as the Germans had demanded, Australia lost its mandate and they received all of their old colonies back.[56] Another anonymous author looked at problems of the New Guinean workforce in promoting the progress of the population.[57] E.W.P. Chinnery published a brief anthropological report on his experiences of touring New Guinea, focusing on native practices of sorcery, magic and religion and the summoning of ancestral ghosts.[58] Chinnery was later hired on the basis of these experiences as Minister for the Interior, to implement Prime Minister John McEwan's plans to manage Aboriginal affairs.[59] He argued that 'the Australian aborigine is not inferior to the natives of Papua or New Guinea'. Such reports were common enough. Alexander Rentoul described his successes in 'taming head hunters and cannibals to accept the white man's burden and abandon their care-free ways', and described searching the jungle until, at the end of the day, having a translator meet with some 'near naked savages'.[60]

Aside from this explicit 'white man's burden', race remained a consistent topic in the new journal. This included the White Australia policy, the Northern Territory and colour prejudice. Herbert Gepp argued that the lack of settlement of Northern Australia, even prior to white settlement, was to do with the inhospitable nature of the territory. The primary barriers to white settlement were tropical diseases and that women did not want to live there. For women to want to settle in the Northern Territory, improvement to living conditions would be needed including 'suitable types and colours of [women's] clothing and underclothing must be continually studied and improved'.[61]

Following up on this argument, Ernest Scott suggested that Asians did not want to settle in Australia in any case, rendering changing Australian immigration procedures irrelevant. He argued that 'the supposition that there are thousands of Asiatic eager to people Northern Australia is sheer nonsense'.[62] Although this minimised the threat of invasion, it also negated the need to allow Asian immigration legally. He gave the example of the Japanese government rejecting a South Australian proposal, although the South Australian and Queensland government had also considered bringing in Indians and Pacific Islanders to develop the Northern Territory, with the schemes falling over primarily due to fears of non-white immigration on behalf of the population.[63] Scott concluded that anyone thinking that the 'empty' spaces of Australia were suitable to settling British immigrants were deluding themselves and thus all immigration to Australia should be kept at a minimum.

In an interesting moment of dissent, K.C. Masterman, writing in 1938, gave a forerunner to what was to become a rejection of explicit imperial racial doctrines after WWII when arguing that 'one of the most striking results of the revolt against reason which has been the main characteristic of the last few years is the recrudescence of race prejudice'.[64] He lamented the treatment of Jews in Europe and pointed out the hypocrisy of Americans decrying this same hatred when 'drawing the line at negroes'. He carried on further suggesting that the successes in New Zealand of Maori villages would be replicated in Australia if they were given a chance.[65]

What was new in this journal, though, and perhaps a result of the AIIA's focus on East Asian affairs, was consistent analysis and commentary beyond the Northern Territory, South Pacific, and the empire. Articles appeared that were written from around Asia, including India, the Philippines, China, Japan, as well as US and UK policy in the region. Occasionally, local, non-Australian authors would give their perspective, particularly in the case of imperial possessions like India.[66] Several reports appeared over the pre-war life of the journal of Japan's colonial policies and its naval build-up. Although this work was written in a more descriptive style, it was written from the perspective of gathering facts to improve Australia's position.[67] An American, Wilbur Burton, wondered whether the US would allow the Philippines to become a Republic and argued it may be better off, given growing Japanese aggression, becoming a Dominion of the US.[68] Elsewhere, Syed Amjad Ali, a future Pakistani Ambassador to the US, argued for India's involvement in the war as a means of defending India from invasion.[69]

The focus of *Austral-Asiatic Bulletin* was broader than that of its contributions to *The Round Table*. Out of the original vision, a new stream of thought had emerged in which Australia began to look towards Asia with a modified version of Curtis' imperial gaze. Throughout the commentary though, the maintenance and development of Australia's small colonies and the fantasy of control and influence over Asia were ever present. Over the course of WWII, *Austral-Asiatic Bulletin* came to focus far more on the destruction in Europe, the Australian war effort and the Southward advance of the Japanese. This perhaps made the name of the journal outdated and led in some part to its change to *Australian Outlook*. The sense of abandonment by Britain in WWII has been thought of as the beginning of a more independent Australian foreign policy. The chosen 'great and powerful friend' of Australia shifted from the UK to the US. This was perhaps not an entirely ground-breaking change, but it did lead to Australia becoming far more engaged with the world, rather than having its foreign policy dictated from London.[70] WWII was also a major hanging point in IR theory globally, as well as in political and imperial ideologies around the world. While the backlash against the horrors of Nazism led the imperial powers to abandon their explicitly racial doctrines, Australia kept its colonial possessions and continued the White Australia policy until its gradual demise throughout the 1970s.[71]

With the development of this journal, Australian IR had moved on from solely engaging with the colonial world, as was done in *The Round Table*, and its own settlement to examine and engage with the rest of Asia. In doing so, though, its fantasy of gathering facts to better the world was soaked in its anxieties about Asian settlement and invasion. This produced an attempt to understand Asia to soothe Australia's invasion anxieties and ultimately with the desire to exert influence and control.

LOOKING BEYOND ASIA: *AUSTRALIAN OUTLOOK*

The *Australian Outlook* replaced the *Austral-Asiatic Bulletin* in 1947. This was not due to any failures of the previous journal, but more so that each branch of the AIIA could feel ownership of the publication, by not maintaining the Victorian group's chosen name. Part of the reason might also have been that a journal focused solely on Asia could not allow sufficiently detailed commentary on the changing world order after WWII. The opening editorial was written by R.J.F. Boyer and argued that:

> The day is long past when the issues covered by the Institute are matters of intellectual and group concern only. The Institute is designed to leave its mark to some good purpose on the actual turn of events. It does so not by espousing any policy – indeed, it is strictly prevented by its constitution from endorsing or propagating any point of view. It does aim, however, to strike firmly at the heart of the problem by setting up means whereby research into international issues may be carried out and information of a factual nature may be disseminated, and also to act as a forum wherein those competent not only to give information but to express views may do so without any limitation and without unwanted publicity.[72]

The editorial continued that the journal would 'act as a unifying influence among our widely separated branches, giving us a cohesion which is difficult to achieve by other means'. The idea of this publication as creating greater unity and a shared outlook on the world is a repetition of the original idea of the construction of the original *Round Table*. Once more, the collection and dissemination of facts for the betterment of politics remained the primary goal of the institute.

In concluding the editorial, Boyer repeated a common facet of Australian foreign policy discourse that Australia should punch above its weight in international affairs, arguing that 'Australia's influence is, and must be, more than commensurate with the size of her population, and it is urgent that that influence should be wisely and nobly exerted.'[73] *Australian Outlook* became a common outlet for Australian scholarship on international affairs. It published articles of far greater depth than *Austral-Asiatic Bulletin*, where work was generally very brief, and perhaps more like a news service with some analysis. It also began to print almost all the articles with the names of the author. The type of scholarship in this case shifted and was somewhat less focused on Asian events, but the content was generally similar. The White Australia policy was a common subject, as was the maintenance and benefits of colonial rule over the islands of the South Pacific. Race and hierarchy continued to be central themes, with decolonisation treated with caution and suspicion.

With the change in focus, Asia receded somewhat as the subject for the journal's analysis. The construction of a world order, given the founding of the UN, received considerably more attention than was the case in the previous iteration of the journal. Eggleston remained a prolific influence as he was in *Austral-Asiatic Bulletin*. Early in the journal's existence, he published a three-article critique of the UN's charter, looking at various elements of the organisation's founding. In one interesting example, he looked at the trusteeship provisions in the UN, and the organisation's general support for decolonisation in a critical light. He opened with a narrative of imperialism as beginning with European navigators and that 'Empires have been established, the primitive peoples have been exploited and, in some cases, enslaved.'[74] This system could not be maintained indefinitely though, as:

Some of the dependent peoples have developed self-consciousness and demand the recognition of their rights or attention to their needs. The problem would be relatively simple if these dependent peoples were capable of self-government, if they were educated and literate and had a developed social and economic organisation. But these conditions do not exist. Many of these people are in the primitive tribal stage without definite organisation and leaders.[75]

There is little urgency to decolonisation here, and no acceptance that the European 'stewardship' of these places might have been responsible for the state of poverty and low literacy levels, or 'primitiveness' of the societies in question. Despite this, Eggleston critiqued the foundation of the UN trusteeship provisions on the basis that:

> It is, in my opinion, idle to say that these people can stand by themselves in a modern world. There is a rather naive view to be found in some countries like the United States of America that every people has the right to govern itself, and that it has inherently the capacity to do so. This is not true.[76]

This takes the suggestion rather further, from the liberal social Darwinist position that some people were not ready for self-government, but could be improved through imperial tutelage, to seeing some racial groups as static and who could never advance or govern themselves.

Walter Crocker also critiqued the UN's new role in the world in an article published in *Australian Outlook* when he was working as a Chair in International Relations at ANU. He argued against the principle of one state one vote, which at the general assembly could result in 'minority rule', with small, poor states given the same status as larger, powerful states. He critiqued this on two terms. The first, and most important, being contribution to the budget. Wealthy states, he argued, which provide the bulk of UN funding, should have a greater say in UN votes. The second, however, was the more amorphous contribution to civilisation: 'Judged either by contributions to the budget or by contributions to civilization, or even by mere population, the rule of unweighted voting which has been justified in the name of democracy and of the majority means rule by a minority.'[77]

Some depictions of Australian foreign policy still fell within ideas of Greater Britain and Commonwealth unity. H.A. Wolfson's appraisal of Australia's relationship with the Commonwealth suggested that most Australians would see conflicts with Britain as 'familiar quarrels'. He also pointed to an independent streak within Australian identity, going all the way back to Curtis. He drew a parallel between Australia's response to Curtis' imperial federation in the 1910s and the contemporary call for a Commonwealth foreign policy, arguing that Australia had sought in both cases to make its own decisions on the scope of imperial obligations and maintain control of its own defences.[78]

The original method of IR, the analysis of social facts of colonies for the maintenance of imperialism, continued as a theme as well. One author, W.E.H. Stanner, summed up the need to take a more empirical approach to the diversity of colonies in determining their readiness for self-rule, suggesting that 'It begins, I believe, with an effort to analyze by sociological methods the social facts of particular colonies.'[79] Belshaw described what he saw as a new spirit of development and progressivism in South Eastern Papua but tempered his optimism with a sense that there was not yet the administrative skill in the province necessary to allow self-government.[80] Although the South Pacific was a common subject,[81] it was not until *Australian Outlook* that the settlement of the Northern Territory was no longer seen as an appropriate topic for IR. Australian IR had become a mix of events at the global level, the role of the Commonwealth, analysis of events in South East Asia and the ongoing colonial project in the South Pacific.

ESTABLISHING IR AT THE AUSTRALIAN NATIONAL UNIVERSITY

As *Australian Outlook* was devised, it was obvious that there had been something of a scholarly community developing in Australia since the 1920s at least. By 1950, this had developed into a distinct academic discipline which was to be housed in its universities. The first Australian School of IR was to be created with the establishment of the ANU in Canberra. IR was housed within the ANU's Research School for Pacific Studies. Douglas Copland, one of the key founders of the AIIA, was chosen as the ANU's Vice-Chancellor, a position he took up in 1948. A new focus on international affairs was one of the founding goals of the ANU, with the training of cadets for the Australian foreign service, which grew rapidly throughout the Cold War, a part of its mandate.[82] When departing his role as an Australian diplomat in China, he commented that the School of Pacific Studies would 'keep me in active touch with many phases of Chinese life and scholarship'.[83] Pacific Studies was defined not just as focusing on Australia's immediate Pacific north, though this was a significant topic for study, but as focusing on East Asia as a whole.

Eggleston and Crocker were both central to the establishment of ANU and its school of IR, and Eggleston was key to hiring Crocker. The centrality of Australia's identity and its focus on Asia was shown by the institutional structure: the ANU's Department of International Relations was to be a section of the School of Pacific Studies. Even within this institutional setting, Australian IR's focus on its region was central and institutionalised.

Crocker was convinced, at least partly by Eggleston, to take up Australia's first professorship in IR at Canberra instead of a professorship in History at Adelaide University, where he was from. Crocker had worked as colonial administrator in Nigeria for many years, where he was critical of British colonial administration. Despite his criticisms, he believed in imperialism and the white man's burden, arguing that it would have been better for most of Africa 'if the colonial powers had carried on their work for another generation or two'.[84] In 1949, he became Australia's first Professor of International Relations, taking up the Chair in the School of Pacific Studies.[85]

Eggleston laid out the priorities for the school in a memorandum on the School of Pacific Studies and the methods that he sought to use, which was forwarded on to Crocker. They drew quite clearly from Curtis' original framing of what the scientific study of international affairs was to entail. Eggleston's memorandum advocated the detailed gathering of 'facts', its circulation around the department for review, and the belief that knowledge could create reality, rather than just describe it. The methods for the founding of IR were repeated here once again. The extent to which Eggleston still believed in the Round Table vision, however, is debated by Neville Meaney and Cotton.[86] Eggleston seemed to no longer believe in Australia's purely British character, thereby departing from the Round Table's ideology.[87]

These methods were tied to a set of issues that the School of Pacific Studies should focus on:

> The questions I have mentioned are of the highest scientific interest and they give rise to problems which can only be solved by scientific investigation. The political approach to these problems will be fumbling and opportunist unless there is a body of research which elucidates, first the facts and, then, speculates on the way in which they may be dealt with. It would, in my opinion, be a mere evasion if we were to refrain from including these subjects in the School simply because they have political aspects.[88]

These problems were bound with an idealistic call on its academics that:

> the faith of the Social Scientist is that, if we can formulate reliable scientific conclusions they will be a guide to human conduct and that informed conduct will increase the effectiveness of social life and lead to progressive solution of our problems. The importance of the schools can thus hardly be over-estimated, even though success during the present world crisis seems rather a forlorn hope.[89]

With this, even if Eggleston no longer believed in imperial federation, he still sought to improve world order by studying it. As such, he had still not let go of its method.

Eggleston's memorandum on the School of Pacific Studies opened with its key priority as 'the development of communities from the primitive stage to a stage in which they will be able to take their places in the modern world'. He commented that:

> Those who know anything of colonial development know that the process is likely to be slow ... The dependent nations are impatient and demand some voice in their affairs as soon as possible, and so the study of these various stages should be made and the experience of native states like Tonga and Samoa should be carefully studied.[90]

He had suggested elsewhere that Australia's policies in its colonial possession of New Guinea was to 'rely considerably on the anthropological research' of the School of Pacific Studies.[91] Further priorities included the ideal means for distributing aid, comparing constitutions of colonies and mandates in the Pacific, race relations in the Pacific Area, and a review of the process of decolonisation states in the Pacific Area as well as the integration of the community in Malaya. One priority explicitly reserved for the Department of International Relations was to be 'the equilibrium or balance of power of Forces in the Pacific', including the 'basic geopolitical factors' of 'population, natural resources, industrial developing and ideas and movements'.[92]

As we have seen, race was a foundational concern for the establishment of IR around the Dominions. We will close, then with a consideration of how race played out in early Australian IR. At this time, race was being written out of IR's agenda.[93] Bearing in mind the suggestion that it was necessary to study the 'equilibrium' or balance of world politics, how did race play out at ANU under Crocker's Chair? The immediate dismissal of race was not entirely the case in Australia, or at least for Crocker. He had hoped to give a major public lecture on the subject, but instead had it published following his departure for India to work as a diplomat. We can see from his analysis of race and international affairs that he felt race was still an issue in IR, though not as a biological concept but as a residual issue. Crocker argued that 'it is essential, then, to understand the factors that operate to disturb the equilibrium in international affairs, both by the material difficulties they create and by the emotionalism and the irrationality they provoke'.[94] This was based on his experiences working in India as a diplomat but also revealed his approach to scholarship. Indeed, Crocker saw decolonisation as more significant than the Cold War, suggesting that 'In the long run, however, the biggest effects will be, I believe, the independence of the colonial peoples and the emergence of Asia and Africa.'[95] Asia, however, was especially pertinent to Australia, stating that 'the awakening of Asia is, in particular, an immensely important fact of today, and one with which Australia will have to be more and more concerned.'[96]

To understand the argument, we must first consider the historical narrative on which it rested. Crocker argued that the supremacy of the white man was not based on race but had been primarily technological, and through superior technology 'he dominated the world through three or four centuries'. He began his history of different races by sketching out a hierarchy, with Africans and red Indians on the bottom, followed by Asians and then Europeans. His narrative was one of racial development. He argued that all races could learn from one another – specifically that Indians and the Nigerians could learn anything from the British, and that they had done so successfully. He placed this within Rudyard Kipling's framework. He argued that:

> The Historian of the future, free of our feelings and preoccupations, will see the period of European colonial rule as much more than a matter of loot. He will see it as a contrivance by nature for a vast Point four or Colombo Plan programme, whereby the technology invented and applied by Europe was spread over the world.[97]

Although he acknowledged that injustice, cruelty and oppression were part of this, he placed it as part of the normal abuse of power due to ignorance among colonisers. More important than this though is that 'the emotional attitude of the present generation of freed ex-colonials, while it is understandable, is at the same time incomplete'.[98] He concluded by agreeing with Albert Schweitzer, a French medical doctor and philosopher, that the emotion of anti-colonialism ignored the value of the 'tutelage' given by Europeans to their colonies, which far outweighs elements of exploitation and oppression by colonial powers. Of course, Crocker saw the British as the best and most sensitive colonial administrators, particularly in India.[99]

This is not so much an erasure of race but a simultaneous excision of colonial violence and of race as a biological concept. If race is not a biological concept and the Europeans had successfully completed the 'white man's burden' in bringing the non-white races to their standard of civilisation, then why did Crocker still see race as an issue for international affairs? His concern for international affairs and the 'emotionalism' engendered by this process, then, might lead to conflict and division by disturbing the equilibrium of international affairs. Crocker built the argument that saw race as a key element of contemporary international affairs. He argued that 'race relations are even more potent than population pressure in arousing irrationality and emotionalism'.[100] Interestingly, as an opponent of the White Australia policy, he included Australia in this analysis, though only very briefly and without considering the implications that Australia might be needlessly afraid of non-white immigration. For the most part, he dwelled on his experience in India and West Africa, where he had spent much of his career.

He drew on his own experiences here, as living among the 'non-white' had taught him how 'passionately the non-whites are preoccupied with resentments about colour, and about slights, real or fancied, over colour … many non-whites live in a nightmare world of wounded self-esteem'.[101] Africans had a worse experience of this, because they had further to go, and as a result are 'still going through the stage of being treated as a chimpanzee that can ride a bicycle or that can even pour tea out of a tea pot, though occasionally lapsing into drinking it out of the pot instead of first pouring it into the cup'.[102]

Crocker dismissed Indian thoughts on race relations and its anti-racist foreign policy as based on this partiality:

> The average Indian, beguiled by the diatribes of his delegates at the United Nations, and sharing the human frailty of seeing the beam in his colonialist neighbour's eye while missing the mote in his own, would be astonished to learn what the thousand or so African students in India think about Indian race prejudice.[103]

He defines the threat to equilibrium of racial prejudice as based on irrationality of postcolonial states:

> Indians probably complain more, partly because of their greater sensitiveness, which is part of their charm, partly because their own caste system … predisposes them to imagine comparable caste restrictions being imposed against them by the white races, and partly because they are ethnologically or historically largely white in origin. It is Indian exclusiveness in India, incidentally, that makes African students, now brought there in some numbers, feel that they are being discriminated against by Indians because of their colour.[104]

He concluded: 'but the point to drive home is that the preoccupation with colour was, and still is, most passionate even if most irrational'. Here, racial discrimination is placed with the Indians rather that with white nations. The adoption of an 'objective', rationalist IR framework is used in scholarship to dismiss the concerns of Indians as an emotionalist passion. The dismissal of explicitly racial and imperial doctrines in Australian IR is not clear at this point. The irrationality of the postcolonial state means that it might be a threat to international order.

We can begin to see in the 1950s the assertion being made that race does not matter in IR as something biological or civilisational. Explicit racial doctrines were less obvious in this new school of Australian IR. Yet, the implication was still that race does not matter to international affairs except as causing the impartiality of non-white people. By abandoning race as a scientific category and absolving the Europeans from colonial violence, Crocker could turn race into a partiality with which only non-white peoples were afflicted. In doing so, he still claimed an objective viewpoint on international affairs that only white people could access.

A WHITE AUSTRALIAN IR

A distinctive set of people studying the international, most of whom were in some way affiliated with the Round Table and who carried on through the AIIA, existed in Australia from Curtis' original visit to the 1960s. Although the ideology shifted gradually, the method of study remained relatively intact. The study of Australia and its place in world affairs through the Round Table meant initially a focus on Australia's position within the British empire, on shared identity with the Dominions. At this time, Australia's Others under IR's gaze were primarily its nearest neighbours, its colonial projects, and those within: its own settlement, its immigration policy and its Aboriginal population. Curtis' vision in Australia led not just to a desire to keep the empire together, though that was a continual concern of Australian IR. With the foundation of the AIIA, these preoccupations were very much kept, but the study of East Asia became a priority alongside them. The Round Table's ideology of building an imperial federation no longer held such resonance for Australia after WWII because Australia had felt abandoned by the empire over the course of the war. We may debate the extent to which Australia's switching its 'great and powerful friend' from London to Washington was a major transformation. Regardless, however, the point at which we close our narrative of IR in Australia, the study of the international was still enmeshed in Australia's imperial projects in the South Pacific, and it still held on to its original mission.

4

South Africa: Race Relations, the International and the Rise of Apartheid

Among the multiplying origin stories of the discipline of IR, one claims that the ideas and institutions that 'birthed' IR were first developed in South Africa. But, as will become plain in what follows, the country's embrace of the discipline in the twentieth century was halting, hesitant, and often very ham-handed. We argued in Chapter 1 and elsewhere that the work of the Round Table societies drew on lessons learnt during the reconstruction of South Africa after the Boer War of 1899–1902.[1] The very making of the Union of South Africa provided the template for all the subsequent schemes of the Round Table.[2] But here lies the first of many paradoxes that mark the present pathway: after their formation, Round Table societies flourished throughout the commonwealth-in-the-making. But, for much of the 1910s and early 1920s, the Round Table Society was non-existent in South Africa, except a few members who formed one group for the purpose of furnishing an article for the journal, *The Round Table*. Key Kindergarten members such as Patrick Duncan and Hugh Wyndham remained in South Africa, they busied themselves in political work and found little sympathy for another English-driven project in South Africa. Indeed, the enthusiasm for schemes of imperial federation or Organic Union were at a low ebb.

While the founding of SAIIA is a key topic of the chapter, the deeper interest here is with the ideas which brought this about. As we have argued, these began with the idea that conceptual framings of the social and its ordering – to whit, social science – could make the world a better place. So, as 'the international' emerged as a discreet domain of knowledge, it was intended to order a world in flux and, simultaneously, strengthen the hold of an empire on which (it was hoped) the sun would never set.

In looking at South Africa, we might hope to venture into the domain of 'non-Western' IR thought. This, sadly, could not be further from the case. As we will see throughout, South Africa's multicultural context developed, if anything, even whiter, more racialised and masculinised strains of thought. As we noted in Chapter 1, the thought emerging from the engagement between South Africa's various cultural groups led to an explicit civilisational hierarchy in which Africans were seen as static and in need of permanent imperial tutelage coupled with segregation. While Australia's international thought drew heavily on immigration restriction, South Africa's form of segregation was already in practice at home. Indeed, in South Africa, the study of the international had to compete for space with scholars more explicitly studying 'race relations'. Moreover, the domain of the international was used continually as a place-holder for the white, masculine, Anglo-Saxon view of the world, and this was especially so in South Africa.

Having already covered the early history of our thought collective in South Africa in Chapter 1, we begin here with the effort to restart the study of the international in South Africa in the 1920s. South African thinkers, in concert with the Round Table and SAIIA, looked at the racial template that the country provided and mapped this onto the international. With the formalisation of apartheid in South Africa after WWII though and the hiving off of the domestic from the international in the mind of IR scholars and practitioners, a darker stream of thought emerged. With the international becoming seen as the space of exception, South African IR thinkers and practitioners used the idea of sovereignty to turn race relations into a domestic matter, and continuously resist international calls for boycott against the country because of its race relations.

THE LETTER: RESTARTING THE STUDY OF
THE INTERNATIONAL IN SOUTH AFRICA

The flutter of hope for the study of the international in South Africa came in the form of a letter from the first Vice-Chancellor of the University of Cape Town, Professor John Carruthers Beattie (1866–1946). On 30 January 1928, Carruthers Beattie addressed a letter to the RIIA. In it, he queried the 'possibility of an attempt ... to form an association for the study of problems of African people'. His immediate interest seemed largely of a technical nature. He enquired after the 'origins of ... [the RIIA] ...; how members are elected, how the financial means are provided and what the organisation is generally'.[3] Carruthers Beattie confessed that his interest in these matters was fired by an article entitled 'Honolulu', which he had read in the December 1927 issue of the journal, *The Round Table*.

Mainly, the Honolulu piece itself was an account of the participation of a 15-member delegation of the RIIA who had travelled to the conference of the IPR. Their journey had taken them through Canada where a 'Canadian

Honolulu' group had joined for a series of meetings, which had laid the plans for the establishment of the CIIA.[4] However, Carruthers Beattie appeared less interested in the study of international issues, but rather (as he expressed it) in seeking 'knowledge of the work done in different parts of Africa ... [to find] ... the solution of native (sic) problems'.[5] We will pause here to reiterate a point fundamental to the pages of this book. Racial coding ran – as it continues to – through the conceptualisation and, indeed, through the routines of the study of IR.

Hopes of establishing control over the idea of 'race' and the social problems presented by 'race relations' came increasingly to occupy South African political discussion after WWI.[6] 'The native question' – as it was called – was largely hidden by the whites-only imaginings around the formation of the South African Union in 1910, while the war itself had deferred efforts to deal with the issue.[7] However, the Native Affairs Act of 1920 drew the 'native' issue back towards the policy agenda. An urgency was added to this by the deepening black radicalisation both in the country and across the world. In response and with an eye to contributing and controlling it, academic interest was keen to gain 'knowledge' of the 'native races'.

This crossing between the academic and applied end of race and its study was not new in South Africa. Local educationalists such as the Columbia-trained Charles T. Loram (1879–1840), later Sterling Professor of Education at Yale, and Alexander W. Roberts (1857–1938), an Edinburgh graduate, had accessed policymaking (and bureaucratic thinking) through their participation in the Native Affairs Commission – a government advisory group that was mandated to provide answers to 'the native question'.

Such early encounters were driven by the idea that academics could offer both a language and a method to explain and manage the social world. Through increasingly well-established 'imperial networks of knowledge', the social sciences took hold within South Africa's fledging university system. This helps explain how the first Chair in Social Anthropology – in the world, let alone the empire – was established at the University of Cape Town in 1921. On the invitation of the Prime Minister Jan Smuts, the Cambridge-trained anthropologist Alfred Radcliffe-Brown (1881–1955), was appointed professor. This is a shining example of the metropolitan-periphery relationship in matters of culture and knowledge and is a forerunner to what would happen in IR.

The new appointee's understanding of the importance of the discipline to the country was soon to become plain. In the year following his arrival, readers of the *South African Journal of Science* were able to read his view that 'Anthropology' aimed to provide 'scientific knowledge' about the 'mental, moral and social life' of the 'native races'.[8] Such faith in the social sciences is typical of the interwar years: indeed, the founding of IR as a discipline is attributed to this belief. Less well appreciated today, however, is that the categories used in the social sciences were somewhat porous – rather than, as today, sealed off one from another.

So it should be no surprise that in a world which was looking to the 'science of the social' to solve its 'many ills', the analytical categories of 'race' and 'the international' would become fused together as the worry around a 'world race problem' arose.[9]

THE THINKING: RACE IN THE SOUTH AFRICAN IMAGINARY

Although the US and the UK had failed to institutionalise their 'special relationship' under the auspices of a single institute of international affairs, the two sides of the divide had already agreed on the broad architecture of a 'racialised' attempt to secure world order. Much of the form this eventually took hinged on understandings over race that were provided by Anthropology. But these were not static, and thinking on understandings of race were shifting. The urge to become what Radcliffe-Brown had called 'science of man' drove anthropologists to eschew the 'historical approach' to explanation in favour of a 'functional' one – if the former was interested in the evolution of societies through a chain of civilisations, the latter viewed societies as autonomous cultures. As one of the pioneers of this new thinking, Radcliffe-Brown noted that the latter inductively formulated 'the general laws that underlie the phenomena of culture'.[10] Influenced by Boasian thinking,[11] this approach considered societies as largely self-contained but unequal, an approach which plainly strengthened policy arguments about the importance of segregation. In South Africa this understanding had a particular resonance because it was seen as more enlightened than the assimilationist arguments which rested on an evolutionist belief in the natural superiority of whites. As the leading authority in the field, Saul Dubow, has put it, in post-WWI liberal circles "'civilization" was replaced by "culture", while "progress" became synonymous with "differentiation", and individualism was subsumed into the collective interests of "racial groups"'.[12] The new vocabulary positioned segregation as a 'progressive' philosophy, locating it as a 'middle way' between the 'repression' of the defeated Boer Republics with their Old Testament understandings of race, and the 'assimilation' – evolutionist approach – which had been championed in South Africa by the so-called Cape-Liberals.

But, and this road was to lead to apartheid, there were two understandings of 'segregation' in South Africa. One was a 'hard segregation' – an ideology which was championed mainly by Afrikaner Nationalist leaders who had already called for the abolition of non-racial Cape Franchise, and favoured the introduction of legislated segregation including the imposition of an industrial 'colour bar', which would exclude blacks from certain categories of work. The second was a more benign position on the issue of segregation. This carried incorporationist and 'protective' undertones and was under-pinned by the idea that people deemed incapable of directing their own affairs should be governed by others who were capable of doing so.

In the coded, race-infused language of the age, the latter position drew public policy on segregation more towards the paternalism offered by the notion of 'Trusteeship'. This approach was to provide societies viewed by empires as 'unready' for self-government with a new role, that of colonial overseer. But, for all its claims of progress, Trusteeship enabled toxic forms of segregation, which were covered over by the patina represented by the idea that these societies would eventually 'evolve' into self-governing territories. Of course, the idea (certainly, the legitimacy) of the policy of Trusteeship was questioned throughout the life of the LoN. After WWII, the system moved under the auspices of the UN, but still emphasised that the societies were not ready for self-governance.[13] As we will see in Chapter 5, the system was important to New Zealand's ideas of their place in the world, including in the NZIIA's study programme.

As Smuts was one of the key proponents of the idea for the Paris Peace Conference, it held special resonance in South Africa. The benign segrega-tionists, whose point of view was advanced in the pages of *The Round Table*, attempted to separate the economic and political aspects of segregation. Economic segregation, as an article by Harold Butler, who later became the Director of the International Labour Organisation, argued, was detrimental to the interests of both whites and blacks. Rural segregation had already limited the supply of labour to the South African mines, industries and white-owned lands. Despite what was called the 'poor white problem', South African white population was inadequate to fill the demand for labour. As a result, further segregation and the imposition of a 'colour bar' to labour, especially in urban areas, was neither helpful for whites nor for non-whites. The economic functions of wages and labour control, Butler argued, should be left to the market to determine. A consequence of this was an increase in wages of African workers, but this would in turn increase the consumer buying capacity, making the South African economy more diverse and stronger as a whole. Butler said little about political equality, only suggesting that whether Africans become politically equal to whites in the distant future, or co-exist through free cooperation in economic matters while retaining racial purity and political and social segregation, was uncertain, but for any future to be economically viable it was imperative that functions of the economic sphere be left to the market.[14] On political equality, the South African Round Table group assiduously pushed for retaining black vote in the Cape, which was based on property qualifications. Property qualifications were the correct measure of civilisation rather than race, they argued.[15] This, a classic social Darwinist position, was also echoed in the Trusteeship idea. But they were also staunchly opposed to full political and social equality. As Richard Feetham wrote in *The Round Table*: 'The reckless extension of political privileges to any class or race without reference to its political experience or capacity is apt to result in the wholesale purchase of its votes by bribery or the wholesale denial of its rights by force.'[16]

On Trusteeship, Jan Smuts had been strongly influenced on this matter by two founder members of the Round Table, Curtis and Kerr. The former's 1918 article, titled 'Windows of Freedom' (which was also published in the journal, *The Round Table*), made a deep impression on Smuts, who had called upon Kerr's help in drafting the two Articles of the League's Charter which dealt with Trusteeship. So, it was a belief – and, indeed, a policy – which would mark an early path in the study of the discipline of IR combined remarkably well with both segregationist and evolutionary ideas on race. The overriding principle, as written in Article 22 of the League's Charter, was that governance of these territories was to become 'a sacred trust of civilization'.[17] The system matched the static racial hierarchy, with the lowest class of mandates being Pacific Island colonies and South West Africa. South Africa gained control of what is known today as Namibia. Australia governed New Guinea and Nauru. New Zealand governed Samoa. Societies in Asia, such as Syria and Iraq, were given higher levels of self-government as a result of their 'standard of civilization'.

While Anthropology increasingly viewed the world in terms of 'culture', early IR was familiar with the categories of 'nationalism' and 'race'. A historicist approach in IR emphasised evolution towards an organic 'national' polity where burden of acceptability rested on the successful union of states like the US in the eighteenth century, of Canada in the nineteenth century, and Australia in the early twentieth century. These were, of course, settler colonial societies ruled by white elites who had either cowed Indigenous people or, quite simply, obliterated them.

As Anthropology focused on domestic societies, IR was interested in finding ways in which different nations and races could be integrated in a wider community – this was, of course, called 'the international'. For both disciplines, the Union of South Africa provided a model of the task at hand – here was a single space that integrated segregationist and evolutionary thinking in Anthropology and drew from functional and historicist approaches towards the international.

THE LEADER: JAN SMUTS AND THE SAIIA

This understanding points directly towards the founding of the SAIIA and, as we will see, provides the backdrop to its work. But its founding was to be closely tied to mythology around Smuts and, because this is so, we must spend some time with his thinking on three closely linked issues: race, Africa and the idea of the international.

Lauded as an 'International Statesman' after the Paris Peace Conference, Smuts was invited to deliver the 1929 Rhodes Memorial Lectures at Oxford.[18] Under the title, 'Some World Problems', the occasion provided a palette on which to expand and expound his thinking on the ideas which were shaping a changing world. In one lecture, entitled 'Native Policy in Africa', Smuts advocated the territorial and institutional separation of Europeans and non-Europeans within the same country – the latter, almost as a matter of common sense, would be under the supervision of 'Europeans'. Drawing from South Africa, he positioned segregation as a global template arguing that '[w]herever Europeans and natives live in the same country it will mean separate parallel institutions for the two'.[19] This is because, he contended, the African 'has largely remained a child type, with a child psychology and outlook'[20] and went on, in the same patronising manner, to suggest that '[n]o other race is so easily satisfied, so good tempered, so carefree'.[21] Consequently, 'a race so unique, and so different in its mentality and its cultures from those of Europe, requires a policy very unlike that which would suit Europeans'.[22]

For Smuts, effective public policy on the issue, therefore, ought not to either 'de-Africanise the African and to turn him into a beast of the field or into a pseudo-European'[23] – both of which had been tried in the past in South Africa, and ended up badly. 'If Africa has to be redeemed', Smuts argued,

> if Africa has to make her own contribution to the world, if Africa is to take her rightful place among the continents, we shall have to proceed on different lines and evolve a policy which will not force her institutions into an alien European mould, but which preserve her unity with her

own past, conserve what is precious in her past, and build her future progress and civilisation on specifically African foundations.[24]

Crediting Cecil John Rhodes with 'this ... orientation of African policy', Smuts elaborated on the two main ideas of a policy which was first enunciated in the notorious Glen Grey Act of 1894: 'white settlement ... [supplied] ... the steel framework and the stimulus for an enduring civilisation, and indigenous native institutions ... [these were needed] ... to express the specifically African character of the natives in their future development and civilisation'.[25] Through a policy of 'indirect rule' – another policy fetish of the 1920s which had come through Lord Lugard's administration elsewhere in Africa – the scheme would secure territorial and institutional segregation, but not economic.[26] And for the practice of international relationships, he added, the same policy – segregation – should be used to solve the 'world race problem'.[27]

The Rhodes Lectures hid a wider ambition – one that was expansionist, almost imperial – in its vision. This was the desire to create a single white-ruled state that would run from Cape to Kenya – Smuts called this 'Greater South Africa'. Interestingly, this was an ambition that was also associated with Rhodes and also intrigued Milner's Kindergarten which had, on one occasion, defined 'South Africa' as extending from 'Lake Tanganyika to the Cape of Good Hope – this would comprise eleven colonies and 8,000,000 inhabitants of which 1,100,000 would be white'.[28] But this particular ambition – also called an 'organic union of the African Highlands'[29] – had received a setback as the whites in Southern Rhodesia (now Zimbabwe) had voted against incorporation into the Union in a Referendum held in 1924.

On this issue, as in others, Smuts' own people, the Afrikaners, differed with him. Explaining this difference, an article in the increasingly authoritative The Round Table argued that Afrikaners favoured 'an inverted Dixie line ... drawn by international agreement, more or less along the tenth degree of south latitude ... [this would separate] ... the Colour-bar States of White Africa to the south of it from the Colour-blind States of Black Africa to the north'. Based on this, an 'internationally sanctioned' divide could be drawn between a 'European Africa' and an 'African Africa'.[30] As we will see, this notion of two 'Africas' – one 'White-ruled'; the other 'Black-ruled' returned again and again to the IR agenda in South (and Southern) Africa.

Smuts and his supporters continued to hope that a greater white-ruled Dominion would be the inevitable result of 'a unified native' policy.[31] Interestingly, even liberals in the country supported this position. 'In the view that I take of South Africa in the wider sense of the term (that is Africa south of the equator which is capable of European settlement) such a Greater Union is bound to come if the European peoples are able permanently to maintain themselves', wrote the influential liberal thinker Patrick Duncan.[32]

This admixture of 'race' and 'the international' also influenced British thinking on colonial policy, especially on the evolving situation in Southern and Eastern Africa.[33] The Hilton Young Commission (appointed by the Colonial Office in 1926 to investigate the possibility of a closer union of British colonial territories in East and Central Africa) envisioned a 'closer union' of the white settler colonies in Eastern Africa along the model of a South African Union; their report advocated segregation in the issue of settler-native relations.[34] A South African Union extending up to Kenya was still a far-fetched idea, but the vision found strong endorsement in the deliberations at Chatham House.[35]

So it was that the ideas of colonial trusteeship, reflecting the Smutsian vision of global segregation along racial lines, remained the most viable solution to the problem of what the African-American scholar W.E.B. Du Bois had called the 'global colour-line'.[36]

THE REPLY: CHATHAM HOUSE AND SOUTH AFRICA'S RACIAL THOUGHT

Notwithstanding (or perhaps because of) Smuts' increasingly global authority in these matters, Chatham House was already researching and analysing them, and indicated so in their reply to Carruthers Beattie's letter. But for the denizens of Chatham House, the letter itself was more important than the questions it posed. This was because for many in their number, South Africa – the very place where they had honed their political and intellectual skills – had been 'lost' for the project of empire. But Carruthers Beattie's exploratory letter to Chatham House had created a sense of excitement and surprise – and the opportunity of sharing 'scientifically based' research.

The RIIA's work on race, Africa and the international was directed by Hugh Wyndham, who had left South Africa in 1923 after living in the country for 20 years.[37] As Secretary of the Chatham House African Study Group, he had written a paper entitled 'Colour Problem in Africa'. This turned on a taxonomy of approaches to the issue by colonial governments. In North Africa, he reported that the French had used a model of 'la politique d'assimilation' (or assimilation of the lower culture into the higher culture); in Southern Africa, the Portuguese followed a policy of 'miscegenation' which ensured a cohesive settlement through inter-racial marriages. Wyndham contrasted these with the model of 'co-optation' or 'la politique *d'association'* which was practiced in South Africa. This approach, he suggested, was based on 'mutual toleration of two populations and co-operation in economic development'.[38] According to him, the approach allowed for developing separate 'native areas' as well as encouraging 'natives' to work for the Europeans outside of their designated 'areas'.[39]

In the paper, Wyndham recommended a continent-wide implementation of the South African solution to the race issue, as well as championing the use of new anthropological understandings of African societies to train administrators. These would serve as active field workers 'where the information and experience afterwards acquired by them should be collected and made available to others'.[40] Together with the teaching, the pedagogy should be mediated by a lingua franca which 'must be evolved to serve as the medium ... [with which to communicate] ... African culture'.[41] This crossing of the several divides turns to the issue of how knowledge is applied and provides a justification for the creation of an institute.

A city that Wyndham knew well, Cape Town, was proposed as the location for the institute to train African 'administrators', but London, too, was interested in establishing the International Institute of African Languages and Culture – later called the International Africa.[42] Its brief was to 'scientifically' study African languages and cultures, and to actively promote the functional view of Anthropology.

Indeed, in his Rhodes Memorial Lectures, Smuts had proposed setting up yet another institute – one which would study the native policy. Together with Kerr, he had visited the US to garner funds for the proposed institute which would be located in Oxford. However, Smuts' close ties to this project may well have ruined its chances of succeeding. American philanthropists thought it unadvisable to have the South African-like doctrine of segregation propagated through an institute dedicated to the study of Africa even if this were located in a distinguished place of learning.[43]

These initiatives suggest a growing interest in the establishment of institute-driven knowledge to bear on social problems, which is one of the reasons why Carruthers Beattie's exploratory letter to Chatham House had created a sense of excitement and surprise.

On receiving the news from South Africa, Wyndham expressed the hope that some degree of cooperation would be found between the South African interest and the African Study Group. Another member of the Kindergarten, Curtis, reported that he had already talked with members of Chatham House, who were resident in South Africa, about starting a local branch for studying the issue of race.[44] Pushing the case further, Margaret Cleeve, the Assistant Secretary at Chatham House, also informed Carruthers Beattie that the African Study Group at Chatham House was specifically studying these issues.[45]

Despite this excitement, Carruthers Beattie's initiative reached a dead end. The reasons why this happened are not particularly clear, as neither Carruthers Beattie's nor the Chatham House archives reveal the full story. What is clear, however, is that the RIIA did contact other liberal-inclined academics in South Africa, but despite continuing enthusiasm, this early initiative came to nought.[46]

One possible explanation for this was the formation of the South African Institute of Race Relations (SAIRR) in Johannesburg in 1929. This was the brain-child of its first director, the liberal activist and thinker J.D. Rheinallt Jones (1884–1953), who was born in Wales. The hope of the SAIRR was that South Africans might be better informed on the issues facing them by the 'scientific' study of issues related to race and native policy: its founding, however, seemed to bury the establishment of a local institute which was concerned with understanding the other worry of the time, that is, 'the international'.

Nevertheless, the idea of South Africa linking with Chatham House was reignited the very next year, when the London-born historian at the University of Cape Town Eric A. Walker (1886–1976) visited England. By this time, Walker has been loosely associated with both Chatham House and the Round Table movement. He had also attended meetings of the RIIA's African Study group and anonymously contributed articles to *The Round Table* journal.[47] So, when the Director of Chatham House approached Walker with a proposal to open a branch in South Africa, the latter was 'prepared to cooperate'.[48]

Parallel initiatives helped to expedite the process, too. Chatham House was committed to organising a conference on relations between the members of the-then fledgling British Commonwealth. One of its aims would be to establish affiliates or branches of Chatham House in New Zealand, South Africa and India. As we have seen, such institutes had already been built in Canada and Australia.

Unable to participate in a preparatory meeting, Walker turned to the Montagu Burton Professor of International Relations at the London School of Economics, Charles Manning (1894–1978) to attend in his stead. The meeting, which took place in London, resolved to invite delegations from the Dominions to a meeting to be held in Toronto in September 1933. Charged by the London meeting to organise a South Africa delegation, Manning travelled to the country of his birth in order to do so.

On arrival, he discovered that South Africa was caught up in a crisis associated with international finance: the effective abandonment of the 'gold standard' by the US in 1933. The resulting spike in the cost of South African goods had devastating effects on the South African economy. Manning was forced to confront some unsettled business of the Boer War, namely, the tension between Afrikaners and their English counterparts over the association with the empire. Walker had to assure the country's Prime Minister, J.B.M. (Barry) Hertzog, that 'there was nothing sinister in what was projected' by linking up with the London-based RIIA.

This offers an interesting insight both into South Africa's (then wholly white-based) parliamentary politics and the effect of these on the emerging issue of the country's international relations. Hertzog was an Afrikaner Nationalist who had studied in Amsterdam and was committed to distancing the country from the British empire. Interestingly, though, he was timid in his opposition to empire when compared to some of his decidedly pro-German Cabinet colleagues. Almost certainly, Manning's approach was to reassure the Prime Minister that the linkage to the Chatham House initiative was an intellectual, and not partisan, one.

As we shall see, however, the explanation that the institute's work was – or could be – 'non-partisan' would continue to haunt the work of those interested in developing the field of international relations in South Africa for decades to come. But Manning returned to Britain 'knowing that my self-imposed mission had totally, or very nearly, failed'.[49]

But all was not lost.

THE RIPOSTE: FOUNDING THE SOUTH AFRICAN INSTITUTE OF INTERNATIONAL AFFAIRS

In July 1933, an all-white South African delegation – representing both English and Afrikaans speakers – participated in the RIIA's conference in Toronto. Here, the view was expressed that there was 'a lack of people with sufficient leisure to undertake the formation of an African (sic) Institute of International Affairs', and reference was made to the difficultly of the great distances between possible centres of activity in South Africa. The latter has been dealt with in Canada by the establishment of branches: this model would be adopted in South Africa too.

Far more troublesome for the South Africans was the nature of the relationship with the RIIA. Some members, like Eric Walker, were in favour of opening a branch of the Royal Institute. But others preferred the option of an autonomous institute on the lines of Australia and Canada – this meant seeking 'affiliation' with Chatham House.[50]

As we have noted, six months after the Toronto meeting, Chatham House decided on the 'establishment in each Dominion of a scientific and non-political organisation' which would serve as branches of the RIIA.[51] Each branch was required to abide by two fundamental requirements: memberships must be confined to British subjects and the institute must not express an opinion on any aspect of international affairs. Both of these requirements touched on the thorny issue of 'impartiality' in the study of IR, especially in South Africa. Indeed, they illustrated the contradictions which ran through the early discipline's claims to its 'scientific basis': it is no surprise, then, that in a divided South Africa they gave rise to some complications.

On 12 May 1934 more than 60 white men met in the Senate House of the South African Parliament to consider the formation of SAIIA. After the passing of a motion, a National Executive Committee which carefully balanced the interests of the-then two recognised language groups, English and Afrikaans, was elected. But would this be a balancing act sufficient for the institute to survive, let alone thrive?

Although the Constitution sought affiliation with Chatham House, rather than choosing to become one of its branches, a major issue arose over membership. The SAIIA had kept this open to 'Union nationals and other British subjects' but it had reserved the power to admit members who were neither. Indeed, one such member had already been admitted – this was the Stellenbosch-based academic, H. ver Loren van Themaat, who was a Dutch national and was an elected member to the National Executive.[52]

Chatham House had several concerns about the decision on membership made in South Africa. An early one was that one of the publications available to the membership, the *Report on Foreign Affairs of the Empire Parliamentary Association*, was a confidential document to be circulated only among British subjects.[53] How was this to be squared with the possibility that non-British nationals could become 'Affiliated Members' of Chatham House through their membership of the proposed South African institute?

Hurdles like these were seemingly overcome when the RIIA received funding from the South African-based Abe Bailey Trust. This bequest was conditional on the RIIA's membership being limited to British subjects only – this seemed to seal the issue for the South Africans. Non-British subjects could not be affiliated with Chatham House. Ironically, then, it was the conditions attached to funding from a South African mining magnate which prevented certain South African citizens from becoming affiliated with Chatham House. Faced with this, three possible procedures were available for Chatham House: (i) to reject affiliation with the South Africans and seek, instead, a looser form of cooperation; (ii) to devise some formulae for partial affiliation where only British subjects of SAIIA would be recognised as affiliated by Chatham House; and (iii) to ask SAIIA to devise some different arrangement. Chatham House decided on the latter option.[54] They recognised, however, that it was a difficult matter to settle, especially because 'the offending clause (to include non-British citizens as Members of the SAIIA) had been written into the Constitution ... and a foreigner elected to the Council'. A leading figure in Chatham House 'was anxious at all costs to avoid a breach when I was there, particularly as no one wants to see a separate Dutch (read: Afrikaner Nationalist) South African Institute set up'.[55]

Quite obviously there were two factions within the National Executive of the SAIIA: English and Afrikaner. Gey van Pittius, who was on the South African institute's Executive Committee, was reported to have said that the Afrikaners were hesitant to link with Chatham House in any way that connoted a 'relationship between an inferior and a superior body'. He hinted that Afrikaners would secede from the South African institute if it was aligned with Chatham House on a 'superior-inferior' basis. Suspecting that the institute was 'an instrument of imperialist intrigue', he claimed that Afrikaner members of the executive 'were never consulted in advance and have been given no opportunity to approve the constitution'. They could only approve a constitution that restricted the membership of the local institute to South Africans alone. If this was not accepted, the Afrikaners will launch a separate institute which would seek membership with the International Studies Conference.[56]

It is important, momentarily, to reflect on this difference because it offers an insight into early approaches to the issue of partisanship within the discipline. Curtis had argued that 'any attempt to study international affairs at meetings which were open to aliens would end in futility'. Underpinning this was the view that a 'country which committed itself to the policy of admitting foreigners to its discussions from the very outset would not get far with the genuine study of those problems'. This principle, Curtis argued, was central to Chatham House becoming, and being recognised, 'as a place of genuine research', and SAIIA would be able to emulate Chatham House only if it kept its membership restricted to British subjects.[57]

Not only did this kind of thinking indicate the partisan nature of early study of IR but, as the unfolding South African case suggested, it was impossible to sustain such a position in a heterogeneous country. Indeed, cast in the grammar of South Africa's own tragic politics, this was an attempt to enforce apartheid in the study of the discipline.

However, in order to reach some middle ground with their opponents, an agreement was proposed to confine the membership of the SAIIA to South African nationals. All South African nationals were *ipso facto* British subjects, although newly arrived British immigrants were not South African citizens. Afrikaner support for this compromise was gained to include this in a proposal to revise the Constitution.[58] But although the crisis was over membership of the SAIIA and the link with the RIIA was moving towards an agreement, relations with Chatham House would remained tense for several decades.

The first public event was organised by the Cape Town branch of the SAIIA on 9 February 1935. Smuts himself had agreed to deliver the inaugural address – but eventually the speech was read by Patrick Duncan as Smuts had fallen ill. In the speech, Smuts spoke in the most eulogistic terms of institutes of international affairs in general and the founders of the South African institute in particular.[59]

Soon, however, the problem of membership was eclipsed by the challenge of inactivity. While eight branches were envisioned, only four were seen as practically possible: Cape Town, Pretoria, Johannesburg and Stellenbosch. However, the latter three never really took off. The hope lay in Cape Town, and it was effectively the sole branch of the SAIIA.[60] In the earliest years, the institute functioned from a temporary room in the offices of the *Cape Argus*, the local afternoon newspaper.

The approach of the Cape Town branch to the issue of membership seemed to confirm that it would be restricted to South African nationals. However, the archives at Chatham House are unclear as to what actually happened to the issue in the Constitution that was adopted on 6 May 1936. That said, we are certain that the emergency powers of the Executive to appoint non-British subjects were scrapped, but whether the membership was restricted to only 'Union nationals' or 'other British subjects' were also allowed is a matter that still needs clarity.[61] In 1961, after South Africa left the Commonwealth, 'the Institute's affiliation to the Royal Institute' ended.[62]

Despite the new Constitution and setting up of the institute through the Cape Town branch, in the first few years it was largely inactive – only organising occasional discussion meetings. The explanation may be that its finances were very limited. In June 1936, the Institute had only £16 in hand.[63] It did however send a delegation to the second unofficial British Commonwealth Relations Conference held in Sydney in 1938.

Most of the branches did not function during WWII, but at its end the institute's activities were reinvigorated following a donation from mining magnate and politician Harry Oppenheimer, who would go on to become its National Chairman.

THE RESULT: SAIIA AND APARTHEID

With the war in Europe over, thoughts turned to the future of the SAIIA. Although its roots were in Cape Town, where the local branch was most active, it was increasingly plain that the country's centre of gravity had moved to the Witwatersrand, especially to Johannesburg, which was increasingly South Africa's financial capital.

In September 1944, the central offices of the institute were moved to Johannesburg with a full-time secretariat. Major Louis Kraft, an English-speaking, Belgian-born intelligence officer in the Defence Forces of the Union of South Africa, was released from government service to take up the position of General Secretary of the institute. Fund-raising was to be one of his major priorities and the hope was expressed that the institute could become a 'popular movement' rather than a selective one, as was the Royal Institute.[64]

But the figure of Smuts loomed large over the institute, its life and its future. A towering international figure, he wrote the first draft of the Preamble to the Charter of the United Nations. Nevertheless, he was defeated in South Africa's General Election held in September 1948 by the pro-apartheid (Reunited) National Party which was led by his childhood friend, Daniël F. Malan. Two years later, at the age of 80, Smuts died of a heart attack. For several years thereafter was the challenge of finding a suitable way to memorialise the life and celebrate the legacy of one of the 'Greatest South Africans' of all time – as Smuts was named, alongside Nelson Mandela, in 2004.

On a visit to the US in the early 1950s, Dr W.J. (Bill) Busschau, who had moved from the economics profession to become a South African industrialist, visited the Woodrow Wilson School of Public and International Affairs at Princeton University. As Princeton had recognised America's 28th President, Busschau believed that Smuts could be honoured in Johannesburg. With singular determination, he reimagined the idea – if not quite the purpose – of the SAIIA. To do so, he mobilised local business to raise money to build a neoclassical building – to be called 'Jan Smuts House' – on the campus of the University of the Witwatersrand as a living memorial to the late Prime Minister. Operating from this as a base, the SAIIA would be linked to the university through the establishment of an (academic) Chair of International Relations – also to be called in honour of Jan Smuts. The combination of research, academic study and public outreach certainly bolstered the intellectual respectability to local IR and gave a fillip to the work of the SAIIA. However, if Busschau hoped that this schema might draw South African IR away from its roots in the imperial form of the discipline towards an American tradition, he was wrong – more than 60 years after the founding of Jan Smuts House, IR in South Africa remains largely under the spell of empire.

The measure of the SAIIA's work should be judged in terms of its research (which began with purpose after the move to Johannesburg); the measure of its political acceptability might be gauged by its approach to the issue that dogged – as it continuous to – the country, namely, race. In a brochure issued in August 1971 by the SAIIA, a list of its publications reveals that the greater weight of these return (as it were) to the issues in the 'Greater South Africa' debate which were raised by Smuts in his Rhodes Memorial Lectures at Oxford in 1929. Simply put, the question remained, 'how is a European (read white) state to survive in Africa?' Although somewhat freed of the overt racial bias of the Smuts position, this work shows an undercurrent of concern – and, at times, sheer anxiety – at the formal decolonisation of the continent and how this encroached on the issue of race in South Africa. Understandably positioned against the backdrop of Cold War ideology, the work is largely cast in 'realist' thinking but with no acknowledgement of the implicit biases that this position carried. Interesting, too, is that most – if not all – of this work was produced by white English speakers, almost all of whom are men. It is difficult to escape the conclusion that there was no analysis of international relationships outside of this self-selected group – certainly, no opinions or expertise in the domain of IR seemed to exist outside of this episteme.[65]

In no small part, the explanation for this is to be found in the same document where, on a separate page, a listing of the SAIIA's 'Corporate Subscribers and Donors' appears. Listed are 38 of the-then leading South African corporations but only three of these are drawn from the (by that stage) increasingly robust Afrikaans-speaking business community.

This conclusion is unavoidable: for most of its existence, the SAIIA used the chimera of 'impartiality' to avoid dealing with the central issue that both South Africa and the discipline of IR faced – this, of course, was race. It is instructive to note that on the one occasion the SAIIA worked in partnership with the South African SAIRR was in 1979, almost 50 years after the founding of both. This was a symposium on the topic of sanctions against

South Africa, which was held in the headquarters of the SAIIA, Jan Smuts House.[66] The institute was then directed by John Barratt, son of a missionary who had read History at the universities of Witwatersrand and Oxford; he has come to the position after seven years' service in the South African diplomatic corps. However, there is some evidence that the SAIIA had earlier worked with the South African Economic Society and the Institute of Bankers of South Africa.[67]

RACE, APARTHEID AND THE INTERNATIONAL IN SOUTH AFRICA

The question of 'how did the international come to South Africa?' remains wholly unexplored in the country. We have touched on several themes in this chapter – all of which need to be linked together if this question, as it must, is to be answered. There is a sense in which South Africa holds a special place in the history of IR – not exceptional, but 'special'. It was here, as our work has shown,[68] that a proto-form of the discipline emerged in the late Edwardian period. This was marked by two central features of the discipline – exclusion on the basis of race and the claim of impartiality. Both of these are manifestly in the tradition of the Curtis Method.

The first of these, the issue of race, has been a central theme of this book. White men made IR what it was – and what it largely continues to be. In doing so, the discipline's South African forefathers – the young men in Milner's Kindergarten – saw no place in the emerging 'international' for people who were not white. Their 'international' was for whites only. This same message moved – almost seamlessly – into the deliberations around the LoN through the idea of Trusteeship, as we will see, and, thereafter, into the formalised discipline.

The second, impartiality, was of course the child of an understanding that 'science' was a kind of 'royal road' – to twist the famous phrase from Karl Marx. But, as we have shown, the 'impartiality' was on offer only to white British subjects. Approaching the international, all others could only exercise partiality, and so their views could not be authenticated by science. Elsewhere in the empire, this may not well have mattered, but in South Africa it did. This was because Afrikaners, although recently defeated in the Boer War, had both experienced international relations and enjoyed voice, if not quite agency in its making. In this sense, the racial hierarchy and segregation that crystallised into apartheid was present in the early study of IR.

Yet, South Africa's special place in IR comes, too, from the fact that during the apartheid years it was a state – a place, if you like – exiled from international relations.[69] The fact that this was first pointed out at a conference organised by the SAIIA says something about the recognition of the issues that Human Rights were bringing to IR in the late 1970s and, especially, to white-ruled South Africa's place in it. South African IR was able to use the newly found 'space of exception', the international, to defend the country from global criticism. With this, South Africa's role in IR had come full circle. South Africa had housed the thought collective that went global, inscribed the racialised idea of 'Trusteeship' into world order, spread a network of institutes around the world, and then returned home, to defend its approach to race relations as a 'domestic' matter. South Africa's IR thought was deeply enmeshed in its racial politics. It was not necessarily that different from Australia's case that we discussed in Chapter 3. We will turn our attention now back to the Antipodes, to look at New Zealand, where a small group of Round Tablers believed they had developed a better, kinder model of race development and empire-building.

5

New Zealand: Exceptionalism and Isolation in the South Pacific

New Zealand's position in the empire was somewhat akin to that of Australia: seeing itself as a white, British colony, vulnerable to invasion and resistant to Asian immigration. In this chapter, we will see that New Zealand's IR thought mirrored only some aspects of Australia's. New Zealand's study of international affairs was motivated by different anxieties, which shifted its focus. It had a small population, was even more isolated than Australia, and it had signed a treaty with its Indigenous Maori population. For the most part, the Round Table movement and the New Zealand Institute of International Affairs (NZIIA) were less tethered to Curtis' vision than in Australia. The NZIIA itself was slower to be formally instituted than its Australian and Canadian counterparts. And, in part because of its greater interest in the Pacific, it was more closely tied to the IPR.

Few studies of IR's history in New Zealand have been published. Usefully, James Cotton unpicks the relationship between the IPR, the LoN groups, Curtis and the Round Table. However, Cotton suggests that the NZIIA was influential, and its analysis as situated within New Zealand's political and ideational context. He treats the NZIIA and its analysis as avowedly internationalist, 'though sometimes compromised by racial anxieties'.[1] As we saw with our earlier studies of Australia and Canada, the assertion of New Zealand's internationalism neglects the ways in which early New Zealand IR was itself doing domestic racial analysis and was linked to New Zealand's own imperial projects. A clear-cut division between internationalism and imperialism does not necessarily reflect the ways in which internationalism was itself imperialist, and the ways in which internationalism erased settler colonialism from IR's analysis.

White New Zealand tended to believe that it held some special genius for imperialism as it had signed a treaty with its Indigenous Maori people, while Australia refused to do so. This led to New Zealand producing a narrative of itself as the ideal imperial power for the South Pacific. Numerous leaders, including Governor George Grey (1812–1898), Premier Sir Julius

Vogel (1835–1899) and Premier Robert Stout (1844–1930), all presented a vision of New Zealand as an empire in its own right, seeking to convince Britain to allow it to colonise the South Pacific. In the late 1800s, Prime Minister Richard Seddon (1845–1906) promoted the idea of New Zealand as 'the Britain of the South Pacific'. Seddon sought to convince the world that the Cook Islands, Niue, Fiji and Tonga all desired to be part of New Zealand, and was furious when Britain rejected much of his plans, allowing Hawaii and Samoa to be seized by the US and Germany, respectively. He believed, as was common at the time, that New Zealand's successful incorporation of the Maori peoples had meant that it had a special ability for colonial governance.[2] New Zealand was granted governance of Niue and the Cook Islands and was able to gather something of an empire for itself, gaining a LoN mandate for Western Samoa, which became a consistent theme in New Zealand's early IR scholarship. Seddon also toyed with the idea of joining an imperial federation, but ultimately was unable to convince a largely isolationist public of the benefits of joining such an organisation.

These themes of settlement, expansion, isolation and smallness produced a particular strain of IR thought in which colonial expansion was debated alongside themes of racial development and imperial organisation. By the late 1940s, however, New Zealand's IR thought was quite different from that of Australia and South Africa. Though it drew on matters of domestic race relations as part of its analysis of the 'international', it did so in a different fashion. New Zealand's narrative of itself as exceptionally good at imperialism was central.

New Zealand, though, was a very small polity, and the institute itself struggled for funding throughout its existence. The newly formed NZIIA was handicapped by the size of its public. It had a limited membership base and suffered from small attendance at its events in Wellington. It lurched from one grant to the next for decades, and, at one point, was forced to use all of its funds to keep afloat. It eventually found stability by becoming part of VUW, and taking funds from the New Zealand government. As a result of these factors, it did not produce what we might think of as a typical IR journal such as *International Journal* or *Australian Outlook*. Rather, it had a quite prolific pamphlet series and produced the magazine style *New Zealand International Review* in 1976.

We will begin with Curtis' trip to New Zealand in 1911, which he made after his 1910 visit to Australia, and where he had a surprisingly strong influence on New Zealand's political discourse.

FOUNDING THE ROUND TABLE IN NEW ZEALAND

On his visit, Curtis had little trouble meeting with those near the top of New Zealand's politics. He found numerous differences between Australia and New Zealand's attitude to empire, which would go on to shape Curtis' scheme for Organic Union and the patterns of thought in New Zealand's international thought. Early on his tour, Curtis considered differences in attitude and atmosphere between Australia and New Zealand. He noted a difference in the 'moral atmosphere' of the two, alongside a split between the North and the South Islands of New Zealand. He believed this to have been caused by the dominance of the Church of England driving settlement in Canterbury and the Church of Scotland driving settlement in Otago. In contrast, the transportation of convicts had 'injured Australia both in blood and in tradition'.[3] This meant that Australian newspapers had to produce New Zealand only editions should they wish to sell there, as the Australian tone of discourse would not be tolerated in New Zealand.

Of course, the goal of his tour was not just to study the politics of the Dominions, but to drum up support for imperial federation and the Round Table. As such, he was keen to bring up the concept of imperial federation and the nature of imperial defences. One of the major concerns in New Zealand was the anxiety produced by the idea of Australia forming a federation. Mr Beauchamp, the Chair of the Bank of New Zealand, argued that New Zealand could do more good for the empire on the outside of Australia, as a counter to Australia's 'anti-imperialistic tendencies'.[4] Despite this, he found 'heart and soul' support for his scheme in Christchurch putting together a Round Table group based around its president Sir George Clifford.[5]

In his diary, Curtis commented on various meetings that he had in New Zealand with those who rejected his imperial defence scheme. He was, however, able to recruit some of these doubters to his scheme. One member of the Christchurch group, Professor Blunt, a history and literature scholar, Curtis saw as a doubter, and described Blunt as having 'a low view of human nature in general and of New Zealand nature in particular'.[6] Another, W.H. Montgomery, told Curtis that New Zealand should save its money for local development, rather than paying for its own imperial defence. Curtis derided this as a 'little New Zealand' point of view. Montgomery reportedly saw Australasia's real danger as being 'the Mongolian races' and that they needed their own fleet for their own defence.[7] One man, whom Curtis only referred to as 'Reece', believed that Britain had reached the 'zenith of her power' and that without the Dominions' assistance 'the Empire will come a cropper'.[8] The day after this dinner, however, Curtis noted that he had been able to convince Montgomery of his own position, and Montgomery eventually joined the group in Christchurch. This group was to provide the first article for *The Round Table* but was not quite able to produce it in time for publication in the inaugural issue.

Curtis was able to meet with Prime Minister Joseph Ward (1856–1930), who had led New Zealand to Dominion status in 1907 and who along with Seddon had advocated for imperial federation since the 1890s.[9] Ward and Curtis discussed Maori racial development, with an eye to comparing the situation in New Zealand to that of South Africa. Ward suggested to him that the Maoris had been 'managed for the most part through their own members in Parliament', and that this was crucial to their development. Curtis noted that the suggestion would be impossible in South Africa due to white public opinion there, and that Ward did not seem to know this. Here, we can see that New Zealand had a greatly different situation with its own domestic race relations than South Africa and, indeed, Australia. The discussion of Maori politics was all that Curtis noted in his diary with regard to Ward, perhaps as Ward was known as being supportive of imperial federation. Still, that the Round Table was influential in New Zealand can be seen in Ward's presentation at the Imperial Conference of 1911. Ward called for the creation of an imperial parliament which, as Keith Hancock and J.E. Kendle have argued, was clearly influenced by the plans of Curtis.[10]

Aside from these matters of race development, Curtis also discussed some of the difficulties raised for imperial defence, based on political concerns but also in the ways naval officers were trained. As he put it to one target of his project, the 'absence of responsibility in external affairs was really one of the factors contributing to the deterioration in the moral outlook of the dominions'.[11] For the most part, however, Curtis had little difficulty convincing New Zealanders to support his cause and finding writers for *The Round Table* as well as people to promote it. If anything, based on his diary, the rivalry with Australia was the most significant limitation he faced in gaining support within New Zealand. This rivalry would go on to prove a problem for his project of imperial unity, and it would later sour relations between the NZIIA and the AIIA.

NEW ZEALAND IN *THE ROUND TABLE*

The first year of New Zealand's articles in *The Round Table* set out the foremost concerns of the colony and narrated New Zealand's concerns with imperial order for its fellow Dominions. The first discussion of New Zealand in *The Round Table* sought to achieve this through a historical narrative of New Zealand settlement, so as to ground subsequent analysis and to give New Zealand's perspective of possible changes to the imperial structures.[12] The narrative began with the discovery of New Zealand by the Dutch in 1642, coupled with a quick dismissal of Dutch claims to ownership over the territory. It then moved swiftly on to Cook's visit in 1796 and the surveying of the islands. Until May 1841, New Zealand was governed as a dependency from New South Wales. Plans were made for incorporating New Zealand and Australia into a larger federation taking up the South Pacific. After this brief historical narrative of New Zealand's settlement, the analysis went on to cover in a narrative fashion what were seen as the most important international issues facing New Zealand: political progress, settlement, the 'native question' of the Maoris, defence and New Zealand's participation in imperial conferences. These all remained consistent themes of New Zealand's IR.

As part of the discussion of imperial conferences, this first article set up a key ideational clash between New Zealand and Australia. New Zealand was described as comfortable with imperial federation, but keen to draw a distinction between itself and Australia. One author argued that 'many in New Zealand were hoping it would become a sister state to Australia in a far wider reaching federation, and they were not prepared to sacrifice this expectation for the small advantage offered by immediate incorporation in the huge continental state'.[13] The author described geographical concerns about the isolation and the distance between Australia and New Zealand, but also that New Zealand had a different history of colonisation and that it 'clung tenaciously to the idea of independence'.[14] As we will see throughout the chapter, New Zealand had many of the same concerns as Australia, but with some differences in emphasis, particularly with regard to its Maori peoples.

Race was a crucial part of the analysis of the politics and external relations of New Zealand and a constant theme of the early analyses. One article stated that '[t]here is no doubt that there exists in New Zealand a strong antipathy to the yellow races of the East'. This was accounted for as 'partly a natural race prejudice, partly economic, for the New Zealand worker objects to the cheap labour of the Asiatic', as well as 'partly the result of the strong anti-Asiatic agitation in the neighbouring Commonwealth, which, unlike New Zealand, has territory bordering Asiatic seas and not easily exploited by white labour, and which has already experienced to some degree the horrors of mixed white and yellow population'.[15] As was the case in Australia, it was believed that England did not fully understand the concerns in New Zealand about immigration, closing that '[t]his feeling, unreasonable though it may appear to the people of the old country, is real, and has influenced the way in which the British-Japanese agreements of 1902 and 1905 are regarded here'.[16]

Settlement was followed by an analysis of the race relations between the Maoris and the white colonisers of New Zealand. The analysis began: 'Unfortunately, peace has not brought to the Maoris blessings equal to those it brought to the *pakeha* [white man].' Following colonisation, 'disease and depopulation have followed, and a race which in 1800 numbered over 100,000 has now shrunk to fewer than half that number.' The situation was placed in more positive terms, producing a narrative of the Maoris' racial progress:

> The Maori, for his part, is on excellent terms with the white; mixed marriages occur in all grades of society; stringent laws control the sale of alcoholic liquor to the native race; while education, along academic, technical, agricultural, and domestic lines, is at last slowly fitting them to take a place in the elaborate scheme of European civilization.[17]

The status of the Maoris would go on to be a constant consideration of New Zealand's IR, and was used as a means of arguing for New Zealand to take more control of the South Pacific.

The racialised nature of the geopolitical concerns which animated the scholarship in *The Round Table* was made very clear in New Zealand. One discussion opened with the threat that Japan was posing to New Zealand, suggesting that: 'Nothing that has happened during the last three months has done more to arouse in New Zealand a sense of their imperial responsibilities than the activity of the Japanese in various parts of the Pacific.'[18] The need to control external affairs was explicitly tied to the imperial mission and animated by the concern of an opposing potential empire. Repeating a common line from Australian scholarship, the author noted that 'People in England can scarcely realize the attitude of New Zealand and Australia towards the coloured races.'[19] These racial fears of invasion and of 'coloured labour' produced particular geopolitical anxieties.

The narrative of US colonisation of Hawaii here demonstrates the style of analysis, with the threat of 'peaceful invasion' by the Japanese in particular through the hiring of cheap and effective labour. 'The American capitalists who had invested millions in Hawaiian sugar plantations naturally looked about for cheap labour. The native Hawaiians were too lazy, so it became necessary to import labour from abroad.'[20] As a result of this, 'Japanese were poured into the territory in such numbers that they are now the dominant people'.[21] As they were prepared to sell goods for less, there was also the belief that the 'white ... Trader [will] be driven completely out of business'.[22]

This led to the concern that Japan might wish to take over New Caledonia, an island colonised by the French which was only 800 miles from Australia. The island was seen as empty space and colonisable, because 'no effort ha[d] been made to people it with good and hardy settlers'.[23] At this stage, geopolitics were couched in imperial and racial terms, with territory not populated with 'advanced' racial stocks viewed as *terra nullius*.

A great deal of New Zealand's publishing with *The Round Table* at this time was expressed through its fears of Asian immigration. This was connected to concerns about the possibility of imperial unity. One author noted that '[t]he unity of the Empire may depend on feeling, and be the better for symbolical expression, but concrete problems arise which demand practical measures and machinery for dealing with them. Such a one is the question of Asiatic immigration.'[24] As with Australia, New Zealand saw Asian immigration as a threat to its very existence. It is here that the nature of imperial unity became clearly to do with race. The possibility though that intensity of feeling over New Zealand's whiteness would disrupt the imperial unity was raised and dismissed.[25] The author then quoted a *New Zealand Herald* article, which argued that Chinese and Japanese people were not interested in coming to New Zealand, and so India's connection to the empire meant that Indians were the more likely threat:

> India may claim for the Hindus certain privileges as British subjects, but if the right of entry to New Zealand is among these, then the issue must be faced squarely at the next Imperial Conference. As a self-governing country the Dominion has an inalienable right to determine the character of her immigration and to refuse whom she will.[26]

Around this time, India became seen as a problem for those pushing any idea of imperial unity. Curtis himself had become convinced that India needed to be part of any imperial federation or imperial parliament.[27] This same ambivalent dynamic, in which India was central to imperial prestige but rejected as an equal partner, had helped sink the idea of 'Greater Britain' some decades earlier.[28] This was also tied to the discussion on imperial federation. Henry Richards, Chief Justice of the United Provinces of Agra and Oudh, spoke in New Zealand about the attitude of Indians towards federation, arguing that they would not accept any control from the Dominions.[29] The intense racial anxiety felt by New Zealand and Australia was a central problem for the project of imperial unity that Curtis had undertaken. The unwillingness to accept any non-white immigration meant that Indians could not travel freely throughout the empire, and ensured that they could never feel the equal of white imperial subjects. At the same time, India would not accept having its affairs dictated to it from New Zealand and Australia as well as from London.

CURTIS' RETURN IN 1916

WWI was of course a major focus of New Zealand's IR, taking up a great deal of its analytical space. It stirred up patriotic sentiments, with one author opening that: 'There is literally no sacrifice which New Zealand is not prepared to make for the maintenance of the Empire.'[30] It was also noted that Maoris were just as keen to sign up for the war effort as were the Europeans. More importantly for us, however, is the effect it had on the Round Table's efforts to provoke imperial unity. With the Round Table groups up and running in New Zealand and producing continual commentary on New Zealand's role in the empire, Curtis returned to tour once again, and to speak on the merits of his plans in 1916. He did so as part of a tour relating to his 1915 book *The Problem of the Commonwealth*. The central thrust of his argument on the tour was that the Dominions had to claim control of their foreign policy, but within his framework of Organic Union. On this trip, he evoked both his successes in South Africa and the course of WWI to argue for the importance of an Imperial Convention, leading to an imperial parliament. He was also able to gather very positive press coverage and to engage with the groups he had set up on his original visit. He spoke in Wellington on 1 August 1916, and then in Christchurch and Dunedin, before returning to Wellington for a few weeks.

The *Evening Post* described his approach as 'admirably clear, candid and concise'. The paper agreed at least with the first element of his commentary – that an Imperial Convention had to follow WWI, though it stopped short of endorsing an imperial parliament. The newspaper editorialised that 'we should all be able to agree upon this step as a necessary condition of any real progress towards an effective imperial unity'. In particular, Curtis' comment that the UK needed its own 'Dominion government' to look after its own affairs as New Zealand and Canada already had was popular, as it would place the Dominions on an equal footing with the UK.[31] *The New Zealand Times* gave a similarly favourable review of Curtis' arguments.[32] Curtis drew directly on his experiences in South Africa, claiming both that the foundation of the South African Union had been brought about by his group's efforts, and that he had predicted German aggression in Southern Africa.

He gathered support from the crowd by evoking the war, arguing that 'the flower of [New Zealand's] manhood' was being spent abroad, and that this must ensure that the Dominions should rise up the imperial hierarchy.[33]

The Dominion newspaper later editorialised that Curtis' book was commendable and ought to be read, but warned of troubles of imperial taxation and where India and Egypt might fit inside his scheme to reorganise the empire.[34] A few days later, Heinrich. F. Von Haast, a Christchurch lawyer and prominent Wellington Round Table group member, who went on to play key roles in the NZIIA, including writing many of the New Zealand articles in The Round Table,[35] responded to these questions in a letter to the newspaper.[36] He copied Curtis' response to the question of race and empire, commenting that 'there could be no fusion between East and West' and that there would be evil effects from 'pouring the new wine of modern European ideas into the old bottles of a static Oriental civilization'. It was necessary instead to avoid mixing 'Asiatic and Anglo-Saxon blood' and that the Round Table did not advocate granting 'full Imperial franchise to the colour races of the Empire, which are not yet ripe for self-government'. He reiterated Curtis' argument that the white races had only assumed 'trusteeship' over the subject races, and that they would eventually claim self-government.[37] Curtis was able to convince several members of the New Zealand government as to the merits of his plan for imperial reorganisation, though it is unclear from his diary if he was able to convince the Defence Minister upon their meeting.

NEW ZEALAND AND THE SOUTH PACIFIC

In New Zealand's imagination, the matter of the subject peoples within the empire was more about the South Pacific than it was about 'big picture' questions about India and Egypt. That New Zealand had a key role to play in the South Pacific had become even more than an orthodoxy after WWI – it became a reality. Towards the conclusion of WWI, one Round Table author argued for New Zealand to take control of its own colonies, commenting that 'The peril of Australasia is regarded as the peril of the whole Pacific, and the peril of the whole Pacific is not considered to be distinguishable from that of the whole Empire'.[38] The answer for the New Zealand Round Table groups was clear: New Zealand had to take on its own civilising mission in the South Pacific. This was seen in The Round Table as one of the two issues that united all of New Zealand, alongside opposing Asian immigration.

Indeed, with the establishment of the LoN, and the seizing of German colonies around the world, 'mandates' became central to world political order. Western Samoa became a 'class c' mandate (the lowest developed class of mandate), and was granted by the League to New Zealand. Samoa would become a focus of New Zealand's publishing in *The Round Table* for many years, with discussion emphasising its racial development, progress and administration. Debate initially fell on whether or not New Zealand should be directly involved in external colonisation of islands in the South Pacific, or if these societies should be Crown colonies. With Western Samoa proving far more difficult a project for New Zealand, however, this ended up being a more challenging question for the New Zealand Round Table groups than they had expected.

Here, the various forms of status of societies became the crucial discussion in New Zealand's IR. The concepts of empire, Dominion and colony, alongside the idea of different empires clashing with one another, were the two major issues for international relations. New Zealand's IR considered what the relationship between civilisational units within imperial hierarchies could or should be, as well as the clashes between empires. The grant of Samoa as a mandate caused something of an ideational debate in New Zealand, as it seemingly changed the status of the Dominion itself. At the same time, a debate on the utility of imperial federation was taking place, which was far more normative, looking at reorganising the empire to make it more stable, efficient and long-lasting. The framing of both of these debates was deeply racialised.

Samoa proved to be very difficult for the New Zealand administration, and the course of events there, if anything, dispelled the idea that New Zealand had a special knowledge of imperialism. The New Zealand backed administration faced resistance from the Mau, a political organisation seeking independence, for almost the entirety of its existence. The Mau were an anti-colonial political organisation, who practised passive resistance and came to prominence in the late 1920s.[39] They were led by Ta'isi Olaf Frederick Nelson (1883–1944), who was allowed some influence under German rule but was alienated by the New Zealand administration. In 1929, New Zealand military police fired upon a peaceful demonstration, killing eight people. In 1935, the Mau were recognised as a legitimate political organisation, which lessened the urgency of the political crisis in the colony, though independence was not granted until 1962. In a move that very few former colonial powers undertake, Prime Minister Helen Clarke apologised to the people of Samoa during a visit to Apia on the 40-year anniversary of independence.

The anonymous articles in *The Round Table*'s approach to the resistance in Samoa was to defend the colonial administration. The immediate response in 1927, when Mau first came to political prominence to the extent that they were banned as an organisation, was to defend the gentle, benign and reasonable nature of the colonial mandate:

> In view of what has since been said about militaristic tyranny and 'the methods of Moscow,' it is only fair to say that the mild and fatherly tone of the warning is quite in keeping with the reputation that Sir George Richardson enjoys in his own country. The general impression in New Zealand that, if he had erred at all, it would not have been in the direction of severity, has since been confirmed by one who served under him as a volunteer and afterward was his official superior as Minister of Defence.[40]

In 1928, as the Mau began a campaign of passive resistance and challenged colonial rule, it produced a detailed but dry narrative seeking to establish the facts on the ground in Samoa, which was rather gently in favour of the New Zealand government's position and dismissive of 'native' concerns. Here we see the imperial method of gathering 'international facts' to build reality in action. The situation in Samoa was mediated by the Mandates Commission in Geneva, whose report favoured New Zealand. The report was published by *The Round Table*:

> This charge the Commissioners regard as a mere repetition in general terms of the main charge that the Administrator had failed to pay due regard to the customs and feelings of the people of Samoa. On a review of the whole evidence they hold it to be unfounded.[41]

The Round Table group's approach was purely dismissive of the Mau's concerns:

> The Commission had left no room for doubt in any impartial mind about the benevolence and forbearance of the Administrator, the purely selfish and mischievous character of Mr. Nelson's agitation, and the transparent absurdity of supposing that the action of the natives whom he had deluded and inflamed was prompted by genuine grievances or spontaneous resentment.[42]

There was no consideration at this point of what the resistance of the Samoans meant for the idea that New Zealand had a particular genius for colonial government. Rather, the analysis was more limited to threats, with one article closing: 'patience cannot last forever … the change in the administration is the last chance that will be given the Mau natives'.[43] The difficulties of this colonial project would do significant damage to the idea that New Zealand could be the Britain of the South Pacific. As we will see below, after the establishment of the NZIIA one of its first publications was a critique of New Zealand's colonial administration in Samoa.

FOUNDING THE NEW ZEALAND INSTITUTE
OF INTERNATIONAL AFFAIRS

Just prior to the establishment of the NZIIA, the AIIA's Frederic Eggleston and Douglas Copland complained to Chatham House about the low quality of the studies coming out of the Dominions in the Round Table.[44] That same year, Frederic Eggleston wrote to Chatham House to say that the Round Table was failing in its mission. The articles from the Dominions were mostly reports on domestic affairs, with very few specific foreign policy analyses emerging from the Dominions, as the original idea had been. H.V. Hodson, in his role as editor of *The Round Table*, closed the matter by apologising to the New Zealand group, in a slightly backhanded fashion. He commented that he had been unaware of the 'special circumstances' in New Zealand. These special circumstances were 'the dearth, in New Zealand, of big subjects interesting to the outside world'.[45]

Despite, or perhaps because of, the complaints over the work being done in New Zealand, the NZIIA was formed in 1934. The New Zealand branch of the IPR was founded in 1926 and gathered crossover in its membership with the NZIIA.[46] The NZIIA was formally established in 1934, replacing the Round Table groups, but not merging with the IPR until 1939. It is well worth noting that women were not allowed to be full members.[47] Its first goal of study was simple enough: 'to study international relations particular in so far as these affect New Zealand and the British Empire and also the inter-relations of the constituent parts of the British Empire'.[48] It followed the Chatham House model and was hence not to express an opinion as to the course of international affairs. The foundational meeting also recommended a constitution based 'on similar lines to those of the [AIIA] and of the New Zealand Branch of the Institute of Pacific Affairs [sic]'. It also recommended that 'the Institute should arrange for close co-operation with the New Zealand branch of the Institute of Pacific Relations in particularly, and also with such bodies as the League of Nations Union'. There was a great deal of crossover in the membership of each of these bodies. Based only in

Wellington, there were simply not that many people engaged in the study of international affairs. The NZIIA's dues-paying membership in 1936 was just 36 people.[49]

The establishment of the NZIIA was done simply by the New Zealand Round Table changing its name to 'New Zealand Institute of International Affairs' in 1934.[50] Despite its small numbers, the institute immediately had members in high places. The inaugural executive of the NZIIA was extremely diverse in terms of its politics. William Downie Stewart (1878–1949), former New Zealand Finance Minister, was the institution's first president.[51] He was a member of the Reform Party,[52] but had close sympathies with the Labour movement. H.F. Von Haast was its vice-president, and Walter Nash (Finance Minister from 1935 to 1949 and Prime Minister from 1957 to 1960), Robert Campbell Begg (leader of the New Zealand Legion, who moved to South Africa in 1937),[53] F. Martin-Smith and G.R. Powles (a military leader who went to a significant diplomatic career) made up its Council.[54] Downie Stewart and Nash were also inaugural members of the New Zealand branch of the IPR. Nash had previously led New Zealand's delegation to the second IPR Conference in Honolulu in 1927, and was also a member of the League of Nations Union. Nash went on to become Labour Party Prime Minister from 1957 to 1960 and was a pacifist in WWI. He was motivated to study international affairs by both his pacifism and his desire to help the world's poor.[55] Campbell Begg, however, would prove a particularly controversial member of the NZIIA. At the time, he was president of the 'New Zealand Legion', a group that emerged out of frustration with the conservative side of New Zealand politics. It was seen as fascist by those on the left of New Zealand's politics. It advocated individual self-reliance and greater independence from Britain. It was evidently clear at this point that the NZIIA, though closely affiliated with Chatham House and operating along its model, could hardly follow through on Curtis' vision of Organic Unity.

Shortly after its founding, the institute began to hold academic seminars addressing some element of international affairs every two months or so. The topics in the first year included the Abyssinian Crisis, the rise of National Socialism in Germany, Australia's relations with New Zealand, a study of German colonial claims in Samoa by General H. Hart, the more general 'impressions of world affairs' by G.H. Schoelfeld and 'recent impressions of Japan' by F. Martin-Smith. Most of the talks were given by members. A study group led by Von Haast, Wood, Sprat, Stevens and Powles was to complete a memorandum on the Commonwealth and collective security, at the request of Chatham House.[56] They were unable to complete the task, however, holding a discussion of the topic instead, bemoaning that 'the small number of active members continuously resident in Wellington makes it difficult to pursue any particular Study or Research'. As a result, 'the Institutes' activities have ... been confined to holding occasional meeting and hearing addresses'. By July of 1936, the institute had just 36 members, many of whom were not based in Wellington.[57] This at least meant that, in its first year, the NZIIA was able to save money by hosting its events in the houses of members, though it was noted that 'with increasing membership the institute could not expect this assistance in the future'.[58]

In the years between the formation of the NZIIA and its merging with the IPR, a series of scholarly addresses were given to the institute. J.H. Luxford spoke on his goodwill mission to Samoa, trying to find shared political ideas with the Mau. Luxford reportedly had 'the highest admiration for the German administration', arguing that the islands had actually been more peaceful under German than New Zealand's rule and blamed in some part the 'present government of New Zealand' for current troubles in Samoa.[59]

A Round Table session on New Zealand's defence revealed the continuing salience of the Round Table's original formulation to the NZIIA's agenda. Discussion focused on four topics: should New Zealand prepare to defend itself; should New Zealand assist the empire in the event of war; should there be any compulsory military training for citizens; and what is the duty of good citizens in matters of war.[60] There was broad agreement that New Zealand needed to assist in providing for its own defence, but within the framework of the British empire. One speaker, Mr Mawson, described himself as a 'realist' and argued that the Dominions 'were and would be guided entirely by economic self-interest'.[61] Within this, though, he assumed that New Zealand would always be a part of the empire and should take part in any defence of the empire, no matter where in the world it was fought. There was some slight friction, however. Mr Weston's opening remarks, perhaps confusing gendered pronouns, stated that 'Her [New Zealand's] attitude should be that of an affectionate son towards his father.' Mr Free objected to this, saying it was 'sentimental' and 'risked provoking a dangerous spirit of the "my-Empire-right-or-wrong type"'. He conceded that New Zealand might well see international affairs differently from the UK, and that it was the US that was more likely to defend New Zealand from the Japanese.[62]

Over the next few years, the NZIIA heard a great variety of topics, most of them focused on the domestic and international affairs of particular states or regions. An Indian speaker, P. Kondana Rao, also visited to speak to the institute. Rao had worked for V.S. Srinivasa Sastri for over a decade, and toured extensively in Canada with the CIIA.[63] Rao's talk was focused on political order in India, particularly decrying the ongoing role of the princely states, who he saw as pro-British and anti-democratic. He also discussed his distrust of the UK Conservative Party's goals in India. Topics, though, were not just limited to the empire. They included the Far-East, Russia, Germany and Canada. The focus was far less on specific imperial projects than in Australia, and there was far more emphasis on seminars and discussions rather than publications. The NZIIA was not able to publish a journal, partly due to its low membership and limited finances. Most meetings had around 20 to 30 attendees.

The study of international affairs in New Zealand was, in some ways, more independent than that of Australia. Because of its small membership, the institute had to incorporate a broader body of opinion than in Canada, simply because it could not afford to lose the membership and patronage. One talk in particular, by H. Duncan Hall, simply titled 'Some aspects of the International Crisis', proved quite divisive. Begg commented on the talk that he 'disagreed with almost everything Mr Duncan Hall had said'. He began with the Italian-Abyssinian conflict, arguing that 'Abyssinia was but a congeries of savage tribes' that 'should never have been a member of the League'.[64] He believed that sanctions against Mussolini's Italy were entirely unfounded and the Abyssinians to be primarily responsible for the brutality of the conflict. He went on to suggest that German feeling over the demilitarisation of the Rhineland was justified, and the situation was analogous to Germany demilitarising south east England had they won WWI. He continued that 'Dictatorship in some form, was natural to the German people', and that Hitler and Mussolini would abide by international agreements. Furthermore, that 'Hitler had abandoned some of the policies laid down in "Mein Kampf" and his peace plans should be accepted at face value'.[65] The meeting minutes simply note that the rest of the group did not agree with Begg's analysis. The discussion was summed up by Mr Justice Smyth rather diplomatically, suggesting that Australia and New Zealand should be prepared to defend themselves regardless of events in Europe. Begg departed for a study tour shortly after, and moved to South Africa within a year. He never returned to the institute.[66]

THE IPR JOINS NZIIA

As had occurred much earlier in Australia and Canada, the possibility of merging the Round Table affiliated groups with the IPR was ever present in

New Zealand. In an unsigned letter sent from the New Zealand IPR to Guy Powles, secretary of the NZIIA, the possibility of a merger was put forward:

> So far as I am in a position to judge, there seems to be a fairly widespread feeling that New Zealand is too small a place for the existence, side by side of a number of separate and entirely independent organisations having similar objects, similar instructions and pursuing much the same activities by much the same methods.[67]

The case for merger, then, was fairly simple. There was a great overlap between the membership, and limited funds available for the study of the international from which to draw upon. The author noted that the matter 'has been a live issue in the past but that no action in this direction has been taken because of a certain reluctance on the part of both organisations to lose any of their separate identity.'[68]

An IPR meeting which discussed this also noted that 'for some time past it was pointed out the IPR had lacked effective leadership and direction. There was little real life in the majority of local groups and it has been extremely difficult during the last year or two to arrange for proper representative meetings of the National Council.'[69] The meeting felt that, 'despite the organisational difficulties, they still felt they were continuing to undertake useful research'. Believing a merger would safeguard their research and fix their administrative problems, they unanimously agreed to put together a merger proposal. At the next IPR meeting, the group received a full report of a joint IPR-NZIIA committee on a merger. The New Zealand IPR approved the merger on 25 October 1939, with the institute affiliated to both Chatham House and the IPR. The president remained W. Downie Smith, the vice-presidents were Nash, Von Haast, Cocker, Sutherland and William Edward Barnard (Labour Party member, Speaker of the House in the New Zealand parliament and Chairman of the New Zealand IPR[70]).[71]

Around the time the merger was completed, the NZIIA began to publish some of its own research. Its first publication was a short pamphlet on Samoa, questioning whether or not Samoa should be returned to Germany. In keeping with the tradition of anonymity of the Round Table, it was simply represented as the report of a study group. New Zealand's continued rule was justified in this piece on the basis that 'Samoans failed to evolve a stable political system for themselves' and the situation was still not yet stable enough for government.[72] While acknowledging that New Zealand had struggled to deal with the colony, and that things might have been better under the previous German administration, it still argued for

New Zealand to maintain control, commenting that 'there is a fairly wide-spread appreciation of the success of previous German rule in Samoa, and perhaps, a tendency to disparage New Zealand's own record'. This, they argued, would not be the case were Germany to retake control 'as there would be a natural reluctance to give up a task which New Zealand has always taken seriously, and there would be a feeling that, on account of her racial theories, Germany might not be a trustworthy ruler of natives'.[73]

Perhaps the major pre-war achievement of the NZIIA was its publication of *Contemporary New Zealand* in 1938. This was prepared for the British Commonwealth Relations Conference but which was also published for general readership. It described New Zealand's role in the Commonwealth as retaining the psychology of a colony, as with Australia, but described South Africa and Canada as breaking away. On this topic, it was concluded that 'We are British, and proud of it; and feeling a common nationality, we feel the necessity of a common political system'.[74] This work very much followed the template set by the Round Table, of the circulation of domestic information coupled with foreign policy commentary.[75]

In 1940, NZIIA published a collection edited by I.G.L. Sutherland on the development of the Maoris. It framed the issue as a study of what occurs when 'an industrial civilization' engages with 'primitive cultures'.[76] The approach taken to the issues of colonisation in New Zealand, though, were far different to those in Australia. Sutherland commented:

> The institutions of native peoples now that they have been extensively and objectively studied, are seen to have reason, purpose and values of their own, and the policy which in the past would have swept them away in the name of progress is known to produce results which are almost invariably disastrous.[77]

Here, Sutherland argued that Maori institutions need to be integrated into New Zealand society and respected. Comparing New Zealand's approach with other American Indians, he commented that 'though old policies still continue extensively enough, much effort at undoing harm is today being made in various parts of the world'. In concluding the collection, Sutherland commented that none of the 'issues between the Maori and *Pakeha* … cannot be resolved by tolerance, mutual understanding and active goodwill'.[78]

It is clear from the publication of this study that domestic race relations were seen as a form of international affairs, as was the case in Australia, Canada and South Africa. In New Zealand, though, the scholarship was of a different tone. This goes back to the treatment of the Maoris from the beginnings of colonisation, who were respected in ways that Indigenous Australian were not. The signing of the Treaty of Waitangi, between 500 Maori chiefs and the British Crown, gave the British sovereignty over New Zealand. The Treaty gave the Maoris the rights of British subjects.[79] The meaning of the Treaty has been politically charged in New Zealand ever since.

Another interesting case of the varied political politics within the NZIIA is the role of William Ball Sutch, who became particularly famous for being put on trial (and later acquitted) under the Official Secrets Act following engagement with a Russian diplomat.[80] He published an article on New Zealand in the RIIA's *International Affairs* in 1938, which presents a useful survey of what was seen as IR in New Zealand. He opened, rather than with history, with the population of New Zealand. He began by commenting that New Zealand had a higher percentage population of people of UK origin than the UK itself. 'The native population is small but increasing, and there is no native problem as it is known in other English-speaking countries. There is more of the feeling of trusteeship towards the Maoris than of overlord.' He argued, though, that New Zealand was beginning to lose its sense of Englishness, as 'The New Zealand attitude to the English is largely a sentimental one. Most of them do not know England at first hand. They do not know its slums and its industrialism.' This descriptive work comprised over half the article, before finally asking the research question, 'How does New Zealand regard the Empire and foreign affairs?'[81] Here, the analysis moved on to public perception of imperial affairs, suggesting New Zealand questioned British policy in India and the conduct of the Boer War. Of Western Samoa, he argued that while '[t]he sincerity and zeal of the New Zealand Government's administration cannot be doubted ... there is occasional discontent in New Zealand over the government's treatment of the Mau'.

THE POST-WAR LIFE OF NZIIA
AND ITS STRUGGLE FOR SURVIVAL

Post-war, the NZIIA struggled for funds but became rather more prolific and eventually ensured its stability. Shortly after WWII, J.K. Banks became concerned that the 'inactivity' of the National Council might lead to the loss of a crucial 1946 grant from the Carnegie Foundation. He commented to the National Council that 'we will have no alternative but to disassociate ourselves from the present National Council, and we will officially notify our present bodies the IPR and the Royal Institute, stating the whole position to them.[82]

The NZIIA struggled for money until 1970 when the Ford Foundation provided the institution with a grant of US$100,000 over three years. They then received more money from the Ford Foundation and later from the New Zealand government. Although the New Zealand government had previously been urged not to provide funding to the NZIIA,[83] the Ministry of Foreign Affairs finally agreed to do so. This funding ensured its survival, but meant a change in character of the institute. It could no longer be seen as unaffiliated. Guy Powles stated at a meeting 'that the institute could only survive until April (when the government grant, is paid) by the exhaustion of the reserves accumulated over the past 20 years.'[84] Perhaps unaware of this long-standing reluctance, Powles described the ministry as an 'enthusiastic' funder.[85] The grant caused the institute some anxiety, particularly as it, coupled with its move to VUW, ensured its continued existence. It was able to expand its publications, continuing its regular series of pamphlets, starting a newsletter, and, eventually, in 1976 the *New Zealand International Review*.[86] The *New Zealand International Review* remains something between a magazine and an academic journal. Publishing pamphlets continued to be a focus of the institute, though its records suggest there were consistent concerns about publishing costs.

With its place secured through connections to both the government and a university, the NZIIA's goal remained expanding people's knowledge of international affairs. Interestingly, the opening issue of the *New Zealand International Review* did not contain an editorial detailing the purpose of its publication. By the time something had been established that we might call a journal, IR in New Zealand had drifted even further from Curtis' vision. In its official history, the NZIIA now refers to its 'long and valued associations with VUW and the Ministry of Foreign Affairs and Trade. They are cornerstone partners. Their support is vital to the Institute.'[87] The NZIIA now frames its existence in very different terms, although it claims to police 'the country's performance as an international "good citizen".'[88] Any lofty hopes of shaping the course of international affairs, however, have dissipated. An official pamphlet on the institute, hosted on the website of the New Zealand Parliament, was published in 2012. It has a more realistic aim:

Events outside New Zealand will continue to affect us far more than we can influence them. The need for a better understanding of the world we live in and the forces of change at work is never-ending. This is where the Institute will continue to strive to deliver a unique contribution.[89]

The study of New Zealand IR was shaped by its political environment, alongside its relatively small size and isolation. Curtis found willing participants high up in New Zealand's politics and government relatively easily. *The Round Table* articles focused on settlement, race relations and the idea of New Zealand as its own empire. Over time, its horizons shrunk with the failure of New Zealand's schemes to govern the South Pacific as an empire. Still, issues of domestic settlement were a part of their understanding of the international, with *Pakeha*-Maori relations studied by the group. With this, the institute struggled for funding and to produce research. It drew from a small base of issues, to the extent that they were critiqued by the Australians for being insufficiently 'international'.

Curtis' model was particularly difficult to implement in New Zealand, even though he found it to be one of the more agreeable places to his vision of imperial unity on his initial tour. An elite institute in New Zealand drew on too small a membership to be particularly productive. As such, its membership tended to be relatively small, and it struggled for financing throughout its independent existence. New Zealand's international thought at this time was positioned within the idea that it was a kinder imperial overseer than Australia. In this sense, placing New Zealand's IR history in conversation with that of Canada and Australia is important. New Zealand was far more polite about its imperialism than Australia, believing it had succeeded where other settler colonies had failed. Despite this, ideas of settlement, race, empire, were central to the ways in which New Zealand interpreted the world.

We will now turn to our final case study: India. As with New Zealand, the IIIA found only a limited pool of resources from which to draw on, and was not able to produce much work. This was, of course, for very different reasons.

6

India: The Imperial Discipline
Meets Anti-Colonial Nationalism

India has rich and varied traditions of international thought dating back centuries. The Indian Institute of International Affairs (IIIA), though, as it existed within the orbit of Curtis' projects, found itself unable to produce research or to fulfil its mission. In our final case study, we look at the efforts of the Round Table to bring India into its projects. In doing so, we look at the limits of Curtis' imperial mission as the empire slowly fractured.

A colony is a thoroughly politicised site. Institutions founded on anti-politics, on the pretence of *doing* the science of politics, are often 'scientific advisors to colonialism', as the philosopher V.Y. Mudimbe once termed Anthropology.[1] Accordingly, translating Chatham House's vision of a non-partisan, non-political institute, fully committed to objective and impassioned analysis, to the colony of India reveals the ways in which an avowedly *apolitical* project fundamentally aligns itself with power. Indeed, when the moves towards a Chatham House-backed institute in India started in the 1930s, Indian leaders were already urging Indian intellectuals to channel their 'science' towards 'service'. Speaking at the inaugural conference of the Indian Political Science in 1938, Gobind Vallabh Pant, a prominent Congress leader, said: 'Let us take a vow that the freedom of every state, the independence of every nation will be the objective of the [political] science … this seems to me to be the "*summum bonum*" of political science.'[2]

This chapter will narrate the story of the early years of two key IR institutes in India, faced as they were with the challenge of remaining 'objective'. Telling the story itself is valuable in the context of Indian IR, partly because it is so little known. In most narratives of Indian IR, the academic study of international politics in India is dated to the inauguration of the Indian School of International Studies in 1955.[3] Opened under the auspices of the Indian Council on World Affairs (ICWA), a think tank dedicated to promoting thinking on world affairs, the School moved to Jawaharlal Nehru University in 1970. These narratives then vaguely gesture towards the ICWA as the fount of IR's institutional history in India. But little is discussed about how the ICWA was formed. The political context of the origins of the ICWA has nearly disappeared from public memory, and if it all, it is seen as a product of Nehru's thinking about world politics. The historical record shows otherwise. In fact, the Council was started by a faction from within a pre-existing institute, the IIIA. In the run up to independence, the IIIA and the ICWA battled for legitimacy in an increasingly polarised Hindu-Muslim context, and eventually the 'Indian' institute was taken to Pakistan.

The IIIA's biography follows quite a familiar trajectory for the students of the subcontinent's history – it was born in the capital of United India, Delhi, but met its demise in the capital city of the partitioned Pakistan, Karachi. As we will see in the following pages, the IIIA follows the path of other IR institutes in that it was set up as part of Chatham House's efforts at expansion and opening 'sister' institutes. However, the story is also remarkably different in other ways. The institute is the only one among Chatham House affiliates to have not survived.

But before we go deeper into the origins of the IIIA and the ICWA, let us briskly append an important caveat. The absence of a formalised study of IR does not mean an absence of international thought. This is particularly important to stress with regard to India in this book, because the absence of non-Western narratives on IR is neither because of a lack of thinking and articulation, nor because of fewer avenues for scholarly productions. Indeed, ideas and debates on international relations in India, and by Indians, had a vibrant life in the early twentieth century. In occasional references to Indian contributions to international thought, Benoy Kumar Sarkar's article titled 'Hindu Theory of International Relations' in the *American Political Science Review* in 1919 is often presented as a signature contribution (because it was published in an American journal).[4] This is but one sample from the wide range of perspectives and writings that appeared on international politics. As Rahul Sagar's work shows,[5] there was prolific publishing in journals and magazines, published across India, or by Indians abroad. Revolutionaries like Tarak Nath Das (1884–1958), Lajpat Rai (1865–1928), Har Dyal (1884–1939), V. Chattopadhyay (1880–1937), M.N. Roy (1887–1954), Shyamji Krishanverma (1857–1930); liberals like V.S. Srinivasa Sastri (1869–1946), P. Sivaswamy Aiyer (1864–1946), Tej Bahadur Sapru (1875–1949), Zafrulla Khan (1893–1985); Congress leaders like Annie Besant (1847–1933), Mahatma Gandhi, Jawaharlal Nehru, Ram Manohar Lohia (1910–1967); scholars/journalists like St. Nihal Singh, Benoy Kumar Sarkar (1887–1949), V. Shiva Ram, Lanka Sundaram; and literary writers like Rabindranath Tagore (1861–1941), Aurobindo Ghosh (1872–1950), among others, wrote and published copiously on matters concerning world politics.[6] Journals such as *Indian Review, The Hindustan Review* and *Modern Review* are filled with Indian perspectives on a range of issues, and are invariably informed by India's condition of being colonised. Hence, the institutes did not inaugurate IR thinking in the country. IR's institutional life, if at all, was a spectacular contrast to its lively public life, and that Curtis' model of institutionalising the study of international affairs failed to produce any research in such an environment provides some of the key lessons of this project.

FOUNDING THE INSTITUTE

The question of India, as we have identified in the first chapter, was one of the central issues confronting the Round Table. Indeed, it was an issue on which the members of the London Moot had most vociferous disagreements. Curtis and Kerr had pushed for acknowledging the possibility of equality for India in the future, while others like Brand, Malcolm and Craik had vehemently opposed this notion. But in the meantime, the Round Table became deeply involved in policymaking on India. Curtis wrote a tract on *Dyarchy* during his visit to India, which became a significant influence on the Montagu-Chelmsford Reforms of 1919. These reforms lightly decentralised power in India, and brought in a limited form of direct elections, with limited franchise, as Curtis had urged in *Dyarchy*. They were widely seen as disappointing and insufficient by the Indian Civil Service, who had hoped for independence after India had made such a significant contribution to the empire's defence in WWI.[7]

The Round Table published regularly on India. These articles were written mostly by Indian Civil Service officials. Accordingly, the Round Table's views on India were not very far from the British official ones.[8] However, the Round Table had an influential voice in granting India a seat at the imperial table in the imperial conferences. This made liberals in India somewhat sympathetic to the movement, and the latter, given their reach in the British policy circles, became important channels for granting access to the moderate demands of Indian leaders in the 1920s. For instance, at the 1923 Imperial Conference, the London Moot, and Curtis in particular, played an important role in introducing India's representative Tej Bahadur Sapru to influential leaders and journalists in the latter's campaign against South Africa's racist treatment of Indians.[9] The Round Table's championing of the 'British Commonwealth' was indeed most assiduously championed by liberals such as Sapru and Sastri, who used the theoretical possibility of equality through imperial citizenship as a vehicle to denounce the outwardly racist conceptions of citizenship advanced by South African statesmen such as Jan Smuts. However, these Indians were also critical of the 'cold, pseudo-scientific' approach of the Round Table, viewing the 'British Commonwealth' as a locus of political struggles rather than an epistemic project.[10]

The discussion about opening an institute in India, however, started in an unusual manner. In September 1932, Chatham House received a request for grants from an Indian scholar of international law. Lanka Sundaram, later an Indian parliamentarian, informed Ivison Macadam, the RIIA's secretary, that he had started an 'Indian Institute for International Studies' with 'a view to help India rise in her proper stature in the comity of nations' at Bezawada (Vijayawada) in South India.[11] Sundaram knew the workings of Chatham House well. He had worked in its library, contributed an article to its journal, and published alongside Alfred Zimmern and Charles Manning,[12] both early university professors of international affairs and prominent members of Chatham House.[13] As such, he sought to affiliate his institute with Chatham House. On account of 'the poverty and general unpreparedness of India', he asked Chatham House to fund his endeavour in order to consider matters of international affairs seriously.[14] His aim, he wrote, was to start a library on international affairs in India and 'thus quicken Indian interest in extra-territorial matters'.

Instead of replying to Sundaram, Macadam first approached the India Office. He wanted them to investigate Sundaram and his institute. The request was forwarded to the Madras government, which dismissed Sundaram as 'an ardent Congressman with anti-British views'. Sundaram, who had returned from London after the Round Table Conference, had served as political secretary to Gandhi and been arrested once as an agitator.[15] Chatham House was asked to 'wait and see whether the institute would be able to stand on its own legs before affording it assistance.' The Madras government warned that 'Sundaram himself is a man of no property and no profession, the son of a cook' and that his real aim was to secure himself a 'lucrative appointment'.[16] The India Office accordingly advised Chatham House not to cooperate with Sundaram 'until it is evident that it [his institute] is not likely to fall under the influence of Congress opinion'.[17] Sundaram's request was dismissed.

Sundaram's request, however, put India in Chatham House's scheme of things, and the very next year, when the first unofficial British Commonwealth Relations Conference in Toronto was organised to plan for future institutes, an Indian delegation was also invited.[18] The Indian delegation was led by Arcot Ramaswami Mudaliar (1887–1976), a leader of the Justice Party. Other members were Zafrulla Khan, Mir Maqbool Mahmood and

Laurie Hammond.[19] All the representatives were close to the colonial government and the delegation followed the-then set tradition of including non-official members from the legislative assemblies, a representative of the princely states and a British member. At the conference, the Indian delegation expressed strong interest in opening an institute in India. Mudaliar argued that 'it was very desirable that an Institute should be established in India' consisting of a central institute at Delhi and branches in the provincial capitals. He enquired, however, 'how the high standard of membership of [Chatham House] was achieved and had not developed into a "fashion".'[20] Concerned that such an institute might criticise the colonial government's policies, Mudaliar also wanted to know 'how it had been possible to exclude discussions on purely domestic questions ...'.[21] Minutes do not note the reply to this question, but the query reveals the anxieties about segregating the international from the domestic, especially in the colonial context where the latter is severely contested.

Chatham House expressed its enthusiasm and informed Mudaliar that 38 of its members were in India and hence there was a considerable knowledge-base to draw from.[22] Subsequently, Chatham House held discussions with Girija Shankar Bajpai (1891–1954),[23] Tej Bahadur Sapru[24] and Surendra Kumar Datta (1878–1948),[25] apart from Mudaliar and Zafrulla Khan.[26] Consequently, on 3 March 1936, the Viceroy's House in Delhi played host to a few Indian liberal politicians and serving bureaucrats.[27] It was here that the institute was formally set up. This meeting elected Zafrulla Khan, then a young and dynamic Muslim politician recently drafted into the Viceroy's Executive Council,[28] as the Chairman. The Viceroy was made the ex-officio president. This meeting, in the words of Stephen King-Hall, was made possible through the 'energy and initiative' of Frederick E. James, a European member of the Central Legislative Assembly,[29] who along with M.S.A. Hydari, a member of the Indian Civil Service, was elected as the Honorary Secretary. B. Shiva Rao, Labour leader and journalist, was nominated as the Organising Secretary. Invitations to join were also sent to pro-Congress leaders such as Bhulabhai Desai (1877–1946) and Sarojini Naidu (1879–1949).[30] Although most of its council was comprised of bureaucrats and politicians, the institute avowed to maintain a 'non-political' character, precluding it from 'expressing any opinion, from endorsing any policies, or from conducting any propaganda on any aspect of international affairs'.[31] Its founding statement noted that its sole purpose was 'encouraging and facilitating in India the scientific study of international questions'.

However, the institute's pro-government character was quite evident in its membership. Fearing exactly this, S.K. Datta, the oldest Indian member of Chatham House, refused an invitation to the Executive Council arguing that there was little space for an institution like this in India because it would be controlled by government officials.[32]

At the IIIA's founding, Stephen King-Hall, Chatham House's representative and Chairman of its Endowment Committee, argued that a suitable Secretary General had to be found for the institute's first two formative years. The Secretary General would need to make a prolonged India tour to acquaint themselves with Indian conditions. With scant regard to the Indians present in the room, King-Hall announced, such a person 'should be an Englishman, with experience of the working of Chatham House and preferably only a slight previous acquaintance with Indian conditions'. Moreover, he 'should be unmarried', unless the spouse was effectively 'his unpaid assistant'.[33] Datta noted despairingly in response:

> All things that emanate from Delhi and Shimla, whether it is the Red Cross or the St James Ambulance or the Dufferin Fund or the Boy Scouts, do so from the departments of government. Has it not occurred to anybody to see that an Indian is found and trained for this work ... [appointing an English Secretary General would never be] put forward to a Japanese Committee or a Chinese Committee.[34]

It took seven months to organise the first meeting of the new institute. The occasion was the arrival of a visiting delegation from South Africa, led by the Minister for Interior, Jan Hofmeyr. On 3 October 1936, Hofmeyr delivered an address titled 'A South African looks at the Empire'.[35] Two branches were opened in Calcutta and Bombay. They soon became dysfunctional. Despite the initial fanfare, the institute 'only had odd meetings' leading into WWII. In these meetings, according to B. Shiva Rao, 'the attendance was thin, the discussions on topics were poor and dull, and there was nothing of real interest in these activities'.[36] The Calcutta branch closed down in December 1940, while the Bombay branch 'practically ceased activity'.[37] Furthermore, although the institute had originally envisaged, on the Chatham House pattern, 'research into international problems by individual members and study groups by experts',[38] until the early 1940s it conducted no research.[39] Its only function was to send representations to the International Studies Conferences of 1939 and 1940 and the 1938 unofficial British Commonwealth Relations Conference in Sydney. For the latter, the Indian contingent went without any preparatory work.[40]

In the late 1930s while the IIIA lay dormant, the Foreign Department of the INC sprang into action. The international context could not be more suitable. Imperialist actions in Ethiopia and China and the Spanish Civil War had galvanised the younger leaders of the Congress, particularly Nehru and Subhash Chandra Bose, to link India's struggle for independence with expressions of freedom elsewhere. The need for a foreign wing in the INC was also seen as important from the perspective of anti-colonial propaganda abroad.[41] The Department had been originally proposed in 1928 by Nehru, but no action was taken for several years. When Nehru became the President again in 1936, he set it up and appointed a young Indian doctor from Germany, Ram Manohar Lohia as the General Secretary. Lohia left the Department two years later, replaced by another young Congress man, Dharam Yash Dev. Unlike the institute, however, the Congress Foreign Department was quite active in these years. It produced periodical foreign newsletters and maintained contacts with overseas associations and individuals. One of the key documents it produced was a long pamphlet on the important question of India's participation in the war effort. Lohia, supported by Nehru, argued for economic sanctions as being the most appropriate form of punitive actions against the axis of power. It provided a useful background to intense discussions Congress was to have about war participation in the subsequent years.

In December 1938, the Indian Political Science Association was also formed. In its first meeting, G.B. Pant, as we have pointed to above, advised that the aim of political science should be to strive for the freedom of people everywhere. Warning against a dispassionate assembly of facts, Pant urged political scientists to consider that political science could only have one agenda: social service. In a colonial context like India's, he argued that the fundamental purpose of all social science ought to be working for enhancing the moral values of the state. '[A]ll serfdom should cease and exploitation vanish. That is the moral purpose for which political science should exist, and if it does not exist for that, well, let us bury it together', he stated.[42] The Indian institute was indeed almost buried. WWII brought it back to life, but in a manner that launched it towards its final demise.

REJUVENATING THE INSTITUTE
AND THE EMERGENCE OF THE ICWA

In 1942, WWII had extended to the Pacific, and the British empire felt threatened by Japanese advances. Although the formal entry of the US into the war had come as a huge relief to Britain, American politicians were generally hostile to British imperialism. Elites in Whitehall and New Delhi were worried about pro-Congress propaganda carried out by the India League in

America, believing it could jeopardise American support. The League had argued that until India had a national government, the country's human and military resources could not be fully mobilised for war.[43] G.S. Bajpai, who had recently arrived as India's Agent General, wrote in May 1942 that there was a strong need to counter Indian nationalist propaganda, which found considerable sympathy with anti-British undercurrents in America, shaped by the country's revolutionary spirit and significant Irish population.[44]

An important non-government platform that shaped such opinions was the Pacific Relations Conference, organised by IPR. Its eighth conference was proposed to be organised in September 1942 in the US (subsequently moved to Mont Tremblant, Canada, in December 1942). Edward Carter, the left-oriented Secretary General of the IPR, had visited India in 1935 where several Indians had expressed the hope of opening a National Council of IPR in India. He was, however, told by the Viceroy and S.K. Datta that an Indian IPR delegation would only be of service if 'it is authentically Indian; if it gets its stimulus from the Pacific rather than from England, and if its development is on scientific rather than on political and government lines'.[45] The possibility of such an institute, whose members were mostly Indian and which was driven by its Eastern, rather than imperial, outlook without drawing its patronage and worldview from the colonial government, was impossible at this stage.[46] The IIIA, founded a year after this visit, had validated these concerns. Hence, Carter was keen to invite a delegation of 'more wider and representative group of Indian citizens than those who at present constitute the membership of the Indian Institute'.[47]

Considered 'anti-British', Carter's and IPR's moves in India were viewed suspiciously by the British. Carter had previously funded Nehru's trip to China in 1939 and was allegedly close to the India League.[48] Keen to have the INC represented in the 1942 IPR Conference, Carter had sent an invitation to Nehru to attend (he also considered inviting C. Rajagopalachari, as Nehru had been jailed). Unconfirmed rumours also reached Whitehall that Nehru had been invited to visit President Roosevelt. This made both Whitehall and the Indian government anxious about American support to the war effort.[49]

There was some good news, however. British representatives in America wrote that the failure of Cripps Mission and Gandhi's proposals for non-violent non-cooperation with the Japanese had created an impression that the Congress was unreasonable. Lord Halifax, the British High Commissioner, argued that 'Congress pacifism has aroused impatience and Congress distrust of loan of technical and military aid has caused resentment'.[50] Consequently, Bajpai wrote that 'psychologically, the atmosphere has never been more propitious to educating the American peoples to take a more balanced and detached view of the Indian political situation'.[51] Bajpai suggested that pro-government Indian leaders should visit the US on lecture tours to counter the nationalist propaganda, alongside attending the IPR Conference.[52]

Buoyed by this, Leo Amery, the British Secretary of State, wrote to Lord Linlithgow, the Viceroy, that to prevent invitations to Congress aligned individuals, efforts should be made to secure an invitation to the IIIA.[53] The IIIA would give the requisite air of autonomy to the Indian delegation while at the same time ensuring, as another internal government memo noted, that the 'right kind of Indians attend the meeting'.[54] Olaf Caroe, the Secretary of India's External Department, wrote that 'we should certainly handpick the Indian representatives and do everything possible to stop the Chinese and Americans from talking pernicious non-sense about British imperialism in India'.[55] Consequently, Bajpai, who was friends with Carter, was asked to secure a direct invite to the IIIA. Carter readily agreed, knowing little that the whole delegation was chosen by the Indian government. Linlithgow appointed Ramaswami Mudaliar, who was also then Chairperson of the IIIA, to lead the delegation. The final delegation comprised Zafrulla Khan, M.C. Khanna, Begum Shah Nawaz, K.M. Panikkar, S.E. Ranganathan and N. Sivaraj.[56] Importantly, as advised by Bajpai, the delegates were also to carry out a lecture tour across America to influence American opinion on India.

Despite Carter's wishes, the delegation had an 'official' stamp to it. Indeed, one paper noted that the government 'could find no better set of able propagandists and defenders of the official view'.[57] Carter suggested to Bajpai that Congress delegates should be included in the Indian delegation. E.J. Tarr, the Chairman of the Pacific Council and funder of the CIIA, also emphasised the 'desirability [of] having [a] non-official Indian' on the delegation.[58] But Bajpai responded that the Indian government could not be expected to receive such a suggestion favourably, considering that the Congress had just launched the Quit India Movement.[59] After the Indian government threatened to withdraw from the conference[60] and Chatham House, which served as the IPR's National Council in the UK, expressed concern that its Indian affiliate was deliberately being sidelined by Carter,[61] the Indian delegation was accepted.

Bigger trouble, however, was brewing within the institute in India. Anantrai Pattani, dewan of Bhavnagar state and a member of the institute, wrote to Curtis that the Indian delegation should have included 'best possible personnel to represent [the] Indian branch of the Royal Institute at Pacific Conference' and suggested that people of M.R. Jayakar's[62] and Tej Bahadur Sapru's stature should have been in the delegation.[63] Pattani's telegram to Curtis, although dismissed by the Chatham House Secretary Ivision Macadam as inconsequential,[64] pointed towards more deep-seated problems. Sharp differences had arisen within the institute in the context of an intensifying nationalist movement. A rival faction within the institute, led by people like P.N. Sapru,[65] H.N. Kunzru[66] and B. Shiva Rao, now increasingly resented the pro-government outlook of the institute. The way the Mont Tremblant delegation was picked had proved to them that the institute was only a lackey of the government.

While the Indian delegation went to Mont Tremblant as an official delegation of the IIIA, the dissenters pointed out that the institute had not organised any meeting to confirm these delegates, nor were other members consulted. Further, Mudaliar had ceased to be the Chairman of the institute in October 1942 and had no right to choose the delegation on the institute's behalf.[67] Four out of the seven members, including the secretary, were not even members of the institute.[68] After the government realised these procedural errors, Mudaliar accepted that the delegation did not represent the institute as the Viceroy had appointed him in a personal capacity to the delegation. Indeed, the delegation was funded by the Indian government.[69]

At Mont Tremblant, the anti-British sentiment, especially among the Americans and Chinese, was strong. Carter himself made no bones about it, especially on the issue of imperialism in India. In discussions on the specially convened round table on India in the conference, the dominant mood was anti-British. An internal British memo noted that 'there had been a plan by means of this Round Table a pro-Congress demonstration which would set up ripples, or rather tidal waves, to wash Gandhi and Nehru out of prison.'[70] In response, Mudaliar was forced to give some concessions. He proposed the complete Indianisation of the Viceroy's council and establishing an exploratory commission, which could include foreign observers, for the creation of a constitution-making body. These went further than the Indian government's position and surprised even the British delegates. Back in India, Mudaliar was admonished in departmental communiques for 'speaking with complete irresponsibility', although they acknowledged that this helped the Indian delegation demonstrate independence.[71] Major A.S. Shah, an officer from the External Affairs Department who served as the secretary for the Indian delegation, wrote a scathing report arguing that Carter had strongly canvassed for a pro-Congress point of view in the conference. The IPR report on the Indian Round Table, he alleged, deliberately created an anti-British bias for the reader.[72] Carter, he wrote, was keen on opening a National Council of IPR in India which would be closer to Congress and posed 'a danger of this organisation taking a communal bias and indulging merely in anti-British feelings'.[73]

To counter this, Shah advised that immediate steps should be taken to 'strengthen the existing branch of Chatham House' in India. Its membership should be extended among selected non-officials and, importantly, a permanent secretary should be appointed. The institute should draw up a constitution and strengthen its research credentials by publishing and disseminating studies.[74] He had also accompanied the Indian delegates on lecture tours to America after the conference and was convinced that these lectures had helped greatly in turning the American opinion against 'a class of people [the Congress] who are out to establish a system of government based on antiquated notions of caste and rule of numerical majority'.[75] He envisioned the institute's work helping in furthering such informed opinion nationally and internationally. During the war the funding support for the IIIA, he wrote, would have to primarily come from the government.[76]

Back in India, Caroe wanted to publish Shah's report to discredit the IPR by emphasising its biased nature.[77] Mudaliar, however, advised against publishing it and in turn suggested that the IIIA should apply to become an affiliate of the IPR in order to preclude the latter's plans of creating a pro-Congress National Council in India.[78] The Viceroy supported Mudaliar's suggestion and advised revitalising the IIIA.[79] Accordingly, Mudaliar raised the membership issue with Carter, who told him that the IIIA would have to first reorganise itself according to the IPR guidelines (which included complete autonomy from the government and representation of all principal groups in a country). Carter promised Mudaliar that if such changes were made, the institute would be formally admitted upon an application in this regard before the next meeting.[80]

Meanwhile, differences within the institute became public on 24 August 1943 when Kunzru and P.N. Sapru issued a circular that called for 'the immediate establishment of an independent organisation for the study of world affairs' in India.[81] The circular foregrounded this need on the newly established principles of the Atlantic Charter, especially relating to the future of dependencies and colonies, and more generally, on the need to create a machinery for world peace. Critiquing IIIA's representation at the Mont Tremblant Conference, Kunzru and Sapru noted that 'in view of the urgent need for a thorough study of such questions ... and the importance of India being represented at any Conference that may be held hereafter for their discussion, *by delegations capable of voicing the views and aspirations of the great majority of people*', a new institute was necessary.[82] This statement hinted at the lack of any serious study work being undertaken by the IIIA and its pro-government and non-representative character, which, given the growing likelihood of independence, made the institute increasingly irrelevant.

Stung by these internal criticisms and pushed by the IPR, the IIIA was now keen to revitalise itself. At the behest of the government, many organisational changes were introduced. Sultan Ahmad, the member for Information and Broadcasting Department in the Viceroy's Executive Council, was made the new Chairman of the institute. In November 1943, Ahmad proposed wide-ranging changes in the organisation and working of the institute aimed at increasing the membership, opening new branches across the country and the setting up of a Secretariat with a full-time secretary and clerical staff. These proposals also announced that the IIIA 'would be a body of independent status in no way controlled by any government department or made a subordinate organ of government policy'.[83] Further, on the Chatham House model, Ahmad proposed that the institute should focus on 'scientific research on international questions' and consider the production of a periodical journal overseen by a Director of Research.[84]

Although Ahmad promised institutional autonomy, this was almost immediately compromised when he approached the government for funding. Particularly ironic was that he himself headed the propaganda department of the government. Nevertheless, the finance department quickly agreed to make a grant of Rs. 80,000 per annum for the first two years and an additional sum of Rs. 10,000 for the library.[85] The only substantial non-government support came from Pattani who had promised a sum of Rs. 100,000 for building the new headquarters in Delhi.

Ahmad advanced his new proposals in a stormy meeting of the Executive Council of the institute on 15 November 1943. Chaired by Ahmad, the meeting included P.P. Pillai (Vice-Chairman), Kunzru, Mudaliar, Zafrulla Khan, P.N. Sapru, C. Jahangir, U.N. Sen, N.M. Joshi and Narain Mahtha. When asked to explain his move for forming a rival organisation, Kunzru replied that his dissatisfaction with the IIIA was because 'he saw nothing really Indian in the Institute. Neither in the discussions, nor in the composition either of its council or its general body could he find substantial element representing Indian views or Indian sentiments or aspirations'.[86] Replying to Kunzru's accusations, Ahmad stated that his new proposals met with most of Kunzru's concerns. Kunzru promised to reconsider his decision in a meeting with his friends six days later.[87] This 21 November meeting instead birthed a new institute: the ICWA.[88] Kunzru and P.N. Sapru however continued to be on the Executive Council of the IIIA.

THE STRUGGLE FOR SURVIVAL: IIIA AND ICWA

If the IIIA was based on the Chatham House model, the ICWA 'owed its inspiration to the IPR'.[89] Following IPR requirements, it committed to keeping its Executive Council and the majority of its members non-official (although government officials were allowed to become members). Further, its council was required to be representative of the principal groups and interests in the country. Tej Bahadur Sapru was chosen as president of the Council, and vice-presidents included Congress-inclined politicians and business persons like Vijayalakshmi Pandit (1900–1990), G.D. Birla (1894–1983) and Shri Ram. B. Shiva Rao (1891–1975), the first Organising Secretary of the IIIA, also became the first Organising Secretary of the ICWA. Many IIIA members, such as Pattani, C.P. Ramaswami Aiyer, Sri Narayan Mahata and N.M. Joshi, were also on the Executive Committee of the ICWA.[90]

Over the next two years, the two institutes fought a fierce battle for legitimacy. They began to focus on research. After having published nothing in its first eight years, the IIIA published 17 pamphlets and organised 18 lectures in 1944. Likewise, by November 1945, the ICWA had published three monographs (with two more in press) and eight pamphlets. It had also opened eleven branches across the country and formed two study groups on 'India and Security in the Pacific' and 'Progress towards Self-Government in Dependent Areas' in Delhi and Poona (Pune), respectively.[91] Both institutes started their flagships journals in January 1945. In its founding statement, the IIIA's *Journal of the Indian Institute of International Affairs* stated that new awareness on foreign affairs was needed because 'directly and fully involved in the war, India has become more than ever aware of her place in the world, more than eager to play her part in the world'.[92] In contrast, the ICWA's *India Quarterly*, brandishing its anti-government credentials, retorted: 'The fact that India has had no share in the shaping of her foreign policy is largely responsible for the absence of an effective public opinion here on foreign affairs, but the same fact makes continued vigilance all the more essential.'[93] In this sense, the ICWA and its journal were an attempt to project an international identity prior to independence, in response to the colonial government's effort to control discourse on international affairs. *India Quarterly*'s founding statement also implicitly critiqued the founding canard of Chatham House and its affiliate institutes that scientific study of international affairs *will* lead to peace. The newly recruited secretary of the ICWA and later the doyen of IR in India, Angadipuram Appadorai, wrote in his editorial statement:

For publicists, similarly, to claim that their discussions, however well-informed or dispassionate, will set all things right is a piece of professional pedantry, for it ignores the basic fact that social progress is the result of interaction of several factors of which understanding is just one.[94]

Despite these claims, however, much of the work that appeared in both these journals remained descriptive. This was in contrast to *The Indian Journal of Political Science*, which in its initial years paid particular attention to theorising the state and critically analysing key issues and theories in IR. Several contributions in these early years in this journal look at alternative ideas of state-making.[95]

In addition to research, the contest for legitimacy was fierce at international platforms. The Unofficial British Commonwealth Relations Conferences, organised by Chatham House, and the Pacific Relations Conferences, organised by the IPR, were events that would bestow legitimacy. As an official branch of Chatham House, the IIIA qualified automatically for the former, but a place at the next IPR Conference was still up for grabs.

The ninth IPR Conference was scheduled for January 1945 in Virginia, US. Conscious of the problems of representation in the previous conference and the split that ensued, E.J. Tarr asked Maurice Gwyer, the Vice-Chancellor of Delhi University and former Chief Justice of India, for help in the selection of an Indian delegation of 'five to ten members'. Tarr told him that the IPR had not reached an agreement about affiliation to an Indian institute, and wanted to avoid such a decision given the problems between the two institutions.[96] Gwyer met both Ahmad and Kunzru to devise a mechanism for Indian representation. He first suggested that the delegation be selected from members from both the institutes. Ahmad agreed to this on the condition that the delegation should officially be regarded as one from the IIIA. Kunzru rejected this. Gwyer then suggested a joint delegation without reference to either institute, which was acceptable to Kunzru but not Ahmad. Unable to settle the conflict, Gwyer pointed out to Tarr two major differences between these two institutions which made a solution unlikely. First was the widening gap between officials and non-officials in India, as the independence movement intensified. The IIIA was mostly run by government officials, which was 'mainly ... due to absence of interest in foreign affairs among non-officials'. Second, the ICWA consisted 'almost entirely of Members of one community and similar political complexion [Hindu, upper-caste Brahmin]'. He noted that this had led to the 'possibility of ... communal institutions springing up'.[97] Gwyer correctly sensed that the political fault lines in India were increasingly sharpening on these two issues: the opposition to the British and the communal issue. The pro-Congress Hindu elite was also increasingly anti-British, while the pro-Muslim League Muslim elite was closer to the British Indian government. The two organisations fell on either side of the divide.

Having realised that membership of the IPR would be a step towards legitimacy, both organisations now considered applying separately. The ICWA was the first one to seize the initiative. On 24 March 1944, it sent a letter to Carter requesting the ICWA's affiliation with the IPR. Once the ICWA sent its request, the IIIA was in a bind. If it did not send a request of affiliation to the IPR, the ICWA would be affiliated by default which meant that 'the Indian Institute would have suffered such a blow in the eyes of Indian public opinion that it would with difficulty recover (sic)'.[98] However, both Ahmad and Mudaliar were now against affiliation with the IPR given its alleged bias in favour of the ICWA.[99] The Council, they alleged, had been propped up through an active collaboration with Carter. Hence, Ahmad sought the advice of Chatham House on the matter.

By now, Chatham House had become uncomfortable with the IIIA's closeness to the government. In his reply to Ahmad, Lord Astor, the Chairman of Chatham House, wrote that the grant to the institute from the government was indeed contrary to the principles of Chatham House.[100] Any application made to the IPR might be prejudiced by acceptance of such a grant, he added.[101] He further advised Ahmad that Mudaliar should informally write to Tarr, expressing the institute's intent of joining the IPR, given that the institute had made the desired changes in its organisation.[102] Accordingly, Mudaliar wrote such a letter, insisting that in the previous year the institute had undergone major changes which made it non-official and self-sufficient. He also added that the institute was contemplating surrendering its government funding,[103] which it did in September 1944.[104]

To find a way out of this conundrum, the IPR wrote to Chatham House for suggestions. The latter did not want to let down its affiliate in India nor be seen as partisan in India's internal fight. Through its representative at the IPR, Chatham House advised the IPR not to invite any Indian representation to the conference. It also asked for the decision about affiliation to be postponed until the January conference.[105] The IPR accepted the latter suggestion and wrote to the ICWA that the decision towards affiliation of a National Council in India could only be taken at the IPR Conference in January.[106] However, it was not ready to forgo Indian participation.

Tarr once again requested Maurice Gwyer to nominate a delegation on his own, which he declined.[107] Following this, Tarr wrote directly to Tej Bahadur Sapru and Sultan Ahmad, the respective heads of the two organisations, asking them to send four members each. The ICWA accepted this proposition and appointed Vijayalakshmi Pandit, H.N. Kunzru, B. Shiva Rao and Gaganvihari Mehta.[108] P.S. Lokanathan, the editor of *Eastern Economist*, served as the secretary to the delegation. Sultan Ahmad, however, sent a 'polite refusal'.[109] Ahmad was far less polite in discussions with the Indian government. In a discussion with the Foreign Secretary, Olaf Caroe, Ahmad said that the 'procedure suggested was an insult to the institute which on previous occasion was regarded as the only competent body' and that the 'world council [was] a partisan and sectarian body being inspired partly by "certain American friends connected to the IPR"'. The IPR, Ahmad added, was now 'left with a team made up of all-Brahmin group of one school of thought'.[110]

In a final effort at reconciliation, Tarr wrote to Mudaliar asking if merging the two institutions, since both of them were non-official and worked on the same issues, was a possibility. Alternatively, he suggested forming an 'Indian Council of the Institute of Pacific Relations' with only two corporate members (the IIIA and the ICWA), and each would nominate exactly half the members.[111] Nothing came of these suggestions. Even the British Embassy in Washington saw the institute's tetchiness as springing out of nothing but 'touchiness as to prestige'.[112] Tarr worried that the two organisations were 'digging in for a fight to the death'.[113] They were, indeed.

THE 'FIGHT TO THE DEATH'

While the IIIA was constantly under criticism for its official character, the Indian government and the India Office were keen to keep it alive. Both the India Office and the India External Affairs Department impressed upon Chatham House the need to find funding through alternative channels. In an informal meeting between Olaf Caroe and Margaret Cleeve, the Deputy Secretary of the RIIA, in November 1943, Caroe argued that unless Chatham House provided considerable subsidy from its own funds, government funding was the only feasible source for sustaining the institute. Caroe warned Cleeve that the IPR, which was propping up the rival faction of Kuzru and Sapru, 'would step in and steal the thunder' if nothing was done. The institute, he argued, had not been able to secure any funding from rich Indians, in response to which Cleeve suggested approaching the Rockefeller and Carnegie endowments. Caroe argued that seeking American funding for the institute would be risky in India. In any case, Caroe argued that the institute would need funds amounting to an initial amount of Rs. 100,000 (£7,500), a recurring sum of £3,000 per annum and an additional amount of £2,000 per annum for a competent secretary. Caroe also suggested that it was worthwhile considering moving the institute from Delhi to either Bombay or Calcutta, since in Delhi the institute could not shake off its official character.[114]

Leo Amery and the new Viceroy, Lord Wavell, took keen interest in the attempts to reorganise and revive the institute, especially in the matters of selection of the institute's delegation for the 1945 Unofficial British Commonwealth Relations Conference.[115] But this conference turned out to be the last major conference of the IIIA. The delegation was headed by Zafrulla Khan and included other institute members such as K.M. Panikkar, Mir Maqbool Mahmood and Maharaj Singh. K. Sarwar Hasan, the new Director of Research, served as the secretary. The institute, however, fell back into oblivion after the conference, partly because the two competing organisations were further divided along political and communal lines. The ICWA members were pro-Congress and the ICWA was seen as Hindu-dominated. While the Council's Muslim membership had increased, most of these Muslim members were nationalist and pro-Congress.[116] The IIIA, on the other hand, increasingly became a Muslim (League)-dominated organisation ('with a sprinkling of Europeans')[117] in its day-to-day decision-making although Hindus were still a majority of its membership. Indeed, prominent Hindu members of its Executive Council, such as K.M. Panikkar and P.P. Pillai (former Vice-Chairman of the IIIA), also soon joined the ICWA and 'indulge[d] in vigorous attacks' on the IIIA.[118] Further, since the institute had returned the government funding, it struggled to find alternative sources. Chatham House's attempt to secure funding through a Carnegie endowment failed. Run from one room in Delhi which worked both as office and library, the institute, according to an internal Chatham House note, 'continue[d] to exist but [had] little vitality'. Its secretary, K. Sarwar Hasan, was 'depressed and in consequence tend[ed] to be rather depressing'.[119] The membership remained low.[120] The recently restarted branches in Bombay and Calcutta had once again become non-functional.[121] In contrast, the ICWA grew in substance and stature, and was initially funded by the likes of Pattani and Lala Sri Ram, a Delhi businessman.[122] By the end of 1946, its membership stood at 1,056,[123] and it had 15 active branches across the country apart from the headquarters in Delhi.[124] Although 'non-political' and 'un-official', the ICWA was boosted by the presence of political stalwarts like Pandit Nehru on its Executive Council.

However, it was the Asian Relations Conference of 1947 that sealed the rivalry between the two organisations. The idea for this conference had actually emerged at the IPR Hot Springs meeting in Virginia, where the IIIA had refused to send a delegation. At this meeting, Vijaya Lakshmi Pandit, the ICWA's delegation leader, had complained against how Asian problems were discussed with 'old thoughts in new worlds', critiquing Western countries for not being 'prepared to give up preconceived ideas'.[125] From Hot Springs, Pandit and Shiva Rao went to San Francisco for the inaugural UN conference, and found that the marginalisation of Asian views continued. With a few other Indians in the US – J.J. Singh, Syed Hossain, Krishanlal Shridharani and Anup Singh – Shiva Rao conceived of an IPR-like conference of Asian countries. Soon after his return to Delhi in September 1945, Shiva Rao proposed this idea to the ICWA and subsequently, with the Council's backing, to Nehru.[126] Indeed, convened exactly on the pattern of the IPR Conferences, the ICWA took upon itself the task of organising this massive conference between 23 March and 2 April 1947 that eventually hosted 193 delegates and 51 observers from 34 countries. The successful organisation of this conference (which also produced a short-lived Inter-Asian Organisation, once again on the IPR template) catapulted the ICWA into the limelight.[127] The conference itself further sharpened the divide between the two institutions.

The Muslim League had boycotted the conference. Its newspaper, *The Dawn*, whose editor Atlaf Hussain was a member of the IIIA and was close to Hasan, warned of 'the expansionist designs of Indian Hinduism' and called the conference 'An Asian Fraud'.[128] P.N.S. Mansergh, the Chatham House observer to the Asian Relations Conference, noted that 'prominent figures on each side [spoke] with great bitterness of the rival organisation'.[129] Another observer noted that the ICWA was 'the only organisation on the horizon in Hindustan'.[130] Ahmad and Hasan had decided to move the IIIA to the future Pakistan. Ahmad told Liaquat Ali Khan, the Muslim League leader, that if the institute was not taken to Pakistan 'it will be used against you [Pakistan]'.[131] To do this, Hasan engineered an increase in the pro-Pakistan Muslim membership of the institute. He first got Ishtiaq Hussain Qureshi, Professor of History at Delhi University and an activist for the Pakistan Movement, elected as the Honorary Secretary of the institute in place of F.P. Antia, a Parsee. Thereafter, closer to Partition, Altaf Hussain and Mumtaz Hasan, Liaquat Ali Khan's secretary, and Qureshi helped Hasan to enrol pro-Pakistan Muslim members into the institute.

Under the institute's constitution, the headquarters could be moved anywhere in India through a resolution passed in a general meeting. In a carefully planned move just a few days before Partition, Hasan called a general meeting of the institute where pro-Pakistan members dominated. Altaf Hussain proposed that the institute be taken to Karachi which was still within India. Hindu members in the meeting, such as Kunzru and Pattani, opposed this. Pattani reminded the meeting that he had donated a sum of Rs. 100,000 for a building to be constructed in Delhi. Ahmad replied that this sum would be returned if the institute moved to Karachi. After some arguments, Altaf Hussain pressed for a vote on this resolution. The motion was easily 'carried' and the headquarters of the institute was officially moved to Karachi. Liaquat Ali Khan accordingly provided the facilities and rail wagons for moving the library and furniture of the institute to Karachi.[132]

In Pakistan, the 'Indian' institute operated initially from Hasan's new home in Karachi. Soon three rooms were allocated in the Frere Hall building. With the help of funding from Pakistan's government, Hasan started another institute from the same office, the Pakistan Institute of International Affairs (PIIA), which was officially inaugurated by Liaquat Ali Khan in April 1948. For a brief period, the IIIA and PIIA worked from the same office in post-Partition Karachi. In March 1948, Sarwar also started the PIIA's own journal, *Pakistan Horizon*. Given the ethno-national character of the new state and its subsequent history, the opening editorial of the journal points to a seldom remembered idea of Pakistan:

> The Institute's endeavours will be entirely in keeping with the spirit of Pakistan. For the people of the new state have, as all who know them would verify, an inherent aversion to exclusiveness of all kinds. Their ancient traditions are wholly antithetical to nationalism, whether it be territorial, racial or cultural. So are their modern concepts, as is exemplified in the teachings of their great poet Iqbal, where sublime and soul striking stanzas played so significant a part in the battle for Pakistan.

By now, the IIIA was essentially defunct.[133] Its last official publication was a volume of its journal, *Journal of the Indian Institute of International Affairs*, which came out in the middle of 1947. However, it was difficult to formally dissolve the IIIA because 165 of its 215 members still lived in India. Many suggested to Hasan to let it 'die a natural death'.[134] It is unclear how matters were finally settled, but there is evidence to suggest that an Extraordinary General Meeting was called for in Karachi towards the end of 1948 to formally dissolve the Indian institute.[135]

A COLONIAL INSTITUTE IN A DECOLONISING WORLD

In this history of the origins of the institutes of IR in India (and Pakistan), we have shown that the Chatham House-engineered project of a non-partisan, non-political institute had little chance of success in late colonial India. Unlike in Canada, Australia, New Zealand and South Africa, where the institute membership was broadly constituted by white elites with their own government, an institute of primarily Indian membership could do little independent work, especially when the international as well as the domestic situations were becoming increasingly polarised. During WWII, the Indian government saw the institute primarily as an avenue for propaganda abroad, something that drew away moderate members of the organisation, like H.N. Kunzru and P.N. Sapru. In the 1940s, political fault lines in the country were also drawn rather sharply across the Congress-Muslim League axis. This is especially visible in the projection of the ICWA as a Congress organisation, which would otherwise be ironical given that Kunzru and Tej Bahadur Sapru were two of the tallest moderate leaders (who opposed the Congress on many fronts) of the pre-independence period.

This account also allows us to re-interpret the institutional identities of two current South Asian research institutions, the ICWA and the PIIA. It is interesting that on their websites the two institutes narrate their own stories differently.[136] The PIIA sees itself as an institutional successor to the IIIA, while the ICWA views itself as a *sui generis* institution. Both self-images are partly wrong. The PIIA started while the IIIA was still technically functioning, while the ICWA was initiated by some members of the IIIA as a rival organisation. Some of their motives were certainly ideological – the organisation's closeness to the government, for instance – but communal and nationalist identities and political contexts (the inevitability of independence by the early 1940s) also strongly influenced this break-up. This story helps us place the emergence of these Indian institutes within the global politics of institution-making in IR at the time, especially in the context of Chatham House and the IPR. The Indian story is not a solitary one, but forms a part of the broader politics of the role of institutions in particular forms of knowledge creation.

Finally, while we have established that the origins of the IIIA, the ICWA and also the PIIA are interconnected, it is politics rather than ideas that feature prominently in this story. Research by the two organisations starts only in the mid-1940s, primarily as part of their legitimacy gaining exercise. This period is thick with activity, but for vibrancy of ideas about India's international relations in this period one has to look elsewhere. *The Indian Journal of Political Science* is one such venue. However, since our story is largely tied to the Round Table project, that should be left for another time.

Nevertheless, we can draw some conclusions from this story about the nature of the Round Table, and the history of the study of IR. The relative inability of Indian-origin scholars to receive funding and to publish in key journals, in short, to think within the confines of the Round Table's mission, reveals to us just how intellectually closed off the Institutes of International Affairs model was at this point. Although Indian international thought is rich and, indeed, understudied, the formalised study of an IR discipline at this point was precluded by the imperial nature of its 'scientific' method.

Conclusion: The Past of International Relations and Its Future

To conclude the book, we draw together the loose narrative strands of our five national contexts to look at the ways in which racial thinking contributed to the idea of the international across them. We then turn the idea of decolonising IR and think through what this history says about the future of the field of study and how we can go about making it a more diverse and historically open field.

First, the plural origin stories discussed in this book reveal a complex web of colonial interactions which both connected and cut across different cultural and political contexts. The linking of these different scales, the international/imperial context and the state-level founding of institutes (as 'think tanks', perhaps), reveals to us a differentiated and global discipline at its inception. We began our story in South Africa, with Milner's Kindergarten seeking ways of transforming the world through a thought collective, an institution and a journal. This effort went global, with Curtis imagining at first a series of institutes around the empire, and later a world commonwealth, to be built through institutions – this would be a global thought collective, an academic journal, all engaged in 'world-making'. This project was based on an understanding of racial hierarchies, in which some societies were seen as static and needing benign colonial rule and others as dominant and superior. This project failed on its own terms. Even as it failed to build a world government, however, it created a network of common-purpose thinkers, each engaged from different contexts, thinking about international affairs from an imperial perspective, and seeking to 'improve' international affairs. They most certainly had their disagreements, yet broadly still thought in some ways in line with Curtis' vision of making 'the international'.

Although they each fed off one another and were deeply connected through the Round Table's thought collective (except, perhaps, in the case of India), distinct streams of thought with different emphasis emerged from each context. The institutional stories in particular operated on the dynamics, ideologies and personalities of those in charge and those funding the endeavours. The work produced, however, remained grounded in and shaped by both the original goals and the cultural, political/colonial context from which they thought. In each of the settler colonial contexts, ideas about race were central to the making of the international. This bubbled up in different ways but was nonetheless a consistent theme across different contexts. In India, however, competing claims about studying the international emerged from the political context of late colonial India.

Across the British empire, white men laid IR's disciplinary infrastructure and set out its method. They saw no place in the emerging idea of the international for people who were not white. They kept the study across closed groups. Their international was, initially, for whites only, until their belated, failed, attempt to bring Indians into the inside. Race and racial hierarchy were central concepts at this stage, with Indigenous and African societies assumed to be static and Asian societies seen as needing long-term colonial 'tutelage'.

In Canada, the institute was the site of a struggle between an old guard of imperial federationists and a younger generation of more liberal, even socialist, members who believed that Canada should break free of imperial federation to become an independent voice on the world stage. These thinkers, though, still believed that Canada had a 'special' role to play in the world. Canadian IR, then, became a debate between imperial federationists and liberal exceptionalists, the latter of which sought to control the institute and radically expand its character, membership and structure. Unlike Australia, colonial dispossession was not that thoroughly discussed. Amongst the liberal exceptionalists, Canada's ability to play a unique and positive role was assumed, and its colonial ills erased rather than engaged with. Its own practices of Indigenous dispossession were never questioned. In this sense, liberal exceptionalism was another, albeit kinder, imperial narrative. As a result, Canadian IR paid less attention to domestic questions of race than did our other case studies. Despite this shift, with the establishment of *International Journal* after WWII, there were still echoes of Curtis' original formulation: the gathering of facts to improve world affairs.

In Australia, the initial studies published in *The Round Table* and later publications such as the *Austral-Asiatic Bulletin*, thoroughly blurred the domestic and the international. The original priorities of the AIIA in particular were largely to do with settlement, control and utilisation of Australia's land. Their studies, then, were soaked in the idea of *terra nullius*, the idea of land use as determining ownership, and therefore international affairs was fundamental to the foundation of the Australian state. The lack of (white) population in the Northern Territory was construed as a 'foreign policy threat'. These themes became central to Australia's foreign policy thinking in the 1930s and were very much a feature of Australia's anxieties about the world and existence within it. This sat alongside discussions about imperial governance and politics in East Asia. While this theme dissipated after WWII, the formation of an IR chair at ANU still emphasised the need to study threats from Asia, itself a reflection of concerns about the possibilities of Asian immigration and invasion. With the formation of an IR journal in Australia, *Australian Outlook*, there were still significant echoes of Curtis' original framing as to why we should study international affairs. The story of IR in Australia emerging out of and discussing settler colonial anxieties over land utilisation, however, has not generally been acknowledged in the discipline's understanding of itself. This story in particular shows the need for Australian IR to think about its own origins, and its need for decolonisation.

The South African experience of studying the international was limited by its own obsessions with race. The Round Table struggled to take hold in South Africa despite having been its original geographic setting. After WWII, the SAIIA used the hiving off of the domestic and the international to avoid talking about the society's growing and obvious racism. South African foreign policy thinkers could ask questions like 'how can a European state survive in Africa?', and analyse them from a realist, state-as-actor perspective, using the new framing of IR to avoid the obvious racial and colonial meanings of the analysis.

In New Zealand, the NZIIA struggled for funding and to find thinkers and speakers to engage the study of world affairs. Despite this, the NZIIA did manage to contribute to the Round Table and to Curtis' vision as well as study New Zealand's international affairs. A stream of analysis formed which focused on New Zealand's own 'successful' colonisation of the Maoris. The study of the international in New Zealand took as its starting assumption that the society was 'better' and kinder at imperialism than their Australian counterparts. Throughout each of these examples, racial hierarchies imbued both the analysis and the question of who could speak within the institutions and who could not. IR in New Zealand negotiated race and the international by examining itself and its imperial possessions. The project struggled with New Zealand's difficulties in governing Samoa, which was resisted by the local peoples.

The Indian experience stands apart from our other origin stories of IR in the settler colonies. The RIIA and the Round Table realised a need for certain kinds of Indians to engage in the study of the international. English-speaking, educated Indians had long been seen within the empire as higher up the civilisational and racial hierarchy than Indigenous groups and Africans. The Indian story reveals to us the weaknesses of the Round Table's projects in making an imperial world order, as well as the ways in which this project misunderstood the politics of late colonial India. In all of the other examples examined in this book, only white men were allowed to think about the international. In the IIIA, there was to be white leadership of an institution that was predominantly made up of political elites from colonial India. Many were also members of the INC or the Muslim League. With these political divisions tearing at the institution, the IIIA produced very little scholarship at all. It was made quite explicit within colonial bureaucracy, however, that the institution should not be allowed to think independently about race, empire and the international in the ways that the other institutes were.

As a result, the IIIA had a very different experience, which reveals to us the limits of the RIIA model to function outside of imperial contexts. Attempts at 'objective research' in the colonial context, as Indian critics argued, only served the colonial state. Despite India's exceptionally rich history of thinking about the international, the IIIA was largely unable to produce any meaningful research. Instead, the ICWA formed in opposition to the IIIA, and became an important 'think tank' on international affairs in India. The story of the IIIA, the ICWA and the PIIA tells us a great deal about how the production of knowledge about the international was politicised.

It is well worth considering also the thematic connections between the five stories of IR's institutionalisation. The examples of South Africa, Canada, Australia and New Zealand drew from the same set of narratives for understanding the world through the optic offered by the international. They looked at ideas of race, empire, white exceptionalism, and the tussle between imperial elites and those seeking independence and internationalism. Simultaneously, each emphasised the connection between the domestic, the imperial and ideas about race. In many of these cases, though, even at the end point of our stories, there were still echoes of the original Curtis vision. In particular, we regularly see the idea of gathering knowledge with the purpose of improving international affairs and bringing about world peace. For example, this idea appeared in the foundational editorials of *International Journal* and *Australian Outlook*. Within these ideas of world peace, though, one world government was not necessarily seen as desirable. Instead, it was commonplace for analysts working from Australia, Canada or New Zealand to see their societies as having a 'special' or outsized role to play in the world. By the end of each of our chapters, each of these societies believed themselves to be non-racist. The extent to which this was the case, is, of course, deeply questionable. These societies quickly came to roll their eyes at accusations of racism and see themselves as no longer colonisers. In South Africa the international desires were far gloomier. The aim of colonising further, even spreading the South African state as far north as Kenya and Tanzania, were aspirational goals and, of course, subjects of study.

In India, very little research could be done while thinking within the Round Table's set of ideas. In South Africa, race and the making of the international was even more explicit, with expansionist ambitions across the face of the Southern African subcontinent. In Canada, Australia and New Zealand, by the end of WWII, each set of IR thinkers believed themselves, for the most part, not to be imperialist or racist in their thought. They still, though, believed in their society having an outsized role to play in the world.

Putting these five imperialist stories of IR's origins together gives us a very different perspective on race, empire and the international. As our stories ended, the hiving off of the 'domestic' from the 'international' was becoming a key facet of the study of IR. Making the international state the only actor in the international erased the imperial origins of the discipline and led us to ahistorical theorising which emphasised great power politics. To close, then, we will look briefly at the extent to which this method still exists today, and, finally, what our history says about the possibilities for decolonising the study of IR.

WHAT IS LEFT OF CURTIS' METHOD TODAY?

Most of our stories in this book closed in the 1950s and 1960s. By way of a postscript, though, it is worth looking briefly at what is left of this original disciplinary method and infrastructure today. The institutes discussed here exist in some form, with the exception of the IIIA. *The Round Table* became a Taylor and Francis journal, as has been a major trend in academic publishing. It is still publishing on international affairs. This means the back catalogue of *The Round Table* is archived on their website and university library searches with sufficient subscriptions. If we are to take a cue from the academic literature on the archival turn, this is no small point. The articles dating back to 1910 are positioned deep within the archive of the discipline. They are easily accessible as a result for those with institutional access. If disciplinary history lies somewhere in the archive, and the way that archive is ordered builds the discipline today, these earliest texts remain at the bedrock of the formal study of IR.

Curtis' method was largely empirical, with the belief that studying international affairs would make the world a better place. That the world envisioned was one of permanent empire is what the discipline has largely chosen to forget. This means that it is relatively easy to think of studying international affairs as a path to improving them. This is a marketable idea. For example, the University of Aberystwyth today states that its department was the first ever IR department, and that its 'teaching and research remain true to its founding ideals: to seek greater security, peace and justice in a disordered world'.[1]

We can quite clearly see echoes of streams of thought in our case studies, if not necessarily the same method. They still reflect the contemporary strategic culture, particularly in Canada, Australia and New Zealand. Canada and New Zealand still draw on the idea of themselves as exceptionalist. Australia still produces a great deal of analysis on Asia, much of which is still imbued with a sense of fear of the Other. India's think tanks tend to distance themselves from academic IR debates, and instead pursue India's 'national interest' at all costs. Academic Indian IR is often engaged in recovering Indian international thought, and Indian scholars have made major contributions to the development of postcolonial IR. South Africa is still very much grappling with the aftermath of apartheid, and its academic IR debates often examine decolonisation.

That the institutions examined in this book still exist today and contain echoes of their founding, is not that much more than a curiosity for our purposes here. Their journals publish much excellent research, on the basis of the peer review systems now ubiquitous in academia. Of greater concern is the extent to which theoretical concepts used today still base themselves on Curtis-like ideas. Postcolonial IR scholarship and theory has often noted that the instinct to govern the world still exists in much neoliberal institutionalist IR, such as in studies of the 'Responsibility to Protect', in liberal interventionist literature, and in the English School.[2] Notions of who is a 'responsible' state and who is not are still at play in international governance and in scholarship.[3] The idea of 'revitalising' the UN Trusteeship Council, based on the LoN's mandates system, with which Kerr and Smuts are deeply affiliated, has arisen periodically, particularly in debates on international law, as a means of governing 'failed states', improving humanitarian intervention and even as a way of getting the UN involved in the Iraq War.[4] The UN Trusteeship Council's chamber is still used for meetings, and, interestingly, is often the venue for conferences on the Responsibility to Protect.[5] Of course, this is seldom explicitly racialised in contemporary IR analysis. Nevertheless, they reflect modes of analysis that base themselves on implicit standards of civilisation. This is not that distinct from Curtis' belief that higher civilisations should govern the rest.

Although these instincts still exist in some IR scholarship, perhaps the most obvious place in which Curtis' mission exists today is not the academy, but in today's enormous proliferation of think tanks. Curtis' idea that a think tank could straddle the middle ground between truth and propaganda, and build support for particular polices, has been thoroughly taken to heart by policy elites worldwide. Many of these think tanks are attached to state foreign policymaking. Many are neoliberal in nature, advocating for deregulation, and the spread of neoliberal market economics. Some, such as the Heritage Foundation in the US and the Institute for Public Affairs in Australia, are conservative in nature and produce ideas that are rapidly sucked up into conservative political parties. Some have advocated for regime change wars, such as the 2003 invasion of Iraq.[6]

Think tanks producing knowledge to construct world orders is very much still with us today.

DECOLONISING THE DISCIPLINE

When we began writing this book, we had hoped we might find moments of resistance, or dissent, in the manner of Vitalis' analysis of the Howard School in the US[7] that might give us a clearer sense that an anti-imperial or decolonised IR might be possible. There were, however, only some moments of dissent that we found throughout the story in these pages. In Canada, the debate between an explicitly imperial IR and a more independent version of Canada's role in world affairs still relied on the assumption that Canada had a special and outsized role to play in the world. In the case of India, even though there are long-standing and vibrant traditions of international thought from that cultural context, the institute in question was unable to produce research within the confines of the Chatham House method and instead fought over legitimacy.

Numerous scholars have looked at the possibilities and difficulties of decolonising the study of international relations. Perhaps closest to what we have done here is what Meera Sabaratnam noted as the need for challenging Eurocentric historiographies as part of decolonial strategies.[8] Elsewhere, the late Lily Ling reminded us that decolonising IR means finding a 'cross-cultural model of understanding that accepts multiplicities'.[9] In her early collection, Branwen Gruffydd Jones notes that IR is largely an Anglo-American social science and that this needs to shift for IR to be decolonised.[10] Bearing in mind these themes, what can we learn about decolonising the discipline from the history that we have recounted here?

For critical IR scholars, at first glance, the implications of our tale(s) might appear bleak. One of the more obvious implications of the history that we have examined here is that IR's colonial history is deeper and darker than previously understood. And yet, we also reveal that colonial societies, and non-Western contexts like South Africa, were important in producing the formalised study of IR. Understanding IR's history as not just Eurocentric, but also imperial; as studying the non-West and Indigenous groups so as to control them, and specifically silencing the voices of non-white men and women, gives us a better sense of both the discipline's history outside the US and the UK, and indeed what we are up against when we want to decolonise a deeply colonial discipline.

First, the key finding of our history here is to challenge the idea that IR has always been an (Anglo-)American social science. These nationally focused histories which emphasise the US and the UK, though not ahistorical by any means, miss the role of empire in making the international. Traditions of thinking, studying and researching about the international were strongly informed by both local and imperial contexts.

Aside from showing the need to study a far broader spatial scope when understanding disciplinary history, our study here also shows just how deeply enmeshed IR's history is with race and empire. It is hard to miss the centrality of race in any imagination of Empire/International from its settler colonial frontiers. One of the key results of the study, therefore, is a greater understanding of how imperial ideology historically informed IR's knowledge production. IR's analysis, as it emerged from these institutions, was often engaged in the study of non-white peoples from an explicitly colonial and race development perspective. The Round Table's project, then, was always about what we might call today the 'Global South'. It studied non-white peoples. It was about them. Many of its ideas came from interactions in South Africa. Much of its study was explicitly colonial, such as of the settlement of the Northern Territory in Australia or New Zealand's holding of Samoa. Making this a racially diverse project was anathema to its very purpose.

IR is far from alone in its need to have a reckoning with its imperial history. Anthropology's relationship with imperialism and racial categorisation is well recognised. As Irene Gendzier has shown, Development Studies has its own connections to ideas of race development which emerged after WWII.[11] Questions of who can and who cannot be 'trusted' to govern themselves have, in this sense, been central to world politics for centuries.

As we have shown here, such questions are deeply buried in IR's origins, in ways which are yet to be acknowledged. They remain implicitly central to liberal humanitarian political discourse today.[12]

So, what is the way forward? First, better understanding where the discipline came from, across different cultural and historical contexts, will assist in decolonising IR. Critical IR scholars have thoroughly critiqued the Eurocentric origins of IR. They have looked at non-Western ways of seeing the world. By finding, telling and analysing stories of the idea of institutionalising the study of the 'international' and the ways in which it found its way around the world, what meanings were attached to it, and how its early institutions were set up can help us to understand why the study of the Eurocentric study of international affairs has been so hard to shake.

Telling more stories of the origins of IR helps us to imagine a decolonised IR because it shows how different the discipline could be and denaturalises the end point of its study of great power politics. One of the key calls for this book, then, is for more scholars around the world, from new and diverse cultural or national contexts, to take up critical historical disciplinary studies of IR. We have looked at three settler colonial societies here, at how the international arrived, how it was thought about and studied and institutionalised. In each of these cases, themes of race, colonisation and empire played different roles in their analysis of the international. We have also examined some 'non-Western' contexts. In South Africa, where a white minority ruled like they were running a settler colony, the most brutal, racist form of IR emerged. In India, the formalised study of the international managed to exclude Indian international thought at its foundation. Understanding the disciplinary and institutional reasons for why the formalised study of the international rejected the study of Indian international thought tells us a great deal about why Eurocentrism has stuck so defiantly to the study of IR.

In each of the cases examined here, the international was imbued with racial meaning. With the historical moment of decolonisation, notions of sovereignty and non-interference, the systemic disconnection of the domestic and the international, enabled states like South Africa and Australia to claim that the study of IR no longer had racial meanings. This was used to get these societies off the hook. Today, a great deal of IR is indeed still produced outside of these old imperial centres. However, IR is taught, studied and produced across the post-colonised world. Much of this remains tethered to the state-as-actor model, or is designed with the goal in mind of improving the foreign relations of a particular state. In this sense, Eurocentric models of IR are often replicated in postcolonial states, in ways which naturalise the state and its foreign relations. This spread of the discipline alone has been insufficient to deal with some of these issues. This is, at least in part, because the discipline is premised on the forgetting of its colonial history, and its tethering to the state.

We cannot hope to decolonise IR without a deeper and more spatially expansive understanding of its history. Such a transformation of IR, though, will only be possible with a sustained and critical engagement of the discipline's history. Plural and differentiated origins stories can help to imagine a decolonised IR. The stories discussed here have, in most cases, not been told before. Telling a story of origin of IR that is global and networked, which embedded itself around the world across different state contexts, can help us to understand the plural origins of the discipline. IR emerged out of transnational whiteness, but it had origins and meanings outside of this, as it spread across the world.

Building a decolonised IR will need a deeper, more variegated, and culturally nuanced history of the discipline, so as to understand where it came from, how deep the rot is, and what to do about it. It is also crucial to put these histories into a broader global context that can pay attention to who counts, who can speak, and who cannot. If only solely tied to state- or national-level histories, we run the risk of IR still naturalising the existence of the international state and not challenging the foreign policy elites, funders and think thanks who benefit from the hiving off of the domestic from the international. Ours is still a very limited story – after all, we have mostly only looked at white settler colonial states of the British empire. Each context around the world will have a different story.

This disciplinary history gives us a base from which to move forward. The discipline's history has been premised not on ignoring these diverse perspectives, but by silencing them. In our case studies, funders, discursive and national contexts, as well as global politics itself, combined with the foundational concerns of the disciplinary thought collective to produce a means of studying the international which drew heavily on race and empire. They did so not just from the US and the UK, but from ideas formulated at the imperial frontier. The Global South, then, was always important in disciplinary history, but for the purposes of surveillance control – not emancipation.

In order to achieve this, we need a deeper fracturing of the discipline, which opens it up to broader disciplinary perspectives. We cannot only decolonise IR without a diverse understanding of our history combined with a desire to incorporate as many diverse, Indigenous or subaltern voices as possible. This book shows the need for critically rethinking of

IR's disciplinary history. This means breaking open disciplinary history and flooding IR with multiple origin stories and diverse voices from as many geocultural contexts as possible, while continually paying attention to social and cultural hierarchies, who benefits from the study of the international, who is studied, who can speak, and who cannot.

Notes

INTRODUCTION: RACE, EMPIRE AND THE FOUNDING OF INTERNATIONAL RELATIONS

1. Lionel Curtis and W.H. Shepardson, 'Memorandum', Folder 2 (1) – Foundation of RIIA, Paris 1919, Chatham House Archives, London.
2. Peter Lassman, 'Political Philosophy and the Idea of a Social Science', in George Klosko (ed.), *The Oxford Handbook of the History of Political Philosophy* (Oxford: Oxford University Press, 2011), p. 437.
3. Peter Laslett, 'Introduction', in Peter Laslett (ed.), *Philosophy, Politics and Society*, 1st series (Oxford: Basil Blackwell, 1956), p. vii.
4. Lassman, 'Political Philosophy', p. 453.
5. Duncan Bell, 'International Relations: The Dawn of a Historiographical Turn?', *British Journal of Politics and International Relations* 3, no. 1 (2001), 115–26; Gerard Holden, 'Who Contextualizes the Contextualizers? Disciplinary History and the Discourse about IR Discourse', *Review of International Studies* 28, no. 2 (2002), 253–70.
6. Brian C. Schmidt, *The Political Discourse of Anarchy: A Disciplinary History of International Relations* (Albany, NY: State University of New York Press, 1998); Torbjørn L. Knutsen, 'A Lost Generation? IR Scholarship before World War I', *International Politics* 45, no. 6 (2008), 650–74; Nicolas Guilhot, 'The Relist Gambit: Postwar American Political Science and the Birth of IR Theory', *International Political Sociology* 2 no. 4 (2008), 281–304; Nicholas Guilhot, 'Imperial Realism: Post-War IR Theory and Decolonisation', *The International History Review* 36 no. 4 (2014), 698–720; Lucian Ashworth, *A History of International Thought. From the Origins of the Modern State to Academic International Relations* (London: Routledge, 2014); Siba Grovogui, *Beyond Eurocentrism and Anarchy: Memories of International Order and Institutions* (New York: Palgrave Macmillan, 2005). Though not specifically focused on the IR discipline, Or Rosenboim provides an extremely useful and expert discussion of Anglo-American political thinkers around this time. See Or Rosenboim, *The Emergence of Globalism: Visions of World Order in Britain and the United States, 1939–1950* (Princeton, NJ: Princeton University Press, 2017).
7. Robert Vitalis, 'Birth of the Discipline', in David Long and Brian Schmidt (eds), *Imperialism and Internationalism in the Discipline of International Relations* (Albany, NY: State University of New York Press, 2005), pp. 159–81 and Robert Vitalis, *White World Order, Black Power Politics: The Birth of American International Relations* (Ithaca, NY: Cornell University Press, 2015).
8. See, for example, Robbie Shilliam, *International Relations and Non-Western Thought: Imperialism, Colonialism and Investigations of Global Modernity*

(London: Routledge, 2011) and L.H.M. Ling, *The Dao of World Politics: Towards a Post-Westphalian: Worldist International Relations* (London: Routledge, 2014).

9. Vitalis, *White World Order*.

10. Stanley Hoffmann, 'An American Social Science: International Relations', *Daedalus* 106, no. 3, 41–60.

11. See, for example, Schmidt, *Political Discourse of Anarchy*; Ido Oren, *Our Enemies and US: America's Rivalries and the Making of Political Science* (Ithaca, NY and London: Cornell University Press, 2003); Vitalis, *White World Order*; and Jessica Blatt, *Race and the Making of American Political Science* (Philadelphia, PA: University of Pennsylvania Press, 2018).

12. Blatt, *Race and the Making of American Political Science*.

13. Perry Anderson, *American Foreign Policy and Its Thinkers* (London: Verso Books, 2015).

14. A key part of the British anxiety was that the US might be becoming the model for the 'Commonwealth', especially on the racial question. British liberals thought of America as central to the Commonwealth project. Americans also looked at British colonies to find answers for their own problems. For example, American scholars came to South Africa in the mid-1920s to study segregation. For an analysis, see Paul Rich, *White Power and the Liberal Conscience: Racial Segregation and South African Liberalism* (Johannesburg: Ravan, 1984) and Saul Dubow, *A Commonwealth of Knowledge: Science, Sensibility and White South Africa, 1820–2000* (Oxford: Oxford University Press, 2006).

15. David Long and Brian Schmidt (eds), *Imperialism and Internationalism in the Discipline of International Relations* (Albany, NY: State University of New York Press, 2005), p. 4.

16. William C. Olson and A.J.R. Groom, *International Relations Then and Now: Origins and Trends in Interpretation* (London: Routledge, 1991), p. 47; ibid., p. 9.

17. Philip Mirowski and Dieter Plehwe (eds), *The Road from Mount Pelerin: The Making of the Neoliberal Thought Collective* (Cambridge, MA: Harvard University Press, 2009).

18. Brian C. Schmidt, 'Lessons from the Past: Reassessing the Interwar Disciplinary History of International Relations', *International Studies Quarterly* 42, no. 3 (1998), 433–59 and Peter Wilson, 'The Myth of the "First Great Debate"', *Review of International Studies* 24, no. 5 (1998), 10–12.

19. Long and Schmidt, *Imperialism and Internationalism*, p. 5.

20. Vitalis, *White World Order*; John Hobson, *The Eurocentric Conception of World Politics*; Long and Schimdt, *Imperialism and Internationalism*.

21. Vitalis, *White World Order*.

22. John Hobson, 'Re-viewing the Eurocentric Conception of World Politics: A Response to Knutsen, Ling, Schmidt, Tickner and Vitalis', *Millennium: Journal of International Studies* 42, no. 2, 485–514.

23. On race and racism in IR, see Alexander Anievas, Nivi Manchanda and Robbie Shilliam (eds), *Race and Racism in International Relations: Confronting the Global Colour Line* (London and New York: Routledge, 2015); Duncan Bell, *The Idea of Greater Britain: Empire and the Future of World Order, 1860–1900*

(Princeton, NJ: Princeton University Press, 2007); Alexander E. Davis, *India and the Anglosphere: Race, Identity and Hierarchy in International Relations* (Abingdon, Oxon: Routledge, 2019); and Srdjan Vucetic, *The Anglosphere: Genealogy of a Racialized Identity in International Relations* (Palo Alto, CA: Stanford University Press, 2011).

24. Sankaran Krishna, 'Race, Amnesia, and the Education of International Relations', *Alternatives: Global, Local, Political* 26 no. 4 (2001), 401–24.

25. Navnita Chadha Behera, 'Knowledge Production', *International Studies Review* 18, no. 1 (2016), 153–5.

26. Ibid, p. 154.

27. Patricia Owens, 'Women and the History of International Thought', *International Studies Quarterly* 62, no. 3 (2018), 467–81.

28. Thankfully, such a project is ongoing, led by Kimberly Hutchings, Patricia Owens and Katharina Rietzler. We eagerly await the results of their study.

29. T.V. Paul, 'Indian International Relations Studies: The Need for Integration with Global Scholarship', ORF Issue Brief, no. 219, December 2017, available at www.orfonline.org/research/indian-international-relations-studies-need-integration-global-scholarship/ (accessed 28 February 2020).

30. Martin Wight, 'Why Is There No International Theory?', *International Relations* 2, no. 1 (1960), 35–48.

31. On this subject, see Bell, *The Idea of Greater Britain*; Davis, *India and the Anglosphere*; and Vucetic, *The Anglosphere*.

32. It is worth noting that there were courses taught at universities covering IR, and IR-like topics outside of the US and the UK prior to the post-WWII era. See, for example, James Cotton, 'Early International Relations Teaching and Teachers in Australia: Institutional and Disciplinary Origins', *Australian Journal of International Affairs* 67, no. 1 (2013), 71–97.

1. AN EDWARDIAN FANTASY: THE EMPIRE-WIDE ORIGINS OF INTERNATIONAL RELATIONS

1. Lionel Curtis to Philip Kerr, 6 December 1936. Letter reproduced in 'The Lionel Curtis–Phillip Kerr Correspondence', *Annals of the Lothian Foundation* (London: The Lothian Foundation Press, 1991), p. 395.

2. See Walter Nimocks, *Milner's Young Men: The 'Kindergarten' in Edwardian Imperial Affairs* (Great Britain: Hodder and Stoughton, 1968); Deborah Lavin, *From Empire to International Commonwealth: A Biography of Lionel Curtis* (Oxford: Clarendon Press, 1995); J.E. Kendle, *The Roundtable Movement and Imperial Union* (Toronto: University of Toronto Press, 1975); Carroll Quigley, *Anglo-American Establishment* (New York: Book in Focus, 1981); Alexander C. May, 'The Round Table, 1910–1966' (PhD Thesis, University of Oxford, 1995); Andrea Bosco and Alexander C. May (eds), *The Round Table, the Empire/Commonwealth and British Foreign Policy* (London: Lothian Foundation Press, 1997); Andrea Bosco, *The Round Table Movement and the Fall of 'Second' British Empire (1909–1919)* (Newcastle upon Tyne: Cambridge Scholars Publishing, 2017); Jeanne Morefield, *Empires without Imperialism:*

Anglo-American Decline and the Politics of Deflection (Oxford: Oxford University Press, 2014); J.R.M. Butler, *Lord Lothian (Philip Kerr), 1882–1940* (London: Macmillan, 1960).

3. Bosco and May, 'Introduction', in Andrea Bosco and Alexander C. May (eds), *The Round Table, the Empire/Commonwealth and British Foreign Policy* (London: Lothian Foundation Press, 1997), p. xx.

4. See Andrea Bosco, 'From Empire to Atlantic "System": The Round Table, Chatham House and the Emergence of a New Paradigm in Anglo-American Relations', *Journal of Transatlantic Studies* 16, no. 3 (2018), 222–46.

5. Given what we read at the start of the previous chapter, one observation by Curtis in the quote above appears to be in contrast to his assertion for the setting up of an institute in 1919: the role of propaganda. In 1919, Curtis seemed bullish about the role of propaganda – in fact, this was the reason he had argued why an institute of international relations be set up. But in 1936, he seemed to think the opposite. A possible reason for the change of views is perhaps the benefit of hindsight. In 1919, when Curtis seemed bullish about propaganda, the Round Table network, of which he was the 'prophet', still seemed vibrant. The Round Table movement was indeed at the height of its power – Alfred Milner, the patriarch of the group, was the Colonial Secretary in David Lloyd George's cabinet. Philip Kerr, the other half of the Round Table duo, was the prime minister's secretary, and so was Edward Grigg, another Round Tabler. The chief of the LoN section of the British Foreign Office was Robert Cecil, another key member of the Round Table. The prime minister himself had called The Round Table the most influential group in the UK. The key scheme of the Round Table – of Imperial Union – was fairly controversial but was yet to be fully discarded. That happened at the Imperial Conference of 1921. After 1921, the Round Table groups were deprived of a central scheme, but their influence continued to be exerted in policy sphere through institutions like Chatham House. Curtis felt that the Imperial Federation scheme, which we will discuss below, had been sabotaged by too eager propaganda, it had received an almost visceral opposition. Consequently, his own focus in the 1920s moved from Imperial Federation to schemes of British Commonwealth and eventually imaginations of a World Commonwealth/State.

6. Nimocks, *Milner's Young Men*. This section also draws from our work in Vineet Thakur, Alexander E. Davis and Peter Vale (2017), 'Imperial Mission, Scientific Method: An Alternative Account of the Origins of IR', *Millennium: Journal of International Studies* 46, no. 1, 3–23 and Vineet Thakur and Peter Vale, *South Africa, Race and the Making of International Relations* (London: Rowman & Littlefield, 2020).

7. Bosco and May, 'Introduction', p. 1.

8. For more on this group, see Nimocks, *Milner's Young Men*; Lavin, *Empire to International Commonwealth*; Quigley, *Anglo-American Establishment*; Kendle, *Roundtable Movement*; May, 'The Round Table, 1910–1966'; Bosco, *The Round Table Movement*.

9. See Thakur and Vale, *South Africa, Race*.

10. Lionel Curtis, 'The Place of Subject People in the Empire', 9 May 1907, Fortnightly Club Collection, A 146, Wits Historical Papers, Johannesburg.

11. Ibid.

12. Basil Williams (ed.), *The Selborne Memorandum: A Review of the Mutual Relations of the British South African Colonies in 1907* (Oxford: Oxford University Press, 1925).

13. Nimocks, *Milner's Young Men*, p. 97.

14. Lionel Curtis, *The Government of South Africa*, Vol. 1 (South Africa: Central News Agency, 1908), pp. x–xi.

15. Lionel Curtis, *The Commonwealth of Nations* (London: Macmillan, 1916) and Lionel Curtis, *Civitas Dei: The Commonwealth of God* (London: Macmillan, 1938). The US edition was titled *The Commonwealth of God*.

16. The State, 'Association of Closer Union Societies', *The State* 1, no. 1 (1910), 113–16.

17. 'Curtis to Oliver', 15–16 August 1910, Lothian (Philip Kerr) Papers, National Archives of Scotland, Edinburgh, GD40/17/12, f. 149.

18. 'Curtis to Oliver', f. 148.This statement also prefigures the increasingly Christian leanings of their academic writings in the 1920s and 1930s. See Curtis, *Civitas Dei*.

19. 'Curtis to Oliver', f. 148.

20. 'Lord Selborne to Curtis, 8 Feb 1909', MSS Curtis Reel 1: General correspondence and paper, c. 1880–1909, Bodleian Library, Oxford.

21. 'S.A. Atkinson to Lionel Curtis, 10 May 1912', MS Eng. Hist. 777, f. 68, Bodleian Library, Oxford.

22. Quoted in Nimocks, *Milner's Young Men*, p. 134.

23. Ibid., pp. 147–8.

24. Ibid., pp. 147–8.

25. 'Memorandum', MS Curtis 156/1, f. 6.

26. Morefield, *Empires without Imperialism*, p. 8.

27. As Andrea Bosco notes, the coverage given to international over imperial affairs increased from 17.8 per cent in 1918 to 31.5 per cent in 1939. Bosco, 'From Empire', 20, footnote 10.

28. 'Curtis to Kerr, 21 July 1910', Lothian Papers, GD40/17/1, f. 67.

29. Bosco and May, 'Introduction', p. xviii.

30. Bosco, 'From Empire', p. 5.

31. Ibid., p. 12.

32. Curtis, *Civitas Dei*.

33. For instance, a prominent reason for the establishment of the Commonwealth of Australia was the policy of White Australia. Indeed, the Australia Prime Minister Edmund Barton held a copy of Charles Pearson's book *National Life and Character*, which had warned about the impending swamping of the white spaces by non-whites.

34. Marilyn Lake and Henry Reynolds, *Drawing the Colour Line: White Men's Countries and the International Challenge of Racial Equality* (Cambridge: Cambridge University Press, 2008).

35. See Bill Schwarz, *Memories of Empire, Vol. 1: The White Man's World* (Oxford: Oxford University Press, 2011).

36. 'Memoranda', MS Curtis 156/5, Lionel Curtis Papers, f. 60.
37. Ibid., f. 58.
38. Ibid., f. 60.
39. Leo Amery, 'Notes on the Re-organization of Official Relations between the United Kingdom and the Dominions, and on the possible development of the Conference System', Lothian Papers, GD40/17/13, f. 55 (1911).
40. Richard Jebb, *Studies in Colonial Nationalism* (London: E. Arnold, 1905).
41. 'Memoranda', Appendix, ff. 206–7.
42. William Marris, 'India and the English', *The Round Table* 1, no. 1, p. 49.
43. Ibid., p. 47.
44. Ibid., p. 49.
45. Bosco and May, 'Introduction', p. xxviii.
46. 'Kerr to Curtis, 17 April 1912', MS Eng. Hist. c. 823, f. 36.
47. Philip Kerr, 'India and the Empire I', *The Round Table* 2, no. 8 (1912), 623. Although he added, 'it will be long before India can govern herself on democratic lines' (p. 624).
48. Ibid., p. 625.
49. 'Philip Kerr to G. Paterson, 18 April 1912', MS Eng. Hist. c. 826, f. 2.
50. Philip Kerr, 'Memorandum of Representation to India', MS Eng. Hist. c. 826.
51. See 'The Round Table in Canada: How the Movement began. What it hopes to accomplish', 1917, MS Eng. Hist. 822, ff. 45–57, at 51–2.
52. Achieving universal peace through a scheme of world federation was a key theme of Kerr and Curtis' subsequent work. For one sample see Philip Kerr and Lionel Curtis, *The Prevention of War* (New Haven, CT: Yale University Press, 1923).
53. 'The Round Table in Canada', f. 56.
54. 'Lionel Curtis to Valentine Chirol, 27 March 1912', MS Eng. His. c. 823, f. 33.
55. In this book, Chirol had argued that the stirrings of unrest in India were primarily regional (lower Bengal and Maratha strongholds) and Hindu-centred. His thesis was that the unrest wasn't specifically against British misrule, but a result of the import of Western education and ideas. These had helped both reactionary – those who opposed the consequent waning of the Hindu knowledge dominance – as well as revolutionary – those who believed that Western ideals should be realised in India – elements to oppose British rule in India. See Valentine Chirol, *Indian Unrest* (London: Macmillan, 1910).
56. 'Curtis to Chirol, 22 March 1912', MS Eng. Hist. c. 823, f. 21.
57. 'William Marris to Lionel Curtis, 1 April 1912', MS Eng. Hist. 823, f. 21.
58. In June 1912, he was made the Beit Lecturer of Colonial History at Oxford, with H.E. Egerton (who was the first Beit Professor).
59. H.G. Wells, *The Shape of Things to Come* (London: Orion, 2017), p. 5 (originally published 1933).
60. Kendle, *Roundtable Movement*, p. 171. Curtis was reading copiously and discussing his project with several colleagues and fellow imperial enthusiasts. Alfred Zimmern, who had just published his *Greek Commonwealth*, was also recruited into the Round Table.

61. A concise version of Curtis' thesis was sent to Indian civil servants on 27 June 1912. See MSS EUR 136/10, ff. 50–60, India Office Records and Private Papers, British Library, London.

62. On the development of Curtis' views on sacramental state, see Gerald Studdert-Kennedy, 'Political Science and Political Theology: Lionel Curtis, Federalism and India', *The Journal of Imperial and Commonwealth History* 24, no. 2 (1996), 197–217.

63. John Hobson criticised this as 'Prussianism'. See John Hobson, 'New Books: The Commonwealth of Nations', *The Manchester Guardian*, 11 September 1916.

64. 'Whitsuntide Memorandum, 21 July 1914', MS Eng. Hist. c. 779, ff. 37–72, 1–36, at 3–4.

65. MSS EUR 136/10, f. 55.

66. Robert Brand, 'Memorandum by Hon. R. Brand on first part of Round Table Report', October 1912', MS Eng. Hist. c. 777, f. 4.

67. Curtis understood that ideas succeed not because of the solutions they offer, but because of the promises they make. As an anonymous letter written by an Imperial Leaguer in the 1890s advised the Round Table, political ideas gain acceptance of masses not because they solve practical problems, but because they present philosophical ideals. Gospels, not elaborate schemes, win masses. Two of the most successful contemporary ideas – religion and socialism – were cases in proof. Anon, 'Lucubrations on the possibility of a moral and philosophical groundwork for an Imperial Policy, 22 December 1912', MS Eng. Hist. c. 777.

68. Curtis, *Civitas Dei*, p. 882.

69. For a detailed discussion of Curtis' life and thought in this period, see Rosenboim, *The Emergence of Globalism*, pp. 107–14.

70. S.R. Mehrotra, 'Imperial Federation and India, 1868–1917', *Journal of Commonwealth and Comparative Politics* 1, no. 1 (1961), 37.

71. Arnold Toynbee, *Acquaintances* (New York: Oxford University Press, 1967), p. 134.

72. Ibid., p. 135.

73. Dipesh Chakrabarty, *Provincializing Europe: Postcolonial Thought and Historical Difference* (Princeton, NJ: Princeton University Press, 2000).

74. Some years later when he visited India, initially for a few months, he commented on what he saw: 'To fit [the Indians] for self-government needs generations of real education and patient work. And the few thousands of articulates are demanding it within 25 years. I have never seen a more difficult or critical situation, nor one which needed clear and careful interpretation to the other self-governing parts of the Empire. Unless it is understood and handled with strength and care we are in for a cosmic smash such as would throw India back for generations.' See 'Lionel Curtis to Alfred Zimmern, 29 November 1916', MS Eng. Hist. 779.

75. 'Lionel Curtis–Philip Kerr Correspondence', p. 323.

76. The original memorandum, called Brown memorandum, was written by Curtis but was met with some objections at the Moot with suggestions that its opening chapter of 24 pages be revised. Edward Grigg took on the task

of revision and substituted the first 12 pages of Curtis with his own revised document. See 'Lionel Curtis to Edward Grigg, 29 July 1914', MS Eng. Hist. c. 778, ff. 76–9.

77. 'Whitsuntide Memorandum', f. 14.

78. Ibid., f. 22.

79. On the origins of segregation in South Africa, see chapters by Martin Legassick, 'British Hegemony and the Origins of Segregation in South Africa, 1910–1914', pp. 43–59 and Saul Dubow, 'The Elaboration of Segregationist Ideology', pp. 145–75, in William Beinart and Saul Dubow (eds), *Segregation and Apartheid in Twentieth-Century South Africa* (London: Routledge, 1995); and Paul Rich, 'Race, Science and the Legitimization of White Supremacy in South Africa, 1902–1940', *The International Journal of African Historical Studies* 23, no. 4 (1990), 665–86.

80. Howard Pim, 'The Question of Race', 15 November, Fortnightly Club Collection, A 146, Wits Historical Papers, Johannesburg.

81. William L. Honnold, 'The Negro in America, 21 May 1908', Fortnightly Club Collection, A 146, Wits Historical Papers, Johannesburg, 1908.

82. W.S. Weber, 'Can the White Race Continue to Dominate South Africa?, 23 May 1907', Fortnightly Club Collection, A 146, Wits Historical Papers, Johannesburg.

83. For this, see Charles Pearson, *National Life and Character: A Forecast*, 2nd edition (London: Macmillan, 1913) (originally published 1893).

84. Lionel Curtis, *The Government of South Africa*, Vols 1 and 2. The journal *The State* ran from December 1908 to December 1912. Kerr relinquished editorship in mid-1909.

85. Curtis, *The Government of South Africa*, Vol. 1, p. 164.

86. Ibid., p. 109.

87. 'Whitsuntide Memorandum', f. 20.

88. Curtis, *The Commonwealth of Nations*, p. 2.

2.   CANADA: FROM IMPERIAL FEDERATIONISM TO LIBERAL IMPERIALISM

1. A.J.R. Groom and Peter Mandaville, 'Hegemony and Autonomy in International Relations: The Continental Experience', in Robert M.A. Crawford and Darryl S.L. Jarvis (eds), *International Relations – Still an American Social Science? Toward Diversity in International Thought* (Albany, NY: State University of New York Press, 2001), pp. 151–66.

2. K.J. Holsti, *The Dividing Discipline: Hegemony and Diversity in International Theory* (Boston, MA: Allen & Unwin, 1985).

3. Hoffmann, 'An American Social Science'.

4. Vitalis, *White World Order*.

5. Priscilla Roberts, 'Tweaking the Lion's Tail: Edgar J. Tarr, the Canadian Institute of International Affairs, and the British Empire, 1931–1950', *Diplomacy & Statecraft* 23, no. 4 (2012), 636–59.

6. Stéphane Roussel and Greg Donaghy (eds), *Escott Reid: Diplomat and Scholar* (Montreal: McGill-Queen's University Press, 2004); Davis, *India and the Anglosphere*; Ryan Touhey, *Conflicting Visions: Canada and India in the Cold War World, 1946–76* (Vancouver: University of British Columbia Press, 2015).

7. Davis, *India and the Anglosphere*, chapter 3.

8. Kim Richard Nossal, 'Defending the "Realm": Canadian Strategic Culture Revisited', *International Journal* 59, no. 3 (2004), 505–6.

9. Ibid., p. 512.

10. Alexander E. Davis, 'Rethinking Australia's International Past: Identity, Foreign Policy and India in the Australian Colonial Imagination', *Flinders Journal of History and Politics* 29 (2014), 70–96.

11. 'Memoranda', MS Curtis 156/5, Lionel Curtis Papers.

12. Christopher R.J. Rickerd, 'Canada, the Round Table and the Idea of Imperial Federation', in Andrea Bosco and Alexander C. May (eds), *The Round Table, the Empire/Commonwealth and British Foreign Policy* (London: Lothian Foundation Press, 1997), p. 199.

13. Quoted in James Eayrs, 'The Round Table in Canada, 1909–1920', *The Canadian Historical Review* 38, no. 1 (1957), 6.

14. Rickerd, 'Canada, the Round Table and the Idea of Imperial Federation', p. 202.

15. Ibid., p. 202.

16. Ibid., p. 193.

17. Quoted in Eayrs, 'The Round Table in Canada', p. 6.

18. Rickerd, 'Canada, the Round Table and the Idea of Imperial Federation', p. 210.

19. The Round Table, *The Round Table in Canada: How the Movement Began: What It Hopes to Accomplish* (Toronto, 1917).

20. Rickerd, 'Canada, the Round Table and the Idea of Imperial Federation', p. 211.

21. Caroll Quigley, 'The Round Table Groups in Canada, 1908–38', *Canada Historical Review* 43, no. 3 (1962), 204–24.

22. These included: Robert Borden, O.M Biggar, Loring Christie, George Foster, A.J. Glazebrook, Vincent Massey, Newton W. Rowell, George M. Wrong, Joseph Pope and W.S. Milner.

23. Over the years, the IPR organised biannual conferences which discussed issues related to Pacific affairs, before the organisation was accused of communist connections during McCarthy Years in the US, eventually leading to its dissolution in 1960. See Paul F. Hooper, 'The Institute of Pacific Relations and the Origins of Asian and Pacific Studies', *Pacific Affairs* 61, no. 1 (1988), 98–121. Also see Paul F. Hooper (ed.), *Remembering the Institute of the Pacific Relations: The Memoirs of William L. Holland* (Tokyo: Ryukei Shyosha, 1995); Tomoko Akami, *Internationalizing the Pacific: The United States, Japan, and the Institute of Pacific Relations in War and Peace, 1919–45* (London and New York: Routledge, 2002).

24. Quigley, 'The Round Table Groups in Canada', p. 191.

25. In 1930, five out of seven members – Jerome Greene, F.W. Eggleston, N.W. Rowell, Lionel Curtis and James Allen – were Round Tablers or close associates.
26. 'CIIA – Memorandum on its organisation and activities, May 1936', MG MG28-I250, Container 7, File 2, LAC.
27. The Round Table, 'Affairs in Canada', *The Round Table* 1, no. 1 (1910), 71.
28. Ibid., pp. 75–83.
29. The Round Table, 'Canadian Affairs', *The Round Table* 1, no. 2 (1911), 168–81.
30. The Round Table, 'Canadian Affairs', *The Round Table* 1, no. 4 (1911), 482.
31. The Round Table, 'Canada', *The Round Table* 9, no. 33 (1918), 163–4.
32. The Round Table, 'Canadian Affairs', *The Round Table* 1, no. 4 (1911), 494.
33. Ibid., p. 494.
34. The Round Table, 'Canada', *The Round Table* 7, 28 (1917), 774.
35. The Round Table, 'Canada', *The Round Table* 12, 48 (1922), 868.
36. The Round Table, 'Canada', *The Round Table* 13, no. 50 (1923), 398.
37. The Round Table, 'Canada', *The Round Table* 1, no. 44 (1921), 911.
38. For example, see Davis, *India and the Anglosphere*, chapter three.
39. The Round Table, 'Canada', *The Round Table* 13, no. 50 (1923), 401–2.
40. Davis, *India and the Anglosphere*, chapter three.
41. In 2007, it became the 'Canadian International Council', after merging with the Centre for International Governance Innovation based in Winnipeg.
42. 'The Canadian Institute of International Affairs – Handbook, 1935', MG28-I250, Container 7, File 2, Library and Archives Canada (hereafter LAC), Ottawa, f. 15.
43. The Canadian International Council, 'Our History', available at http://thecic.org/about/our-history/ (accessed 29 November 2016).
44. Escott Reid, *Radical Mandarin: The Memoirs of Escott Reid* (Toronto: University of Toronto Press, 1989), p. 74.
45. Roberts 'Tweaking the Lion's Tail'.
46. Ibid., p. 638.
47. Ibid., p. 636.
48. Ibid., p. 636.
49. Ibid., p. 636.
50. Reid, *Radical Mandarin*, p. 75.
51. J.L. Granatstein, 'Becoming Difficult: Escott Reid's Early Years', in Stéphane Roussel and Greg Donaghy (eds), *Escott Reid: Diplomat and Scholar* (Montreal: McGill-Queen's University Press, 2004), pp. 11–22.
52. Ibid., p. 15.
53. A historian, professor and career diplomat, who served as Canada's Ambassador to the US after WWII.
54. Minister of External Affairs of Canada from 1948 to 1957 under Louis St. Laurent, and then Prime Minister from 1963 to 1968.
55. A career diplomat who served as Under Secretary of State for External Affairs, Ambassador to NATO and Canada's Ambassador to the United States.
56. Granatstein, 'Becoming Difficult', p. 14.
57. Ibid., p. 14.
58. Reid, *Radical Mandarin*.

59. Granatstein, 'Becoming Difficult', p. 15.
60. Ibid., pp. 16–17.
61. Escott Reid, 'The future of the Institute: A discussion of the problems and the future of the Canadian Institute of International Affairs', MG28-1250, Container 2, File 13, LAC, f. 31.
62. Ibid., f. 17.
63. Ibid., f. 11.
64. The Round Table, 'Canada and Commonwealth Security', *The Round Table* 25, no. 97 (1934), 112.
65. J.A. Stevenson, 'Canadian Foreign Policy', *Pacific Affairs* 7, no. 2 (1934), 153.
66. Ibid., p. 153.
67. H.F. Angus, 'Canada and Naval Rivalry in the Pacific', *Pacific Affairs* 8, no. 2 (1935), 176.
68. R.M. Fowler, 'Foreword: To First Issue of International Journal', *International Journal* 1, no. 1 (1946), 5–6.
69. Ibid., pp. 5–6.
70. Ibid., pp. 5–6.
71. Ibid., pp. 5–6.
72. Ibid., pp. 5–6.
73. R.M. Fowler, 'A Wider Range of Law', *International Journal* 1, no. 1 (1946), 285.
74. Ibid., p. 286.
75. Willson Woodside, 'UN Progress?', *International Journal* 2, no. 2 (1947), 123.
76. G.V. Ferguson. 'The Challenging World Crisis', *International Journal* 2, no. 4 (1947), 281–6.
77. Malcolm MacDonald, 'Canada, a New Moral Force in the World', *International Journal* 1, no. 2 (1946), 159–63.
78. A.R.M. Lower, 'Canada in the New, Non-British World', *International Journal* 3, no. 3 (1948), 208–21.
79. W.L. Mackenzie King, 'Canadian Citizenship and the Larger World', *International Journal* 2, no. 2 (1947), 95.
80. Ibid., p. 95.
81. Gordon Graydon, 'Canada Deepens Her Roots in the Soil of World Affairs', *International Journal* 2, no. 4 (1947), 316–24.
82. D.C. Spry, 'One Scouting World', *International Journal* 3, no. 2 (1948), 156–9.
83. Edmond Turcotte, 'The World of UNESCO', *International Journal* 1, no. 1 (1946), 365.
84. M.W. Wallace, 'The Human Situation Today', *International Journal* 1, no. 1 (1946), 8–9.
85. Ibid., p. 7.
86. F.R. Scott 'Socialism in the Commonwealth', *International Journal* 1, no. 1 (1946), 26.
87. Ibid., p. 28.
88. Ibid., p 30.
89. Ibid., p. 30.
90. F.E. Dessauer, 'Peace and Law', *International Journal* 2, no. 1 (1946/47), 51.

91. R.G. Trotter, 'Canada as a Colonial Power', *International Journal* 1, no. 1 (1946), 215.
92. Ibid., p. 217.
93. H.F. Angus, 'Immigration', *International Journal* 1, no. 1 (1946), 65–7.
94. H.L. Keenleyside, 'Canadian Immigration Policy', *International Journal* 3, no. 3 (1948), 222–38.
95. H.F. Angus, 'East Indians in Canada', *International Journal.* 2, no. 1 (1946/1947), 47–50.
96. Ibid., p. 49.
97. Davis and Thakur, 'India's Anti-Racist Diplomacy'.
98. Douglas Copland, 'Australia's Attitude to British Commonwealth Relations', *International Journal* 3, no. 1 (1947/1948), 39–48.
99. Ibid., p. 44.
100. Ibid., p. 44.

3. AUSTRALIA: RACE, SETTLEMENT AND UNDERSTANDINGS OF THE INTERNATIONAL

1. Martin Indyk, 'The Australian Study of International Relations', in Don Aitkin (ed.), *Surveys of Australian Political Science* (Sydney: George Allen & Unwin, 1985), p. 426.
2. Ibid., p. 426.
3. J.D.B. Miller, 'The Development of International Studies in Australia, 1933–1983', *The Australian Outlook* 37, no. 3 (1983), 138–42.
4. Richard Devetak, 'An Australian Outlook on International Affairs? The Evolution of International Relations Theory in Australia', *Australian Journal of Politics and History* 55, no. 3 (2009), 343.
5. James Cotton, *The Australian School of International Relations* (Basingstoke: Palgrave Macmillan, 2013), pp. 7–20.
6. A lawyer, politician and diplomat who played crucial roles throughout the life of the Round Table, the AIIA and the founding of the ANU.
7. A historian who lectured in history at the University of Melbourne, before becoming involved in international affairs including the AIIA.
8. An Oxford educated Australian, and who was professor of IR at Syracuse University. He moved back to Australia after working for the LoN, and later studied the Commonwealth and the Mandates System.
9. A historian, now best known for his biography of South African Prime Minister Jan Smuts.
10. An Australian historian who focused on international affairs and foreign policy, and was the founding head of the University of Western Australia's history department.
11. A professor of political science, diplomat, author and journalist, who became involved in Australia's relationship with South East Asia after WWII.
12. A colonial administrator in Nigeria, who held the first Chair in IR at ANU, and then went on to act as a diplomat in India and Indonesia. On all of these thinkers, see Cotton, *Australian School*, pp. 7–20.

13. Cotton has also unpicked the various funding arrangements behind some of the institutes discussed here. The AIIA was founded partly based on funding from American philanthropic institutes seeking to promote foreign policy agendas. See James Cotton, 'Rockefeller, Carnegie, and the Limits of American Hegemony in the Emergence of Australian International Studies', *International Relations of the Asia-Pacific* 12, no. 1 (2012), 161–92.

14. Devetak, 'An Australian Outlook on International Affairs?', p. 342.

15. James Cotton, 'International Relations for Australia: Michael Lindsay, Martin Wight, and the First Department at the Australian National University', Working Paper 2010/2, available at http://ir.bellschool.anu.edu.au/sites/default/files/uploads/2016-08/ir_working_paper_2010-2.pdf (accessed 28 February 2020).

16. Vitalis, *White World Order*; Hobson, *Eurocentric Conception of World Politics*.

17. Leonie Foster, 'The Victorian Imperial Federation League and the Genesis of the Australian Round Table', in Andrea Bosco and Alex May (eds), *The Round Table, the Empire/Commonwealth and British Foreign Policy* (London: Lothian Foundation Press, 1997), pp. 187–8. Cotton also considers Eggleston to be the most important thinker in the 'Australian School'. His work has an extremely useful discussion of Eggleston's intellectual development. See Cotton, *Australian School*, pp. 49–72.

18. May, 'The Round Table', p. 71.

19. Lionel Curtis, 'Dominion Tour Diary', p. 147.

20. Ibid., p. 152.

21. Indeed, the appeal of the ideas of imperial federation were so strong that wealthy Australian-born expatriates who returned to England were key to the formation of the Imperial Federation League in London in 1884. See Foster, 'The Victorian Imperial Federation League', p. 177.

22. Lionel Curtis, 'Notes on the progress of the Movement in Australia', in MS Eng. Hist. 779, f. 153.

23. Ibid. Emphasis added.

24. The Round Table, 'The Australian Situation', *The Round Table* 1, no. 2 (1911), 187–8.

25. Ibid., p. 188.

26. For some later examples, see The Round Table, 'The Draft Protocol and the White Australia Policy – Government Assistance to Exports – the Victorian Labour Government', *The Round Table* 15, no. 58 (1926), 378–834.

27. The Round Table, 'Australia', *The Round Table* 2, no. 8 (1912), 719.

28. The Round Table, 'Naval Policy and the Pacific Question', *The Round Table* 4, no. 15 (1914), 400.

29. The Round Table, 'The Labour Movement in Australia: I. Development of the Labour Movement', *The Round Table* 2, no. 8 (1912), 666.

30. The Round Table, 'Australia', *The Round Table* 2, no. 7 (1912), 542–3. For another example, see The Round Table, 'Australia', *The Round Table*, 4, no. 13 (1913), 162–3.

31. The Round Table, 'Australia', *The Round Table* 6, no. 21 (1915), 158–80.

32. For example, see The Round Table, 'Australia', *The Round Table* 9, no. 33 (1918), 178–93.

33. The Round Table, 'Australia', *The Round Table* 11, no. 42 (1921), 421.

34. The Round Table, 'Australia', *The Round Table* 13, no. 50 (1923), 405–21.

35. The Round Table, 'Australia', *The Round Table* 16, no. 64 (1926), 840.

36. The Round Table, 'Australia: Australian Fiscal Policy – Australian Naval Defence – the New Labour Governments in Western Australia, South Australia and Tasmania', *The Round Table*, 14, no. 56 (1924), 826.

37. The Round Table, 'Australia', *The Round Table* 14, no. 53 (1923), 153–62.

38. 'I. Clunies Ross to Lionel Curtis, 12 February, 1929', Folder 3/6/AUSa – Australian Institute of International Affairs, Chatham House Archives, f. 1.

39. 'I. Clunies Ross to Anon, 22 April, 1929', Folder 3/6/AUSa.

40. 'Tristan Buesst, to Anon', Folder 3/6/AUSa.

41. 'I. Clunies Ross to Lionel Curtis, 12 February, 1929', f. 3.

42. 'Tristain Buesst to I. Clunies Ross, 22 April 1929', Folder 3/6/AUSa.

43. Anon, 'Australian Institute of International Affairs, 14 May, 1930', Folder 3/6/AUSa.

44. 'Neill Malcolm to Professor Chateris, 12 June 1930', Folder 3/6/AUSa.

45. 'Tristan Buesst to The Secretary, RIIA, 6 June 1930', Folder 3/6/AUSa.

46. 'AIIA Commonwealth Council to RIIA Secretary, 18 April 1933', Folder 3/6/AUSa.

47. A London-born, Cambridge educated lawyer who moved to Melbourne to take up the post of Dean of Melbourne University's Law School.

48. Edmund Piesse was born in Tasmania, and served during WWI as an intelligence analyst. His primary interest was in Japan as a possible threat to Australia. He was a member of the Round Table, the IPR and the AIIA. See http://adb.anu.edu.au/biography/piesse-edmund-leolin-8046 (accessed 28 February 2020).

49. An economist originally born in New Zealand, who worked at the University of Tasmania from 1924 to1944 before moving to the University of Melbourne.

50. 'AIIA Commonwealth Council to RIIA Secretary, 18 April, 1933'.

51. AIIA, 'Minute of the meeting of the Commonwealth Council', Folder 3/6/AUSa, f. 3.

52. Anon, 'Introducing "the Austral-Asiatic Bulletin"', *Austral-Asiatic Bulletin* 1, no. 1 (1937), 1.

53. Ibid., p. 1.

54. C.A.S. Hawker, 'Wanted: An Australian Policy', *Austral-Asiatic Bulletin* 1, no. 1 (1937), 4–5.

55. Ibid., p. 5.

56. A Minor Seer, 'New Guinea – Sometime Hence', *Austral-Asiatic Bulletin*,1, no. 5 (1937–38), 20.

57. Anon, 'The Recruiting of Labour in New Guinea', *Austral-Asiatic Bulletin* 3, no. 4 (1939), 17.

58. E.W.P. Chinnery, 'Natives of New Guinea', *Austral-Asiatic Bulletin* 2, no. 3 (1938), 16.

59. Anon, 'The McEwan Memorandum: A New Deal for the Blacks', *Austral-Asiatic Bulletin* 3, no. 1 (1939), 11.

60. Alexander Rentoul, 'Taming the Papuan', *Austral-Asiatic Bulletin* 4, no. 1 (1940), 13.

61. Herbert Gepp, 'The Development of Northern Australia', 1, no. 3 (1937), 10.
62. Earnest Scott, 'Immigration from Asia', *Austral-Asiatic Bulletin* 1, no. 1 (1937), 13. For a similar example, see Anon, 'Editorial', *Austral-Asiatic Bulletin* 1, no. 6 (1938), 6.
63. Davis, 'Rethinking Australia's International Past'.
64. K.C. Masterman, 'Colour Prejudice', *Austral-Asiatic Bulletin* 1, no. 5 (1937–38), 14.
65. Ibid., p. 14.
66. Syed Amjad Ali, 'India and the War', *Austral-Asiatic Bulletin* 3, no. 4 (1939), 18.
67. For example, see 'A Naval Correspondent', 'The Menace of the P.B', *Austral-Asiatic Bulletin* 2, no. 1 (1938), 15.
68. W. Burton, 'The Philippines: Republic or Dominion?', *Austral-Asiatic Bulletin* 2, no. 3 (1938), 13–14.
69. Ali, 'India and the War', p. 18.
70. Davis, *India and the Anglosphere*, pp. 1–16.
71. Gwenda Tavan, *The Long, Slow Death of White Australia* (Melbourne: Scribe, 2005).
72. R.J.F. Boyer, 'Foreword', *The Australian Outlook* 1, no. 1 (1947), 4.
73. Ibid., p. 5.
74. Frederic Eggleston, 'The United Nations Charter Critically Considered: The Trusteeship Provisions', *Australian Outlook* 1, no. 1 (1947), 43.
75. Ibid., p. 43.
76. Ibid., p. 44.
77. W.R. Crocker, 'Voting in the International Institutions', *Australian Outlook* 5, no. 3 (1951), 163.
78. H.A. Wolfsohn, 'Australian Foreign Policy', *Australian Outlook* 5, no. 2 (1951), 67–76.
79. W.E.H. Stanner, 'On the Next Phase of British Colonial Policy', *Australian Outlook* 6, no. 2 (1952), 104.
80. Cyril S. Belshaw, 'Native Administration in South-Eastern Papua', *Australian Outlook* 5, no. 2 (1951), 111.
81. See also Cyril S. Belshaw, 'The Significance of Modern Cults in Melanesian Development', *Australian Outlook* 4, no. 2 (1950), 116–25 and Peter Hastings, 'New Guinea – East and West', *Australian Outlook* 14, no. 2 (1960), 147–56.
82. Frederic Eggleston, 'Memorandum on training cadets in International Affairs, 20 September, 1949', MSS 327, C938p, Series 9 (1.2-5), Crocker Papers, Barr-Smith Library, University of Adelaide.
83. Douglas Copland, quoted in William Sima, *China and ANU: Diplomats, Adventurers, Scholars* (Canberra: ANU Press, 2015), p. 2.
84. Crocker, quoted in Cotton, *Australian School*, p. 218.
85. Cotton, *Australian School*, pp. 209–36.
86. Ibid., p. 72.
87. Ibid., p. 72.
88. Frederic Eggleston, 'Memorandum on the Objectives and Methods of Research in the Social Sciences and Pacific Studies', 1951, MSS 327, C938p,

Series 9 (1.2-5), Crocker Papers, Barr-Smith Library, University of Adelaide, f. 2.

89. Ibid., f. 1.
90. Ibid., f. 10.
91. Frederic Eggleston, 'Memorandum RE the school of Pacific Studies', not dated, MSS 327, C938p, Series 9 (1.2-5), Crocker Papers, Barr-Smith Library, University of Adelaide. f. 1.
92. Eggleston, 'Memorandum on the Objectives and Methods', f. 11.
93. Guilhot, 'Imperial Realism'.
94. W.R. Crocker, *The Racial Factor in International Relations* (Canberra: Australian National University, 1956), p. 4.
95. Ibid., p. 4.
96. Ibid., pp. 8–9.
97. Ibid., pp. 10–11.
98. Ibid., pp. 10–11.
99. Ibid., p. 12.
100. Ibid., p. 12.
101. Ibid., pp. 11–12.
102. Ibid., p. 13.
103. Ibid., p. 13.
104. Ibid., pp 12–13.

4. SOUTH AFRICA: RACE RELATIONS, THE INTERNATIONAL AND THE RISE OF APARTHEID

1. Thakur et al., 'Imperial Mission'; Thakur and Vale, *South Africa, Race*.
2. Kendle, *Roundtable Movement*; Bosco, *Second British Empire*; May 'The Round Table'; Bosco and May, *The Empire/Commonwealth*; Lavin, *Empire to International Commonwealth*.
3. 'Letter from J.C. Beattie to The Director, RIIA, 30 January 1928', Folder 3/6 – SOUa, Chatham House Archives, London.
4. The Round Table, 'Honolulu', *The Round Table* 18, no. 69 (1927), 93.
5. 'Letter from J.C. Beattie to The Director, RIIA, 30 January 1928'.
6. Paul Rich, 'The South African Institute on Race Relations and the Debate on "Race Relations", 1929–1958', *African Studies* 40, no. 1 (1981), 14.
7. As Saul Dubow notes, the 1913 Native Land Act promised segregation, but its implementation was deferred to an unspecified future date. Likewise, the 1917 Native Administration Bill was abandoned. Dubow, 'The Elaboration', p. 39.
8. Alfred R. Radcliffe-Brown 'The Methods of Ethnology and Social Anthropology', *South African Journal of Science* 20, no. 1 (1923), 124-7.
9. Mark Lamont, 'Malinowski and the "Native Question"', in Regna Darnell and Frederic W. Gleach (eds), *Anthropologists and Their Traditions across National Borders*, Vol. 8 (Nebraska: University of Nebraska Press, 2014), p. 74.
10. Radcliffe-Brown 'The Methods'. The need for study of races was important for a number of both national and international reasons. First, the South African

eugenicist J.L. Duerden had highlighted the German eugenicist Karl Pearson's assertion that 'the war was lost [by Germany] because a nation of professed thinkers had studied all sciences, but had omitted to study aptly the science of man'. Application of the science of man in South Africa would mean implementing eugenics-based immigration policies that make sure efficient whites are invited.

11. Franz Boas, *Race, Language, and Culture* (London: Macmillan, 1940).

12. Dubow, 'The Elaboration', p. 32.

13. Antony Anghie, *Imperialism, Sovereignty and the Making of International Law* (Cambridge: University of Cambridge Press, 2004).

14. Harold Butler, 'The African Labour Problem', *The Round Table* 18, no. 71 (1928), 498–521.

15. See South African Round Table Group, 'Native Policy in South Africa', *The Round Table* 26, no. 103 (1936), 528–45; Anon, 'Native Policy in South Africa', *The Round Table* 25, no. 100 (1935), 722–73. This, as Quinn Slobodian has argued, was also the position of later neoliberals like William Hutt. See chapter 5, 'A World of Races', in Quinn Slobodian, *Globalists: The End of Empire and the Birth of Neoliberalism* (Cambridge, MA: Harvard University Press, 2018).

16. Richard Feetham, 'The Colour Question in Politics', *The Round Table* 13, no. 49 (1922), 62.

17. League of Nations, 'The Covenant of the League of Nations', 1918, available at https://avalon.law.yale.edu/20th_century/leagcov.asp (accessed 28 February 2020).

18. Jan Smuts, *Africa and Some World Problems* (Oxford: Clarendon Press, 1930).

19. Jan Smuts, *Plans for a Better World* (London: Hodder and Stoughton, 1940), p. 48.

20. Ibid., p. 37.

21. Ibid., p. 37.

22. Ibid., p. 38.

23. Ibid., p. 38.

24. Ibid., p. 39.

25. Ibid., p. 40.

26. Frederick D. Lugard, *The Dual Mandate in British Tropical Africa. Fifth Edition* (London: Frank Cass, 1965).

27. Lamont, 'Malinowski'.

28. Curtis, *The Government of South Africa*, p. 3.

29. The Round Table, 'The New Problem of Africa', *The Round Table* 17, no. 67 (1927), 447–72.

30. The Round Table, 'Africa from the South', *The Round Table* 21, no. 81 (1930), 126.

31. The Round Table, 'The New Problem', p. 457.

32. 'Note from Patrick Duncan on various questions affecting South Africa', 12 September 1932, BC294 – A54.4.1, Patrick Duncan Papers, UCT Libraries, Cape Town.

33. John Cell, 'Lord Hailey and the Making of African Survey', *African Affairs* 88, no. 353 (1989), 481–505.

34. See J.H. Oldham, 'Report of the Commission of the Closer Union of the Eastern and Central African Dependencies', *Journal of the Royal Institute of International Affairs* 8, no. 3 (1929), 227–59. Oldham also published a response to Smuts' Rhodes Lectures where he argued that the South African precedent was quite incompatible with the British mandate in Eastern Africa. See J.H. Oldham, *White and Black in Africa: A Critical Examination of the Rhodes Lectures of General Smuts* (London: Longmans, Green, 1930). Also Cell, 'Lord Hailey', p. 488.

35. Even South African liberals were sceptical of creating a common state, but agreed that 'a broad policy of Native development should be a joint policy' and 'an unrestricted Customs Union with extension to the North as far as possible should be accepted as a cardinal point in policy'. See W.H. Ramsbottom, 'South Africa and the North', in E.H. Brooks et al., *Coming of Age: Studies in South African Citizenship and Politics* (Cape Town: Maskew Miller Ltd, 1930), pp. 110–28

36. See Curtis, *Civitas Dei*.

37. Ian Van der Waag, 'Hugh Archibald Wyndham: His Life and Times in South Africa, 1901–1923' (Unpublished PhD Thesis, Department of Historical Studies, University of Cape Town, 2005).

38. Hugh Wyndham, 'The Colour Problem in Africa', *Journal of the British Institute of International Affairs* 4, no. 4 (1925), 182.

39. Ibid., pp. 183–4.

40. Ibid., p. 177.

41. Ibid., p. 177.

42. Cell, 'Lord Hailey', pp. 482–3. Such an institute was eventually established in London.

43. Ibid., pp. 486–88.

44. 'Letter from the Ivision Macadam to JC Beattie, 19 March 1928', Folder 3/6 – SOUa.

45. 'Margaret Cleeve to John Beattie, 22 February 1928', Folder 3/6 – SOUa.

46. 'Extract from Letter from S. Herbert Frankel, December 1928', Folder 3/6 – SOUa.

47. For a full list of these anonymous authors, see appendix in May, 'The Round Table'.

48. 'Ivision Macadam to JJ Rousseau, 12 January 1931', Folder 3/6 – SOUa.

49. Charles Manning's letter to Leif Egeland is quoted at length in A.L. Bostock, *A Short History of the South African Institute of International Affairs, 1934–1984* (Johannesburg: South African Institute of International Affairs, 1984).

50. 'Memorandum, 11 October 1933', Folder 3/6 – SOUa.

51. 'Letter from Campbell Stuart to Eric Walker, 7 March 1934', Folder 3/6 – SOUa.

52. 'Letter from Eric Emmett to the Secretary, Chatham House, 22 June 1934', Folder 3/6 – SOUa.

53. 'Letter from Ivision Macadam to Campbell Stuart, 1 August 1934', Folder 3/6 – SOUa.

54. 'Confidential Memorandum – South African Institute of International Affairs, 6 December 1934', Folder 3/6 – SOUa.

55. Ibid.
56. 'Letter from Escott Reid to Ivision Macadam, 23 February 1935', Folder 3/6 – SOUa.
57. 'Copy of letter received from Mr. Lionel Curtis dated 16 February 1935', Folder 3/6 – SOUa.
58. Ibid.
59. Bostock, *A Short History*, p. 13.
60. Ibid., p. 15; Letter from 'Eric Emmett to Campbell Stuart, 16 January 1936', Folder 3/6 – SOUa.
61. In 1938, S.H. Frankel said at the second unofficial Commonwealth Relations Conference that the membership had been restricted to 'Union nationals', but what is intriguing is that in 1944 the amended Constitution of SAIIA allows 'Union nationals and British subjects' to be members. The original emergency powers of the Executive Council to appoint non-British subjects are scrapped. It is unclear if 'and British subjects' was added in 1944; this seems very unlikely as, during the war, the Afrikaner sentiments against English domination were high and allowing British subjects to be members of the institute without being Union nationals would have certainly raised many questions. It seems more plausible that the 1934 original phrase 'Union nationals and other British subjects' remained unchanged.
62. 'The South African Institute of International Affairs, Pamphlet issued by [the] S.A. Institute of International Affairs', Jan Smuts House, Johannesburg, 1971, p. 5. Unfortunately, we have been unable to access the archives of the SAIIA, and so cannot draw this point out further.
63. Bostock, *A Short History*, p. 19.
64. Ibid., p. 25.
65. 'The South African Institute of International Affairs'.
66. David Willers and Sonja Begg (eds), *South Africa and Sanctions: Genesis and Prospects. A Symposium* (Johannesburg: SAIRR, 1979).
67. See Michael Heilperin, *The Role of Gold as a Basis of International Monetary Order* (Johannesburg: The South African Institute of International Affairs, 1961).
68. Thakur et al., 'Imperial Mission'.
69. Peter Vale, 'South Africa as a Pariah International State', *International Affairs Bulletin* 1, no. 3 (1977), 121–42.

5.   NEW ZEALAND: EXCEPTIONALISM AND ISOLATION IN THE SOUTH PACIFIC

1. James Cotton, 'The Emergence of International Studies in New Zealand', *The International History Review* 37, no. 3 (2015), 458–80.
2. Tom Brooking, *Richard Seddon: King of God's Own* (Penguin New Zealand, 2014), pp. 284–319.
3. Curtis, 'Diary', p. 27.
4. Ibid., p. 29.

5. A wealthy resident of Christchurch, best known for his skill at breeding horses. See Mary Mountier, 'Sir George Clifford', in *Te Ara: The Encyclopaedia of New Zealand*, available at https://teara.govt.nz/en/photograph/38959/sir-george-clifford (accessed 29 October 2019).

6. Curtis, 'Diary', p. 78.

7. Ibid., p. 72.

8. Quoted in ibid., p. 73.

9. Around the time of his meeting with Curtis, Ward was seeking to increase the level of financing for the New Zealand navy. See Matthew J. Wright, 'Sir Joseph Ward and New Zealand's Naval Defence Policy, 1907–12', *Political Science* 51, no. 1 (1989), 50.

10. J.E. Kendle, 'The Round Table Movement, New Zealand and the Conference of 1911', *The Round Table* 84, no. 336 (1995), 495–508. Kendle argues that there was little direct connection between Ward's proposals at the conference and his meeting with Curtis.

11. Curtis, 'Diary', p. 87.

12. The Round Table, 'New Zealand Affairs', *The Round Table* 1, no. 2 (1911), 206–29.

13. Ibid., p. 209.

14. Ibid., p. 209.

15. Ibid., p. 212.

16. Ibid., p. 212.

17. Ibid., p. 215.

18. The Round Table, 'New Zealand Affairs', *The Round Table* 1, no. 4 (1911), 527.

19. Ibid., p. 527.

20. Ibid., p. 528.

21. Ibid., p. 528.

22. Ibid., p. 528.

23. Ibid., p. 529.

24. The Round Table, 'New Zealand', *The Round Table* 10, no. 40 (1920), 931.

25. Ibid., p. 931.

26. Ibid., p. 932.

27. Davis, *India and the Anglosphere*.

28. Bell, *The Idea of Greater Britain*.

29. The Round Table, 'New Zealand', *The Round Table* 8, no. 29 (1917), 210.

30. The Round Table, 'New Zealand', *The Round Table* 5, no. 20 (1914), 487.

31. *Evening Post*, Tuesday, 1 August 1916, at ANZ, ALLEN1, 4, M2/49, 'Ministerial Files – Imperial questions: Round Table: Visit of Mr Lionel Curtis'.

32. A Wellington-based newspaper that ran from 1874 to 1927.

33. *New Zealand Times*, 'Imperial Commonwealth, Past and Future Problems' at ANZ ALLEN1, 4, M2/49, Ministerial Files – Imperial questions: Round Table: Visit of Mr Lionel Curtis.

34. Anon, 'The Problem of the Commonwealth', *The Dominion*, 12 August 1916, ALLEN1, 4, M2/49, Ministerial Files – Imperial questions: Round Table: Visit of Mr Lionel Curtis.

35. Cotton, 'International Studies in New Zealand', p. 459.

36. Ibid., p. 459.

37. H.F. Von Haast, 'The Problem of the Commonwealth', *The Dominion*, 18 August 1916, at ALLEN1, 4, M2/49, Ministerial Files – Imperial questions: Round Table: Visit of Mr Lionel Curtis.

38. The Round Table, 'New Zealand', *The Round Table* 8, no. 31 (1918), 650–60.

39. The Round Table, 'New Zealand: The Samoan Commission', *The Round Table* 18, no. 71 (1928), 664–83.

40. The Round Table, 'New Zealand: The Trouble in Samoa', *The Round Table* 18, no. 69 (1927), 194.

41. The Round Table, 'The Samoan Commission', p. 673.

42. The Round Table, 'New Zealand', *The Round Table* 19, no. 73 (1928), 225.

43. The Round Table, 'The Samoan Commission', p. 683.

44. For the details of this, see the file, 'Scholefield Papers – The Round Table Group', at R24491894, New Zealand National Archives.

45. H.V. Hodson to E.P. Hay, November 21, 1932 at New Zealand National Archives ANZ, R24491894, 'Scholefield Papers – The Round Table Group' 2.

46. NZIIA, 'Resolutions as to the Formation of a New Zealand Institute for submission to meeting convened for Saturday 7th July, 1934', in JC Beaglehole Reading Room (hereafter JCBRR), 831, Box 1, Book 3, NZIIA, Minutes of meetings, 7 July 1934–30 July 1937.

47. Cotton, 'International Studies in New Zealand', p. 462.

48. NZIIA, 'Resolutions as to the Formation of a New Zealand Institute for submission to meeting convened for Saturday 7th July, 1934', in JCBRR, 831, Box 1, Book 3, NZIIA, Minutes of meetings, 7 July 1934–30 July 1937.

49. Cotton, 'International Studies in New Zealand', p. 462.

50. NZIIA, 'Resolutions as to the Formation of a New Zealand Institute for submission to meeting convened for Saturday 7th July, 1934'.

51. Stephanie Dale, 'Stewart, William Downie', in *Te Ara: The Encyclopaedia of New Zealand*, available at https://teara.govt.nz/en/biographies/3s35/stewart-william-downie (accessed 30 October 2019).

52. A predecessor party to the contemporary centre-right New Zealand National Party.

53. Paul Goldstone, 'Begg, Robert Campbell', in *Te Ara: The Encyclopaedia of New Zealand*, available at https://teara.govt.nz/en/biographies/4b18/begg-robert-campbell (accessed 30 October 2019).

54. The leadership of the NZIIA was drawn from this small, educated political elite. For a discussion, see Cotton, 'International Studies in New Zealand'.

55. Barry Gustafson, 'Nash, Walter', in *Te Ara: The Encyclopaedia of New Zealand*, available at https://teara.govt.nz/en/biographies/4n2/nash-walter (accessed 30 October 2019).

56. Only very limited discussion of the content of these meetings survives in the NZIIA files.

57. 'Minutes of meeting, 29 July, 1936', pp. 1–3, in JCBRR, Box 831/1/3, Book 3, NZIIA, Minutes of meetings, 7 July 1934–30 July 1937.

58. NZIIA, 'First Annual Report, 27 August 1935', in JCBRR, Box 831/1/3, 'Book 3, NZIIA, Minutes of meetings, 7 July 1934–30 July 1937.

59. 'Minutes of NZIIA meeting, 27 August, 1936', pp. 1–2, in JCBRR, Book 3, NZIIA, Minutes of meetings, 7 July 1934–30 July 1937.

60. 'Minutes of a meeting of the NZIIA, Thursday November 26', pp. 1–5, in JCBRR, Book 3, NZIIA, Minutes of meetings, 7 July 1934–30 July 1937.

61. Ibid.

62. Ibid.

63. 'Minutes of NZIIA Meeting, 29 October, 1936', in JCBRR, Book 3, NZIIA, Minutes of meetings, 7 July 1934–30 July 1937.

64. 'Minutes of meeting 24 June, 1937', p. 50, in JCBRR, Book 3, NZIIA, Minutes of meetings, 7 July 1934–30 July 1937.

65. Ibid.

66. On Campbell Begg's life, and departure to Johannesburg, see Goldstone, 'Begg, Robert Campbell'.

67. 'Unsigned Letter from NZ IPR to MR G. R. Powles, Secretary of NZIIA, 27 August, 1938', in JCBRR, Book 2a, material laid into minute book 2 of IPR, 31 October 1934.

68. Ibid.

69. IPR, New Zealand Branch, 'Minutes of meeting April 20, 1939', in JCBRR, Book 2a, material laid into minute book 2 of IPR, 31 October 1934.

70. Neill Atkinson, 'Barnard, William Edward', in *Te Ara: The Encyclopaedia of New Zealand*, available at https://teara.govt.nz/en/biographies/4b5/barnard-william-edward (accessed 30 October 2019).

71. IPR, New Zealand Branch, 'Minutes of meeting April 20, 1939', in JCBRR, Book 2a, material laid into minute book 2 of IPR, 31 October 1934.

72. NZIIA Study Group, *Western Samoa: Mandate or German Colony?* (New Zealand Institute of International Affairs, 1938), p. 13.

73. Ibid., p. 13.

74. NZIIA Study Group, *Contemporary New Zealand* (Dunedin: Whitcomb and Tombs Ltd, 1938), p. 16.

75. Ibid., p. 13.

76. I.G.L. Sutherland, *The Maori People Today* (NZIIA and the New Zealand Council for Educational Research, 1940), p. 31.

77. Ibid., p. 31.

78. Ibid., p. 440.

79. Anon, 'The Treaty of Waitangi', in *Te Ara: The Encyclopeadea of New Zealand*, available at https://teara.govt.nz/en/treaty-of-waitangi (accessed 2 December 2019).

80. Brian Easton, 'Sutch, William Ball', in *Te Ara: The Encyclopaedia of New Zealand*, available at https://teara.govt.nz/en/biographies/5s54/sutch-william-ball (accessed 30 October 2019).

81. W.B. Sutch, 'New Zealand and World Affairs', *International* Affairs 16, no. 5 (1937), 722.

82. 'J.K. Banks to A.W. Free, National Secretary, NZIIA, Wellington 4th November, 1946', in JCBBR, NZIIA 877/1.

83. See Gwendolen M. Carter, 'Report of Dr. Gwendolen M. Carter on British Commonwealth Relations Conference, 1949', at AEFZ W5727, 22618, Box 152, New Zealand Institute of the International Affairs (sic), 1950. Carter was a Canadian academic interested in African affairs. The New Zealand government paid for her travel expenses. She reported the conference was successful,

but suggested that the government resist funding the NZIIA unless absolutely necessary.

84. NZIIA, 'Minutes of a meeting of the standing committee held on Thursday 27 February 1975', pp. 1–4, in JCBRR, 885/2 Box 27, 1972–77.

85. 'Minutes of the annual meeting of the national council of the NZIIA', 24 April 1976, in JCBRR, 885/2 Box 27, 1972–77.

86. There were initial concerns about both subscriptions and finding advertisers. See NZIIA, 'Minutes of a meeting of standing committee held on Tuesday 18 May 1976', in JCBRR, 885/2 Box 27, 1972–77.

87. NZIIA, 'The New Zealand Institute of International Affairs (NZIIA): Origins, Developments, Prospects', in New Zealand Parliament, available at www.parliament.nz/resource/0000180203 (accessed 29 October 2019).

88. Ibid., p. 3.

89. Ibid., p. 7.

6.   INDIA: THE IMPERIAL DISCIPLINE MEETS ANTI-COLONIAL NATIONALISM

1. V.Y. Mudimbe, *The Invention of Africa: Gnosis, Philosophy and the Order of Knowledge* (Bloomington, IN: Indiana University Press, 1988).

2. Gobind Vallabh Pant, 'Postulates of Political Science', in V.N. Chawla and S.K. Sharma (eds), *Political Science in India* (Jullundur: International Book Company, 1938), pp. 17–24.

3. See the special issue on Indian IR: *International Studies* 46, no. 7 (2009), particularly contributions by Muthia Alagappa, Varun Sahni, Devika Sharma and Amitabh Mattoo. See also M.S. Rajan, 'Golden Jubilee of the School of International Studies: An Assessment', *International Studies* 42, nos 3&4 (2005), 195–204; Navnita Chadha Behera, 'Re-imagining IR in India', *International Relations of the Asia-Pacific* 7, no. 3 (2007), 341–68; Kanti Bajpai and Siddharth Mallavarapu (eds), *International Relations in India: Bringing Theory Back Home* (New Delhi: Orient Longman, 2005), pp. 17–38.

4. Amitav Acharya and Barry Buzan, *The Making of Global International Relations* (Cambridge: Cambridge University Press, 2019).

5. See The Ideas of India website, www.ideasforindia.in/ (accessed 10 December 2019).

6. Martin Bayly, 'The Forgotten Histories of Indian IR', ORF Issue Brief 210, November 2019, available at www.orfonline.org/research/the-forgotten-history-of-indian-international-relations/ (accessed 10 December 2019).

7. For a discussion, see Studdert-Kennedy, 'Political Science and Political Theology.

8. For an extended discussion, see Chandrika Kaul, 'The Round Table, the British Press and India, 1910–1922', in Andrea Bosco and Alexander C. May (eds), *The Round Table, the Empire/Commonwealth and British Foreign Policy* (London: Lothian Foundation Press, 1997), pp. 343–68.

9. Vineet Thakur, *Jan Smuts and the Indian Question* (Pietermaritzburg: University of KwaZulu Natal, 2017), p. 40.

10. See V.S. Srinivasa Sastri, 'V.S. Srinivasa Sastri to Hope Simpson, 10 April 1924', in T.N. Jagadishan (ed.), *Letters of V.S. Srinivasa Sastri* (Madras: Rochhouse, 1944), p. 246.

11. 'Lanka Sundaram to I. Macadam, 20 September 1932', IOR/L/I/1/427, British Library, London, p. 22.

12. Lanka Sundaram, 'The International Status of India', *Journal of the Royal Institute of International Affairs* 9, no. 4 (1930), 452–66. A few other Indians also delivered talks at Chatham House in the 1920s and 1930s, including The Maharaja of Patiala in 1928 and Gandhi in 1931. Sapru and Zafrulla Khan were published in 1933 and Zafrulla Khan again delivered an address in 1937. See The Maharaja of Patiala, 'The Problem of the Indian States', *Journal of the Royal Institute of International Affairs* 7, no. 6 (1928), 38–406; M.K. Gandhi, 'The Future of India', *International Affairs* 10, no. 6 (1931), 721–39; Tej Bahadur Sapru and Zafrulla Khan, 'Indian Public Opinion on the White Paper', *International Affairs* 12, no. 5 (1933), 611–28; Zafrulla Khan 'India's Place in the Empire', *International Affairs* 16, no. 5 (1937), 743–60.

13. See Alfred Zimmern, C.A.W. Manning and Lanka Sundaram, *India Analysed* (London: Victor Gollangz, 1933).

14. 'Sundaram to Macadam, 20 September 1932', p. 23. See also 'I. Macadam to R.A. Butler, 9 November 1932', IOR/L/I/1/427, p. 21.

15. 'Confidential – Public Department, D.O. No. 823-S, 14 December 1932', IOR/L/I/1/427, f. 14.

16. Ibid., f. 15.

17. 'Butler to Macadam, 9 November, 1932'.

18. Anon, 'Meeting on Institutes of International Affairs, First Meeting, Ref. No. T89/20th/140, Canadian Institute of International Affairs, British Commonwealth Relations Conference Toronto, September 11th–21st, 1933', Folder 7/1/1e, Chatham House Archives (hereafter CHA).

19. From 1939 to 1942, Mudaliar served in the Viceroy's Executive Council and from 1942 to 1945 he was a member of Winston Churchill's Imperial War Cabinet. Mudaliar also represented India at the San Francisco Conference of 1945 and became the first president of UNESCO. Zafrulla Khan was a chief proponent of the Pakistan movement and was the first foreign minister of Pakistan. Mir Maqbool Mahmood was the Foreign Minister of Patiala and represented the princely states. Hammond was a former governor of Assam.

20. Anon, 'Meeting of Institutes of International Affairs', f. 7.

21. Ibid., f. 8.

22. Ibid., f. 9.

23. A member of the Indian Civil Service and later the first Secretary General of the Indian Ministry of External Affairs.

24. Eminent lawyer and liberal politician who had served in the Viceroy's Council and represented India at the 1923 Imperial Conference.

25. A prominent YMCA member and member of the Central Legislative Assembly. Earliest Indian member of Chatham House, and the first Indian participant in the IPR Conference of 1929.

26. 'R.C.M. Arnold to Edward Carter, 18 May 1935', Folder 6/2/38, CHA.

27. Politicians included: K.N. Haksar, Akbar Hydari, T.B. Sapru, N.M. Joshi, B.L. Mitter, Kunwar Jagadish Prasad, C.P. Ramaswami Iyer, Purshottamdas Thakurdas, R.P. Paranjpye, P.D. Pattani, Cowasji Jahangir, V.T. Krishnamachariar, J.G. Laithwaite, Chunilal V. Mehta, Edward Benthall and Mirza M. Ismail. Girija Shankar Bajpai, M.S.A. Hydari and E.T. Coates were the bureaucrats.

28. Zafrulla Khan later recounted that he was the 'first and only President of the Institute'. This is untrue. The Viceroy was the ex-officio president, but even as chairman Zafrulla Khan was replaced by Ramaswami Mudaliar in the late 1930s, who was followed by Sultan Ahmad in November 1942. See Zaffrulla Khan, *Reminiscences of Sir Muhammad Zafrulla Khan: Based on Interviews by Prof. Wayne Wilcox and Prof. Aislie T. Embree* (New York: Columbia University, 2004), pp. 136–7.

29. King-Hall, *Chatham House*, p. 105.

30. S.K. Datta, 'Correspondence with the Indian Institute of International Affairs, and related papers', Papers of S.K. Datta, MSS EUR F178/36, IOR and Private Papers, British Library, London.

31. IIIA, 'The Indian Institute of International Affairs: Constitution, 1936, New Delhi', Folder 3/6 – INDa, CHA, f. 7.

32. Datta, 'Correspondence with the IIIA'.

33. King-Hall, 'Note', MSS EUR F178/36, CHA.

34. 'S.K. Datta to Lionel Curtis, 26 May 1936', MSS EUR F178/36, British Library.

35. On Hofmeyr's India visit, see Alan Paton, *Hofmeyer* (Oxford: Oxford University Press, 1964), pp. 245–54.

36. B. Shiva Rao, 'The Indian Council of World Affairs', B. Shiva Rao Papers, II Instalment, Nehru Memorial Museum and Library (NMML), New Delhi.

37. 'Minutes of the Joint Meeting held at 3 p.m. on Saturday 3 March 1945, 10 St. James Square, London', File 3/6 Aus A, CHA, p. 4. Also see 'The Indian Institute of International Affairs: Annual Report of the Council, 1940–41', External Affairs Department, F.118 – F.O/42, No. 1-7, National Archives of India (hereafter NAI).

38. Shiva Rao, 'The Indian Council for World Affairs', p. 13.

39. Ibid., p. 13.

40. H.V. Hodson, *The British Commonwealth and the Future: Proceedings of the Second Unofficial Conference on British Commonwealth Relations* (London: Oxford University Press, 1939).

41. For a thorough discussion of Nehru's internationalisation of India's freedom movement, see Michele L. Louro, *Comrades Against Imperialism: Nehru, India, and Interwar Internationalism* (Cambridge: Cambridge University Press, 2018).

42. Pant, 'Postulates of Political Science', p. 23.

43. A.S. Shah, 'Report: Lecture tours to the United States and Canada by the Indian delegates to the IPR Conference', IOR/L/I/1/1090, File No. 462/94, BL.

44. 'G.S. Bajpai to David Monteath, 16 May 1942', IOR/L/I/1/1090, 462/94.

45. 'Edward Carter to R.C.M. Arnold, 4 April 1935', Folder 6/2/38, CHA.

46. Ibid.

47. 'Indian Representation at the IPR Conference', Folder 6/2/38, CHA, f. 3.

48. 'Viceroy to Secretary of State, 6 May 1943', IOR/L/I/1/1090, File No. 462/94, BL; A.S. Shah, 'Report on the eighth session of the IPR Conference held at Mont Tremblant, Canada, from December the 4th to December the 14th', IOR/L/I/1/1090, File No. 462/94, f. 16.

49. 'Draft telegram for circulation: Secretary of State to Viceroy, No. 2645', IOR/L/I/1/1090, File No. 462/94, TBL.

50. 'Telegram: Washington to Foreign Office, 24 May 1942', IOR/L/I/1/1090, File No. 462/94, BL.

51. 'Bajpai to Monteath, 16 May 1942', f. 2.

52. Ibid., f. 2.

53. 'Secretary of State to Viceroy, 26 May 1942', IOR/L/I/1/1090, File No. 462/94, BL.

54. 'Minute, External Department, 18 May 1942', IOR/L/I/1/1090, File No. 462/94.

55. Ibid.

56. Khanna represented the Hindu Mahasabha. Begum Shah Nawaz represented the Muslim League and Women. Panikkar, scholar, diplomat and Dewan of Bikaner, represented Princely States. Ranganathan was adviser to the Secretary of State and Sivaraj was a last minute addition, at the insistence of the Viceroy, to give a representation to dalits.

57. 'Pacific Delegation: From the National Call, 28 October 1942', EJ Tarr Series, CIIIA Fonds, MG28-I250, Container 3, File 4, National Archives of Canada (hereafter NAC), Ottawa.

58. 'Indian Representation at the IPR Conference', f. 4.

59. 'G.S. Bajpai to David Monteath, 27 August 1942', IOR/L/I/1/1090, File No. 462/94.

60. 'Indian Representation at the IPR Conference', f. 4.

61. Ibid., f. 3.

62. M.R. Jayakar led the Swaraj Party from 1923 to 1925 and was a Federal Court Judge (1937–39).

63. 'Indian Representation at the IPR Conference', f. 4

64. Ibid., f. 5.

65. Eminent lawyer, member of the Central Legislative Assembly and son of T.B. Sapru.

66. Leader of the National Liberal Federation and President of Servants Society of India. On Kunzru's contribution to setting up the ICWA and later the School of International Studies, see M.S. Rajan, 'H.N. Kunzru, A Memoir', *India Quarterly* 34, no. 4 (1978), 441–56.

67. 'Telegram No. 99, 3 November 1942, Information Department, India Office', IOR/L/I/1/1090, File No. 462/94, BL.

68. 'India and the Institute of International Relations Conference', EJ Tarr Series, CIIIA Fonds, MG28-I250, Container 3, File 4.

69. 'Extract from the Official Report of the Legislative Assembly Debates, 10 Feb 1943', IOR/L/I/1/1090, File No. 462/94, f. 2.

70. Anon, 'An impression of the IPR Conference', IOR/L/I/1/1090, File No. 462/94.

71. 'Political Secretary: Note, 6940/42', IOR/L/I/1/1090, File No. 462/94, ff. 117–20.

72. Shah, 'Report on the eighth session of the IPR Conference', pp. 12–14.

73. Ibid., p. 20.

74. Ibid., pp. 20–1.

75. Shah, 'Report: Lecture tours', p. 2.

76. Shah, 'Report on the eighth session of the IPR Conference', p. 20.

77. 'Olaf Caroe to A. R. Mudaliar, 18 May 1943', IOR/L/I/1/1090, File No. 462/94.

78. 'A. Ramaswami Mudaliar, POL (S) 1225, 1943', IOR/L/I/1/1090, File No. 462/94.

79. 'Telegram: Viceroy to Secretary of State, 6 May 1943'.

80. 'Indian Representation at the IPR Conference', f. 5.

81. ICWA, *Indian Council of World Affairs, Constitution, Rules and Activities* (New Delhi: ICWA, 1950), p. 1.

82. Ibid., p. 1. Emphasis added.

83. 'Extracts from Minutes of Meeting of the Council of the Indian Institute of International Affairs, held on Monday the 15th November 1943: Appendix A', IOR/L/I/1/729, File No. 462/16E.

84. Ibid.

85. 'A. Joyce to A.F. Morley, 3 November 1943', IOR/L/I/1/729, File No. 462/16E.

86. 'Extracts from Minutes of Meeting of the Council of the Indian Institute of International Affairs, 15 November 1943', IOR/L/I/1/729, File No. 462/16E.

87. Ibid.

88. B. Shiva Rao alleges that the Indian government tried to prevent the establishment of the Council. Kunzru and P. Lokanathan had met Carter who was in India on a visit to discuss the new body, but the Indian government blackmailed Carter to withdraw from further discussions by making his further journey to Moscow conditional upon him not seeing the duo. Rao, 'The Indian Council of World Affairs'.

89. 'B. Shiva Rao to Edward Carter, 26 July 1944' (intercepted message), IOR/L/I/1/1091, File No. 462/94.

90. 'B. Shiva Rao to Carter, 24 March 1944', Folder 6/2/38, CHA.

91. 'The Indian Council for World Affairs: Constitution, Rules and Activity, 1945', F. 14/19 – CC/46 (Vol. 1), External Affairs Department, NAI.

92. K. Sarwar Hasan, 'Editorial Foreword', *Journal of the Indian Institute of International Affairs* 1, no. 1 (1945), 3.

93. Appadorai, 'Ourselves', *India Quarterly* 1, no. 1 (1945), 4.

94. Ibid., p. 5.

95. For instance, the following articles were published in the first four years of the journal's existence dealing specifically with issues of political theory, state and international affairs. V. Puntambekar, 'The Role of Myths in the Development of Political Thought', *The Indian Journal of Political Science* 1, no. 2 (1939), 121–32; K.N.V. Sastri, 'A Criticism of Streit's "Union Now"', *The Indian Journal of Political Science* 1, no. 4 (1940), 439–41; Dev Raj, 'The Problem of International Peace', *The Indian Journal of Political Science* 2, no. 1 (1940), 81–91; Ilyas Ahmad, 'Aristotle Natural Theory of the Origins of the State', *The Indian Journal of Political Science* 3, no. 1 (1941), 1–12; B.M. Sharma, 'Essentials of a World Federation: A Critical Examination', *The Indian Journal of Political Science* 3, no. 1 (1941), 62–71; M. Yamunacharya, 'The Hindu Theory

of International Relations as Expounded in Kamandaka's Nitisara', *The Indian Journal of Political Science* 3, no. 2 (1941), 127–33; H.N. Raghavendrachar, 'The Origin of the State According to Bhisma (Mahabharata, Santiparvam)', *The Indian Journal of Political Science* 3, no. 2 (1941), 134–43; V.S. Ram and P.N. Masaldan, 'Peace and Collective Security', *The Indian Journal of Political Science* 3, no. 2 (1941), 165–75); N. Kasturi, 'Monroe Doctrine', *The Indian Journal of Political Science* 3, no. 2 (1941), 176–81; M. Abdul Qadir, 'The Social and Political Ideas of Ibn Khaldun', *The Indian Journal of Political Science* 3, no. 2 (1941), 117–26; V.K.N. Menon, 'Utopia or Reality: An examination of Professor Carr's Theory of the Nature of International Relations', *The Indian Journal of Political Science* 2, no. 4 (1941), 384–8; H.K. Sherwani, 'Political Theories of Certain Early Islamic Writers', *The Indian Journal of Political Science* 3, no. 3 (1942), 225–36; C.V. Srinivasa Murty, 'Is Nazism Platonic?', *The Indian Journal of Political Science* 3, no. 2 (1942), 249–55; E. Ashirvatham, 'Liberty of the Individual in War Time', *The Indian Journal of Political Science* 3, no. 3 (1942), 256–69; C.L. Gheewala, 'Was the Hindu State Pluralistic?', *The Indian Journal of Political Science* 3, no. 3 (1942), 237–48; K.V.N. Sastri, 'The Political Theory of Mysore as a Dekhan Power (1700–800)', *The Indian Journal of Political Science* 3, no. 4 (1942), 380–3; V.K.N. Menon, 'Morals, Politics and Machiavelli', *The Indian Journal of Political Science* 4, no. 1 (1942), 1–5; Ilyas Ahmad, 'The Social Contract and the Foundations of Islamic State', *The Indian Journal of Political Science* 4, no. 2 (1942), 132–69.

96. 'E.J. Tarr to Morris Gwyer, 18 January 1944', IOR/L/I/1/729, File No. 462/16E.

97. 'Telegram, Secret 10068, from Government of India, External Affairs Department, to Secretary of State, 22 March 1944', Folder 6/2/38, CHA.

98. 'Sultan Ahmad to Lord Astor, received 30 May 1944', Folder 6/2/38, CHA, London. Also, see 'Sultan Ahmad to Lord Astor, Received 5 February 1944', IOR/L/I/1/729, File No. 462/16E.

99. 'Sultan Ahmad to Lord Astor, received 30 May 1944'.

100. In internal meetings, this concern was expressed strongly. See P.J. Patrick, 'Draft Memo, 17 August 1944', IOR/L/I/1/729.

101. 'Lord Astor to Sultan Ahmad, 20 April 1944', Folder 6/2/38.

102. 'Lord Astor to Sultan Ahmad, 8 July 1944', IOR/L/I/1/729, File No. 462/16E.

103. 'A.R. Mudaliar to E.J. Tarr, 28 July 1944', Folder 6/2/38.

104. 'Ivision Macadam to A.F. Morley, 5 September 1944', IOR/L/I/1/729, File No. 462/16E.

105. Ibid.

106. 'Maurice Gwyer to Ivison Macadam, 4 July 1944', IOR/L/I/1/729, File No. 462/16E.

107. 'A.S.B. Olver to A Morley, 7 December 1944', IOR/L/I/1/729.

108. Mehta pulled out because of personal reasons and was replaced by Abdur Rahman Siddiqui.

109. Ibid.

110. Anon, 'Cypher Telegram, Secret 38620, Government of India, External Affairs Department, to B.A.S Washington, 4 November 1944', IOR/L/I/1/729.

111. 'E.J. Tarr to R. Mudaliar, 16 October 1944', IOR/L/I/1/729.

112. 'George Sansom to EJ Tarr, 23 October 1944', MG28-I250, Container 3, File 10, LAC.

113. 'E.J. Tarr to Frederick Whyte, 16 October 1944', IOR/L/I/1/729.

114. Olaf Caroe, 'Note, 23 November 1943', IOR/L/I/1/729, File No. 462/16E.

115. 'Leo Amery to Wavell, 15 March 1944', IOR/L/I/1/729, File No. 462/16E.

116. Early on, the ICWA lacked Muslim representation (only two members in its Executive Committee were Muslims) and was justifiably attacked for its upper-caste Brahmin character. Muslim membership increased over time. Likewise, it had five women participating in its Executive Council.

117. Anon, 'Note on the Indian Institute of International Affairs, The Indian Council of World Affairs and the Asian Relations Organisation, 19 May 1947', Folder 3/6 INDa 1-2, CHA.

118. Ibid.

119. Ibid.

120. In mid-1948, even though it was defunct and based in Pakistan, the IIIA had 165 members living in India and 50 in Pakistan.

121. Anon, 'Note on the Indian Institute of International Affairs'.

122. Rao, 'The Indian Council of World Affairs'.

123. ICWA, *Annual Report on the Workings of The Indian Council of World Affairs from 1 January 1947 to 31 December 1947* (New Delhi: ICWA, 1948), p. 18.

124. Ibid., p. 12.

125. Globe-Reuter Eastern, 20 January 1945.

126. B. Shiva Rao Papers, II Instalment, Nehru Memorial and Museum Library, Delhi, f. 98.

127. See Asian Relations Conference, *Asian Relations: Being a Report of the Proceedings and Documentation of the First Asian Relations Conference, March–April 1947* (New Delhi: ICWA, 1948).

128. P.N.S. Mansergh, 'The Inter-Asian Relations Conference, 16 April 1947', Folder 3/6 INDa 1-2, f. 10.

129. Anon, 'Note on the Indian Institute of International Affairs', f. 2.

130. 'Excerpts from a recent letter from an American in India, 25 July 1947', MS28-I250, Container 3, File 10 NAC.

131. K. Sarwar Hasan, 'The Pakistan Institute of International Affairs: How It Was Established', *Pakistan Horizon* 61, no. 1/2 (2008), 9.

132. Ibid., pp. 7–11.

133. 'Memorandum on an interview with K. Sarwar Hasan at Chatham House on 5 October 1948', Folder 3/6 – Pakistan, CHA.

134. Ibid.

135. Ibid.

136. ICWA, 'About Us', available at www.icwa.in/aboutus.html (accessed 22 September 2016) and PIIA, 'About Us', available at www.piia.org.pk/about-us (accessed 22 September 2016).

CONCLUSION: THE PAST OF INTERNATIONAL RELATIONS AND ITS FUTURE

1. Aberystwyth University, 'About Us', available at www.aber.ac.uk/en/interpol/about/ (accessed 17 January 2020).

2. Ritu Mathur, "'The West and the Rest": A Civilizational Mantra in Arms Control and Disarmament?', *Contemporary Security Policy* 35 no. 3 (2014), 332–55; Anghie, *The Making of International Law*; R. Paris, 'International Peacebuilding and the "Mission Civilisatrice"', *Review of International Studies* 28 no. 4 (2002), 637–56; B. Bowden, 'In the Name of Progress and Peace: The "Standard of Civilization" and the Universalizing Project', *Alternatives: Global, Local, Political* 29 no. 1 (2004), 43–68. On the English School, see William A. Callahan, 'Nationalising IR Theory: Race, Class and the English School', *Global Society* 18 no. 4 (2004), 305–23.

3. Priya Chacko and Alexander E. Davis, 'Resignifying "Responsibility": India, Exceptionalism and Nuclear Non-Proliferation', *Asian Journal of Political Science* 26, no. 3 (2018), 352–70.

4. See, for example, Tom Parker, *The Ultimate Intervention: Revitalising the UN Trusteeship Council For the 21st Century* (Sandvika: Norwegian School of Management, 2003); Brian Deiwert, 'A New Trusteeship for World Peace and Security: Can an Old League of Nations Idea be Applied to a Twenty-First Century Iraq', *Indiana International & Comparative Law Review* 14, no. 3 (2004), 771–806; and Saira Mohamed, 'From Keeping Peace to Building Peace: A Proposal for a Revitalized United Nations Trusteeship Council', *Columbia Law Review* 105 no. 3 (2005), 809–40.

5. See, for example, International Coalition for the Responsibility to Protect, 'General Assembly Debate on the Responsibility to Protect and Informal Interactive Dialogue', available at http://responsibilitytoprotect.org/index. php/component/content/article/35-r2pcs-topics/2493-general-assembly-de-bate-on-the-responsibility-to-protect-and-informal-interactive-dialogue (accessed 5 October 2017) and Gareth Evans, 'Taking Stock of R2P', available at http://gevans.org/speeches/Speech596.html (accessed 5 October 2017).

6. David L. Altheide and Jennifer N. Grimes, 'War Programming: The Propaganda Project and the Iraq War', *The Sociological Quarterly* 46 no. 4 (2005), 617–43.

7. Vitalis, *White World Order*.

8. Meera Sabaratnam, 'IR in Dialogue ... but Can We Change the Subjects? A Typology of Decolonising Strategies for the Study of World Politics', *Millennium - Journal of International Studies* 39, no. 3 (2011), 781–803.

9. L.H.M. Ling, 'Decolonizing the International: Towards Multiple Emotional Worlds', *International Theory: A Journal of International Politics, Law and Philosophy* 6, no. 3 (November 2014), 579–83.

10. For an early collection, see Branwen Gruffydd Jones, *Decolonizing International Relations* (London: Routledge, 2006).

11. Irene L. Gendzier, *Development Against Democracy* (London: Pluto Press, 2017).

12. Anghie, *The Making of International Law*.

Select Bibliography

Aitkin, Don (ed.), *Surveys of Australian Political Science* (Sydney: George Allen & Unwin, 1985).

Akami, Tomoko, *Internationalizing the Pacific: The United States, Japan, and the Institute of Pacific Relations in War and Peace, 1919–45* (London and New York: Routledge, 2002).

Anghie, Antony, *Imperialism, Sovereignty and the Making of International Law* (Cambridge: University of Cambridge Press, 2004).

Anievas, Alexander, Nivi Manchanda and Robbie Shilliam (eds), *Race and Racism in International Relations: Confronting the Global Colour Line* (London and New York: Routledge, 2015).

Ashworth, Lucian, *A History of International Thought. From the Origins of the Modern State to Academic International Relations* (London: Routledge, 2014).

Beinart, William and Saul Dubow (eds), *Segregation and Apartheid in Twentieth-Century South Africa* (London: Routledge, 1995), pp. 43–59.

Bell, Duncan, 'International Relations: The Dawn of a Historiographical Turn?', *British Journal of Politics and International Relations* 3, no. 1 (2001), 115–26.

——, *The Idea of Greater Britain: Empire and the Future of World Order, 1860–1900* (Princeton, NJ: Princeton University Press, 2007).

Blatt, Jessica, *Race and the Making of American Political Science* (Philadelphia, PA: University of Pennsylvania Press, 2018).

Bosco, Andrea, *The Round Table Movement and the Fall of 'Second' British Empire (1909–1919)* (Newcastle upon Tyne: Cambridge Scholars Publishing, 2017).

——, 'From Empire to Atlantic "System": The Round Table, Chatham House and the Emergence of a New Paradigm in Anglo-American Relations', *Journal of Transatlantic Studies* 16, no. 3 (2018), 222–46.

Bosco, Andrea and Alexander C. May (eds), *The Round Table, the Empire/Commonwealth and British Foreign Policy* (London: Lothian Foundation Press, 1997).

Bostock, A.L., *A Short History of the South African Institute of International Affairs, 1934–1984* (Johannesburg: South African Institute of International Affairs, 1984).

Brooks, E.H., *Coming of Age: Studies in South African Citizenship and Politics* (Cape Town: Maskew Miller Ltd, 1930), pp. 110–28.

Butler, J.R.M., *Lord Lothian (Philip Kerr), 1882–1940* (London: Macmillan, 1960).

Callahan, William A., 'Nationalising IR Theory: Race, Class and the English School', *Global Society* 18 no. 4 (2004), 305–2.

Cell, John, 'Lord Hailey and the Making of African Survey', *African Affairs* 88, no. 353 (1989), 481–505.

Chacko, Priya and Alexander E. Davis, 'Resignifying "Responsibility": India, Exceptionalism and Nuclear Non-Proliferation', *Asian Journal of Political Science* 26, no. 3 (2018), 352–70.

Cotton, James, 'Early International Relations Teaching and Teachers in Australia: Institutional and Disciplinary Origins', *Australian Journal of International Affairs* 67, no. 1 (2013), 71–97.

——, *The Australian School of International Relations* (Basingstoke: Palgrave Macmillan, 2013).

——, 'The Emergence of International Studies in New Zealand', *The International History Review* 37, no. 3 (2015), 458–80.

Crawford, Robert M.A. and Darryl S.L. Jarvis (eds), *International Relations – Still an American Social Science? Toward Diversity in International Thought* (Albany, NY: State University of New York Press, 2001), pp. 151–66.

Crocker, Walter, *The Racial Factor in International Relations* (Canberra: Australian National University, 1956).

Curtis, Lionel, *The Government of South Africa*, Vols 1&2 (South Africa: Central News Agency, 1908).

——, *The Commonwealth of Nations* (London: Macmillan, 1916).

——, *Civitas Dei: The Commonwealth of God* (London: Macmillan, 1938).

Darnell, Regna and Frederic W. Gleach (eds), *Anthropologists and Their Traditions Across National Borders*, Vol. 8 (Nebraska: University of Nebraska Press, 2014).

Davis, Alexander E., 'Rethinking Australia's International Past: Identity, Foreign Policy and India in the Australian Colonial Imagination', *Flinders Journal of History and Politics* 29 (2014), 70–96.

——, *India and the Anglosphere: Race, Identity and Hierarchy in International Relations* (Abingdon, Oxon: Routledge, 2019).

Dubow, Saul, *A Commonwealth of Knowledge: Science, Sensibility and White South Africa, 1820–2000* (Oxford: Oxford University Press, 2006).

Dyer, Hugh C. and Leon Mangasarian (eds), *The Study of International Relations: The State of the Art* (London: Macmillan, 1989).

Gendzier, Irene L., *Development Against Democracy* (London: Pluto Press, 2017).

Grovogui, Siba, *Beyond Eurocentrism and Anarchy: Memories of International Order and Institutions* (New York: Palgrave Macmillan, 2005).

Guilhot, Nicolas, 'The Realist Gambit: Postwar American Political Science and the Birth of IR Theory', *International Political Sociology* 2 no. 4 (2008), 281–304.

——, 'Imperial Realism: Post-War IR Theory and Decolonisation', *The International History Review* 36 no. 4 (2014), 698–720.

Hasan, K. Sarwar, 'The Pakistan Institute of Intenational Affairs: How It Was Established', *Pakistan Horizon* 61, no. 1/2 (2008), 7–11.

Hobson, John, *The Eurocentric Conception of World Politics: Western International Theory, 1760–2010* (Cambridge: Cambridge University Press, 2012).

——, 'Re-viewing the Eurocentric Conception of World Politics: A Response to Knutsen, Ling, Schmidt, Tickner and Vitalis', *Millennium: Journal of International Studies* 42, no. 2 (2014), 485–514.

Hodson, H.V., *The British Commonwealth and the Future: Proceedings of the Second Unofficial Conference on British Commonwealth Relations* (London: Oxford University Press, 1939).

Hoffmann, Stanley, 'An American Social Science: International Relations', *Daedalus* 106, no. 3 (1977), 41–60.

Holden, Gerard, 'Who Contextualizes the Contextualizers? Disciplinary History and the Discourse about IR Discourse', *Review of International Studies* 28, no. 2 (2002), 253–70.

Hooper, Paul F., 'The Institute of Pacific Relations and the Origins of Asian and Pacific Studies', *Pacific Affairs* 61, no. 1 (1988), 98–121.

——, (ed.), *Remembering the Institute of the Pacific Relations: The Memoirs of William L. Holland* (Tokyo: Ryukei Shyosha, 1995).

James Eayrs, 'The Round Table in Canada, 1909–1920', *The Canadian Historical Review* 38, no. 1 (1957), 1–20.

Jebb, Richard, *Studies in Colonial Nationalism* (London: E. Arnold, 1905).

Jones, Branwen Gruffydd, *Decolonizing International Relations* (London: Routledge, 2006).

Kendle, John, *The Roundtable Movement and Imperial Union* (Toronto: University of Toronto Press, 1975).

——, 'The Round Table Movement, New Zealand and the Conference of 1911', *The Round Table* 84, no. 336 (1995), 495–508.

Kerr, Philip and Lionel Curtis, *The Prevention of War* (New Haven, CT: Yale University Press, 1923).

Knutsen, Torbjørn L., 'A Lost Generation? IR Scholarship before World War I', *International Politics* 45, no. 6 (2008), 650–74.

Krishna, Sankaran, 'Race, Amnesia, and the Education of International Relations', *Alternatives: Global, Local, Political* 26, no. 4 (2001), 401–24.

Lake, Marilyn and Henry Reynolds, *Drawing the Colour Line: White Men's Countries and the International Challenge of Racial Equality* (Cambridge: Cambridge University Press, 2008).

Laslett, Peter, *Philosophy, Politics and Society*, 1st series (Oxford: Basil Blackwell, 1956).

Lavin, Deborah, *From Empire to International Commonwealth: A Biography of Lionel Curtis* (Oxford: Clarendon Press, 1995).

Ling, L.H.M., *The Dao of World Politics: Towards a Post-Westphalian, Worldist International Relations* (London: Routledge, 2014).

Long, David and Brian Schmidt (eds), *Imperialism and Internationalism in the Discipline of International Relations* (Albany, NY: State University of New York Press, 2005).

Mathur, Ritu, '"The West and the Rest": A Civilizational Mantra in Arms Control and Disarmament?', *Contemporary Security Policy* 35 no. 3 (2014), 332–55.

May, Alexander C., 'The Round Table, 1910–1966' (PhD Thesis, University of Oxford, 1995).

Miller, J.D.B., 'The Development of International Studies in Australia, 1933–1983', *The Australian Outlook* 37, no. 3 (1983), 138–42.

Mirowski, Philip and Dieter Plehwe (eds), *The Road from Mont Pelerin: The Making of the Neoliberal Thought Collective* (Cambridge, MA: Harvard University Press, 2009).

Morefield, Jeanne, *Empires without Imperialism: Anglo-American Decline and the Politics of Deflection* (Oxford: Oxford University Press, 2014).

Nimocks, Walter, *Milner's Young Men: The 'Kindergarten' in Edwardian Imperial Affairs* (Great Britain: Hodder and Stoughton, 1968).

Oldham, J.H., *White and Black in Africa: A Critical Examination of the Rhodes Lectures of General Smuts* (London: Longmans, Green, 1930).

Olson, William C. and A.J.R. Groom, *International Relations Then and Now: Origins and Trends in Interpretation* (London: Routledge, 1991).

Oren, Ido, *Our Enemies and US: America's Rivalries and the Making of Political Science* (Ithaca, NY and London: Cornell University Press, 2003).

Owens, Patricia, 'Women and the History of International Thought', *International Studies Quarterly* 62, no. 3 (2018), 467–81.

Pearson, Charles, *National Life and Character: A Forecast*, 2nd edition (London: Macmillan (1913) (originally published 1893).

Quigley, Caroll, 'The Round Table Groups in Canada, 1908–38', *Canada Historical Review* 43, no. 3 (1962), 204–24.

——, *The Anglo-American Establishment* (New York: Book in Focus, 1981).

Rajan, M.S., 'Golden Jubilee of the School of International Studies: An Assessment', *International Studies* 42, nos 3&4 (2005), 195–204.

Reid, Escott, *Radical Mandarin: The Memoirs of Escott Reid* (Toronto: University of Toronto Press, 1989).

Rich, Paul, 'The South African Institute on Race Relations and the Debate on "Race Relations", 1929–1958', *African Studies* 40, no. 1 (1981), 13–22.

——, *White Power and the Liberal Conscience: Racial Segregation and South African Liberalism* (Johannesburg: Ravan, 1984).

——, 'Race, Science and the Legitimization of White Supremacy in South Africa, 1902–1940', *The International Journal of African Historical Studies* 23, no. 4 (1990), 665–86.

Roberts, Priscilla, 'Tweaking the Lion's Tail: Edgar J. Tarr, the Canadian Institute of International Affairs, and the British Empire, 1931–1950', *Diplomacy & Statecraft* 23, no. 4 (2012), 636–59.

Rosenboim, Or, *The Emergence of Globalism: Visions of World Order in Britain and the United States, 1939–1950* (Princeton, NJ: Princeton University Press, 2017).

Schmidt, Brian C., 'Lessons from the Past: Reassessing the Interwar Disciplinary History of International Relations', *International Studies Quarterly* 42, no. 3 (1998), 433–59.

——, *The Political Discourse of Anarchy: A Disciplinary History of International Relations* (Albany, NY: State University of New York Press, 1998).

Schwarz, Bill, *Memories of Empire, Vol. 1: The White Man's World* (Oxford: Oxford University Press, 2011).

Shilliam, Robbie, *International Relations and Non-Western Thought: Imperialism, Colonialism and Investigations of Global Modernity* (London: Routledge, 2011).

Smuts, Jan, *Africa and Some World Problems* (Oxford: Clarendon Press, 1930).

——, *Plans for a Better World* (London: Hodder and Stoughton, 1940).

Studdert-Kennedy, Gerald, 'Political Science and Political Theology: Lionel Curtis, Federalism and India', *The Journal of Imperial and Commonwealth History* 24, no. 2 (1996), 197–217.

Thakur, Vineet and Peter Vale, *South Africa, Race and the Making of International Relations* (London: Rowman & Littlefield, 2020).

Thakur, Vineet, Alexander E. Davis and Peter Vale, 'Imperial Mission, "Scientific Method" – an Alternative Account of the Origins of IR', *Millennium: Journal of International Studies* 46, no. 1 (2017), 3–23.

Tickner, Arlene and Ole Waever, *International Relations Scholarship around the World* (London: Routledge, 2008).

Van der Waag, Ian, 'Hugh Archibald Wyndham: His Life and Times in South Africa, 1901–1923' (Unpublished PhD Thesis, Department of Historical Studies, University of Cape Town, 2005).

Vitalis, Robert, *White World Order, Black Power Politics: The Birth of American International Relations* (Ithaca, NY: Cornell University Press, 2015).

Vucetic, Srdjan, *The Anglosphere: Genealogy of a Racialized Identity in International Relations* (Palo Alto, CA: Stanford University Press, 2011).

Wight, Martin, 'Why Is There No International Theory?', *International Relations* 2, no. 1 (1960), 35–48.

Wilson, Peter, 'The Myth of the "First Great Debate"', *Review of International Studies* 24, no. 5 (1998), 10–12.

Zimmern, Alfred, C.A.W. Manning and Lanka Sundaram, *India Analysed* (London: Victor Gollancz, 1933).

Notes on Authors

Dr Alexander E. Davis is a Lecturer in International Relations at the University of Western Australia. He holds an MA in History from the University of Tasmania and a PhD in International Studies from the University of Adelaide. Since completing his PhD, he has worked at the University of Johannesburg and La Trobe University (Australia).

Dr Vineet Thakur is a University Lecturer in History and International Relations at the Institute for History at Leiden University. After completing his doctorate from the School of International Studies, Jawaharlal Nehru University, New Delhi, in 2014, he has worked at Ambedkar University, University of Johannesburg and SOAS.

Professor Peter Vale is Senior Research Fellow at the Centre for the Advancement of Scholarship at the University of Pretoria. He was the founding director of the Johannesburg Institute of Advanced Study, and is Nelson Mandela Professor of Politics Emeritus at Rhodes University. On two occasions he served on the staff of the South African Institute of International Affairs.

Index

Thanks to our Patreon Subscribers:

Abdul Alkalimat
Andrew Perry

Who have shown their generosity and comradeship in difficult times.

Check out the other perks you get by subscribing to our Patreon – visit patreon.com/plutopress.

Subscriptions start from £3 a month.